REVELATION MYSTERY REVEALED

To: Adam Hickman

14/03/17

"Read and Share"

EIVAR GALINDEZ

CONTENTS

3

PROLOGUE

The title "Revelation, Mystery Revealed "follows a significant cause in my life as was through this book of the Bible I came to the knowledge of the truth about the events of the future.

There are many who have written about this portion of Scripture, and all in a superficial way, without going out, without getting wet, trying to look good in front of men but it seemed to me that it is necessary and crucial or critical issues as wars and their order, the correct ordering of the book, the coming of the Lord Jesus Christ for the Church, the mystery of the marriage of the lamb and the mystery of iniquity, among others.

With the help of our God and the respective biblical support in the next books, the whole mystery of iniquity is revealed, the mystery of God the Father and Christ, the mystery of the gospel, the mystery of godliness, God names the seven dispensations and many mysteries.

I thank the Lord Jesus Christ who has dealt with me in a supernatural way and I said things which eye has not seen, nor have entered into the heart of any man. I am amazed that He has chosen me, the most ignorant of the body of Jesus Christ, without doctorates or masters or theological studies to reveal such great mysteries. Of course, do not swallow whole, I done the research and investigated all matters relating to the Bible. **Definitely this is and will be my biggest concern: "know the real truth".**

This book is the product of over twelve years of many fasting, sleeplessness, investigations, much asking, searching studying and asking.

Although many do not seem interested to know when the Lord Jesus Christ will come to lift the church, Jesus himself made it very important because he names it over and over again, the Apostle Paul and the other apostles also found it important and therefore he mentioned it several times in his letters. Today we are millions of people interested to know when the Lord will come to raise the church; for us it is vital to know this secret , now revealed it is necessary to be prepared to be lifted.

There are three theories about the rapture of the church which I studied carefully. But only when was the true interpretation was revealed of each verse involved in the case, was that I knew the truth about this great event. I tried not to leave any verse to drift, to be completely sure of possessing the truth.

First, I thank the Lord Jesus Christ and then those people who in one way or another have contributed to the development of this book, among them Ingrid Flores and the Sisters Marina de Marin, who have checked the grammar. I Also thank my daughter Janna, who transcribed it. Thanks sister Steffany Correa for translating and designing the exterior cover of this book; also want to highlight the immense help they gave me the internet and other sources mentioned.

INTRODUCTION

One of the most important things that the Lord Jesus Christ teaches us is that we must be prepared. What for? For whatever comes, for whatever happens. He emphasizes that we must follow in good times and in bad, in poverty and in wealth, in health and in disease. It also teaches us that we should not fear those who can only kill the body, as our soul cannot be touched.

Finally, we are encouraged with these words: **"He who endures to the end shall be saved".**

In this book you will find answers to the following questions:

1. When does the seventieth week of Daniel start?
2. How do you split the seventieth week of Daniel?
3. When do the seven seals start and end?
4. When do the seven trumpets start and end ?
5. When do the seven bowls of the wrath of God start and end ?
6. Will the church through the great tribulation?
7. When is the church raised?
8. When is the judgment seat of Christ?
9. When does the Antichrist appears on scene?
10. When will we know the name of the antichrist?
11. When does the false prophet come on scene?
12. When is the battle of Armageddon?
13. When is the invasion of China and his followers?
14. When is the trial of the nation of Israel?

15. When is the trial of the nations?
16. When is the millennium?
17. When is the invasion of Gog and Magog?
18. When is the destruction of Damascus?
19. When is the final war?
20. When is the judgment of Satan and the fallen angels?
21. When is the trial before the great white throne or judgment?
22. When is the destruction of the heavens and earth or end of the world.
23. When will there be new heavens and new earth?
24. When does the New Jerusalem descends?
25. When is the wedding of the Lamb?
26. The mystery of the end of Matthew 24:14.

All these questions, explanations, events and more can be found within the pages of this book. I am sure that this book will be valuable morally and spiritually in your daily lives and battles.

I give thanks to the Lord Jesus for having released this mystery that once was hidden certainly through the ages, He has revealed mysteries, pursue revealing and continues until the end of time.

Reading this book of Revelation mixed-up, makes it hard to understand. To order it correctly, we must consider among other things, the narrated events and the possible date for compliance, noting and agreeing with the rest of the prophecies of the Bible.

The book of Revelation is a book that gives personal advice to achieve the salvation of the soul and it also contains seven seals, seven trumpets, seven bowls of the wrath of God and the final judgment; of course all events must be correspondingly sorted.

While the book of Genesis shows us what happened, we could say it was a trip down memory lane by Moses; the book of Revelation shows off what is going to happen through a journey into the future by John.

We have to prepare the church to stand against Satan and his demons, and the only remaining way is empowered by the Holy Spirit.

As we will see later in the match; when speaking of trouble, we note that from the Lord Jesus Christ and continuing with the apostles and prophets , all had to go through tribulations, and great tribulations so that if you were not on the power of Holy Spirit, you could not resist, or endure and as also there was a danger of denying the faith as the apostles themselves did.

The Lord Jesus Christ is preparing an army that we are currently fighting in the flesh, but in the power of the Holy Spirit against Satan and his wicked spirits, so for this constant struggle we must put on the armour of God. (Ephesians 6:10-20).

Here on Earth begins our training which will continue and end when we are caught up to heaven , to rule the earth during the millennium then we will fight the final war, all this will achieve is always taken from the hand of Jesus Christ.

Therefore, we must prepare every day for the great battle considering that the Lord Jesus Christ will prove our knowledge and skills in the great tribulation (Initial three and half years) when we have to face the Antichrist and the false prophet. Then we will really know who God is and who refuses to change his life or that of your loved ones. The same way when we are reviled , exploited , persecuted, tortured , maimed or killed in horrible pain for preaching that we should not receive the microchip and when to just invoke the name of Jesus Christ we will sign our death sentence.

Then, and only then is when you will give value to being a Christian and being with Christ or the devil, or accept invoking his name or denies it saying: "I do not know these Christians; Jesus Christ and don't I even get together with them".

Why be so afraid to suffer for the Name of Jesus Christ? It is because we are not empowered by the Holy Spirit, because until we are not full, we are cowards and deny our faith at every opportunity.

When today we do not suffer persecution and many refuse it when they are dressed indecently, when lying repeatedly, if we do not evangelize to study or work mates, when giving bad example, when changing the gospel for a beer, for sex, power or welfare and for many other reasons; **how will it then be at time of persecution?**

So, beloved pastors, we must prepare to battle Church, persecution, suffering, setbacks, problems; we must say that in this fight we are not alone; because if we struggle alone, we will not resist; but with our mighty Jesus Christ who is with us to strengthen us and make us understand, that we must be glad to be taken into account to suffer for His Name. Knowing that if you do not deny it and if we do not we go back we will receive more accolades, more crowns before the tribunal of Christ. Never the less we will occupy a higher position in the kingdom of God. Is this not enough to encourage you to give your body and your life or that of your family for the gospel of His Name?

We have the promise of Jesus Christ that He will be with us until the end of the world. He will be with us to strengthen us, help us and encourage us through the Holy Spirit who dwells in us. **"For God has not given us a spirit of fear, but of power and of love and of a sound mind".** (2nd Timothy 1:7).

From power, to confront Satan and his hosts of wickedness in love, to preach the gospel truth whatever the cost and own domain, not to succumb to the lust.

The effect produced in the doctrinal position of the believer, in terms of the final events and what will happen in the future will determine how you live your life as a Christian. The position we have with regards to the church and Israel determines its preparation to face the devil and his followers.

The expectation is the coming of Jesus Christ to raise the church, how to present the gospel to those who do not know ... I mean, what is expected of the Bible, how to pray and why to pray. All this is influenced by knowledge or ignorance you have about the "PAROUSIA" and the events of the end times. Undoubtedly, you have to be brave and be watchful about the 70th week of Daniel.

NOTE: I am bound to say that this book does not include the position of His name who believe the church will be lifted before the 70th week of Daniel , because the Bible does not express this, but because they have such a strong tradition for many years there is not even one verse that so confirms this, as discussed throughout this book.

I should also say that there are lots of church pastors who do not believe in pre - millennial teaching and many who have serious doubts about it, or simply do not admit it for fear of being removed from their position. The Lord Jesus Christ in the synagogues was always drawing from the darkness the Main Priests and died preaching the truth, **and if Christ died for the truth, why don't we?.**

I leave in your hands a work that contains many biblical references, which are extremely important to read, to be able to understand the deep revelations written on it; for that reason, this and my other book **"The Holy Spirit",** are the study and spiritual investigation.

HOW WAS THE BIBLE DIVIDED INTO CHAPTERS AND VERSES

Did you know the oldest biblical texts in the original languages were not divided into chapters or verses?

In the "original" there was no separation between words, or vowels, or punctuation, or caption titles that would help locate biblical passages.

You can say it was from the Renaissance when you start editing the first modern books with pages, titles, chapters and indexes. These early printed books imitated manuscripts and offered an extensive and continuous text from the first page to the last, without divisions into paragraphs or stanzas. The Bible has not escaped this rule, although some biblical facts make us think that in the time of Jesus and there was any text division, especially in those passages that were popular and were read cyclically in the synagogues. (Luke 4:17; Acts 13:15; 15:21; 2nd Corinthians 3:14). In addition some of these passages were known by a title referring to its subject. (Mark 12:26; Luke 20:37; Romans 11:2; Acts 8:3). There is evidence that in the S.I A.C. was customary to read the Torah on Saturday morning. We can assume that it was very difficult to use a long text without any divisions that facilitate finding particular passage for public reading.

During the Middle Ages the Masoretes (Jewish scholars setters, preserving the exact text of the Bible), conceived a division in short sentences, but complete sense, which allowed a certain rhythm to the voice of the reader. It should be noted that these divisions were not on the rolls of the synagogue used for worship, the text should not carry any signs added.

CURRENT DIVISIONS

Our current chapter divisions seem to have been drafted in the XI by **Lanfranc**, counsellor of William the Conqueror. At the beginning of the thirteenth century in Paris, **Stephen Langton**, a professor at the Sorbonne, who became Archbishop of Canterbury, developed the outline, and carried out. He established a division into chapters, more or less the same, very similar to what we have in our Bibles printed. Towards 1226, the booksellers of Paris, introduced these divisions into chapters in the biblical text, resulting in what is known as the Bible Parisian. Since then this division became universal.

The first book printed endowed Biblical Poetry and numbered this presentation was that of the Psalms, namely **quintuplex Psalterium** de **Lefevre D' Etaples**, published in 1509, in Paris, by the famous Protestant printer , Henri Estienne, who held the prestigious title of Printer king for Hebrew, Latin and Greek.

Robert Estienne, (or Stephanus), son of Henri, popularized the use of the numbering of verses for the entire Bible. For books of the Old Testament proto adopted Italian Dominican division of the late fifteenth century, **Sanctes Paginus**. And for the deuterocanonical and the entire New Testament developed a new division. It is said that this work was done in the course of a journey on horseback from Paris to Lyons. In 1551 published the Greek New Testament, and four years later he published the entire Bible in Latin. In both cases the verse numbers not in the biblical text, but in the margin. In 1565, Theodore Beza writes the verse numbers within the text itself.

The use of the biblical text divided into chapters and numbered verses allowed since immediately find a passage, whatever the setting adopted by the editing page.

The divisions in chapters and verses are not perfect

Although Langton Estienne and tried to keep a good balance between the number of verses by chapter, in some places the text division is artificial and discussed, as it respects the unity of discourse or story.

Book	N° of verses	N° of chapters	Average Verse per chapter
Genesis	1531	28	30.62
Exodus	1213	16	30.33
Leviticus	859	27	31.81

For example, to some specialists, the transition between chapters 7 and 8 of the Gospel of John is not successful, as the speech does not stop at 7:53, but in 8:1. Therefore Chapter 8 should begin with verse 2. In this case, the situation is particularly complex because 7:53-8:11 text does not appear in most manuscripts, others incorporate it rather differently. The story seems to have been a history preserved first independently and then posted here. The narrative interrupted at 7:52 seems to continue in 18:12.

Another interesting example is found in Psalm 19. Many specialists believe that the last line of verse 4 should be the beginning of verse 5, it refers, as verses 5 and 6, the same protagonist (the sun) that crosses the celestial space and defines the pulse the day and night with their presence and absence.

Finally, note that the numbering of the Psalms in the Hebrew text differs from that used in the Greek version (Septuagint) and Latin (Vulgate). This difference is due to some psalms are divided and others merged. Thus, for example, Psalms 9 and 10 of the Hebrew Psalm 9 correspond to the Greek and Latin versions, while Psalms 114 and 115 correspond to 116 LXX Hebrew texts. The same happens with Psalm 147 of the Hebrew text which is divided into two psalms (146-147) in the Greek version.

Ortega, Ricardo, How the Bible was divided into chapters and verses
http://linajeescogido.tripod.com/Temas % 20of % 20Estudio/Capítulosyversiculos.htm

REVELATION: AUTHORSHIP AND DATE

Authorship and Date

Authorship

The writer tells us that his name is John (1:4), is a servant (1:1), a brother (1:9) and one of the prophets (22:9). He assumed that the seven churches know and writes with the authority of an apostle. The early Christian tradition attributes it to the Apostle John. Justin Martyr (AC 165) said that John the Apostle was the author, the same said Irenaeus (140-202) who was a pupil of Polycarp, who was a student of John, and he said that John the Apostle was the author. Other church fathers who attribute the authorship to John the apostle are: Melito, Hippolytus (AC 235), Tertullian (220), Clement of Alexandria (212), and Origen (185-254).

The great objection to the apostolic authorship is the Greek style, which is totally different from the style of Greek used in the Gospel and in the letters. However, there are also similarities (Morris).

*Reference to logos. (John 1:1 cf Revelation 19:13).

*Legend of the Lamb.
(John 1:29, 36 cf Revelation 5:6).

*The water of life, John 4:10, cf Revelation 8:10, 21:6, 22:1, 22:17.

*He who overcomes(1st John 2:13 cf 2:7, etc... 21:7).

*Keeping the commandments.
(1st John 2:3 cf Revelation 12:17, 14:12).

*Both have very similar ways to Zac 12:10.
(John 19:37, Revelation 1:7).

*An invitation to the thirsty.
(John 7:37 cf Revelation 21:6, 22:17).

*White clothes for angels, John 20:12 (though in Revelation shining angels wear clothes (15:6);
the saints wear white. (3:4,5,18; 6:11; 7:9; and 19: 14).

*A command received by Christ from the Father.
(John 10:18).

Other themes of the gospel:

*The bride and groom. (John 3:29 cf Revelation 19:7).

*The true worshipers. (John 4:23 cf Revelation 11:1).

* The dead shall hear the voice of God and arise to live ...
will rise to be condemned.
(John 5:25-29 cf Revelation 20:11).

* For the Father loves the Son and shows him what
he does. (John 5:20 cf Revelation 1:1).

* I will not lose any of those you have given me, but raise
them up at the last day.
(John 6:39 cf Revelation 7:4 and 14:1).

* My teaching is not mine. It comes from him who
sent me. (John 7:16 cf Revelation 1:1).

* The testimony of two valid.
(John 8:17 cf Revelation 11:3).

* ... is a liar and the father of lies.
(John 8:44 cf Revelation 12:15, and 20:8).

* ... Before Abraham was, I am.
(John 8:58 cf Revelation 1:17-18).

* The thief comes only to steal and kill and destroy.
(John 10:10 cf Revelation 9:11).

* I am the good shepherd. (John 10:11 cf Revelation 8:17)

* The man who loves his life will lose it, but the man who
hates will keep it for eternal life.
(John 12:25 cf Revelation 2:10).

* Whoever serves me must follow me.
(John 12:26 cf Revelation 14:4).

* God's voice sounds like thunder. (John 12:28-29).

* The prince of this world be cast out.
(John 12:31 cf 12:9).

* Come back and take you to be with me that you
also may be where I am. (John 14:3 cf 22:33).

* If the world hates you, keep in mind that it hated me first.
(John 15:18).

* ... anyone who kills you will think he is offering service
to God. (John 16:2).

* ... weep and mourn while the world rejoices.
(John 16:20 cf 11:10).

* In this world you will have tribulation. But trust! I have overcome the world.
(John 16:33 cf Revelation 3:21).

* Holy Father, protect them now by the power of your name. (John 17:11 cf Revelation 7:4 and 14:1).

* I have given them your word and the world hated them, because they are not of the world as I am not of the world.
(John 17:14 cf Revelation 6:9).

* I want those you gave me wherever I am, to behold my glory. (John 19:15 cf Revelation 21:23).

* They shall look on him whom they pierced.
(John 19:37 cf Revelation 1:7).

* I'll be back ... to my God and your God.
(John 20:17 cf Revelation 3:2 and 12).

There are also similarities with the first letter of John (paraphrased):

* Defeat evil. (1st John 2:14).

* Beating the antichrist. (1st John 4:4).

* Overcoming the world. (1st John 5:4).

* Do not love the world or anything in the world.
(1st John 2:15).

* The world and its desires pass away, but the man
who does the will of God lives forever.
(1st John 2:17).

* The last hour and the antichrist.
(1st John 2:18; 2:22 and 4:3).

* Do not be surprised if the world hates you.
(1st John 3:13).

* I write these things to you who believe ... so they
know that you have eternal life. (1st John 5:13).

* The evil one cannot harm the child of God.
(1st John 5:18).

* The whole world is under the control of the evil one.
(1st John 5:19).

* Guard yourselves from idols. (1st John 5:21).

* Continue in him, so that when he appears not be
ashamed before him at his coming. (1st John 2:28).

The second letter of John:

* Such a one is the deceiver and the antichrist.
(2nd John 1:7).

* Look to not lose what you have worked so hard to
be fully rewarded. (2nd John 1:8 cf Revelation 3:11).

Johnson, commenting on 9:11 where the king of the abyss
is called Abaddon in Hebrew and Apollyon in Greek,
stresses that this stylistic trait of giving information in

bilingual terms peculiar to Revelation and the Gospel of John. (John 6:1; 19:13,17, and 20; 20:16). However, see also Mark 5:41 and 5:34; Mt 27:46).

* John is the only Gospel which refers to the spear in the side of Christ. (Revelation 1:7 cf John 19:34).

* John is the only one who uses the word " tabernacle" (purple) skenoo (4 times in Revelation; see 21:3 and John 1:14).

* He calls Jesus the Logos.
(Revelation 19:13 cf John 1:1 and 1st John 1:1).

Who is the author has some importance because if it is the same John who wrote the Gospel of John, clearly expected to be alive until the return of Christ (John 21:21-24, and 1st John 2:18 says, "Is the last time"). If this were so, all the events in Revelation occur over a relatively short period, and all views would be compressed in this time period. What has made the Revelation was so difficult to interpret is the period of time that has passed since the book was written, so that the visions have been   expanded over a period of time much larger. This is how we have four schools of interpretation.

However, the issue of authorship is a secondary issue, in the sense that this book says that its author is God and that is the word of God (Revelation 1:1-2). It is the only book in the Bible that says this. The church has accepted the divine authorship to include it in the canon of Scripture.

(Revelation 1:1-2) The Revelation of Jesus Christ , which God gave unto him , to show unto his servants things which must shortly take place and he sent and signified by his angel unto his servant John, 2 who bore witness to the word of God , and the testimony of Jesus Christ, and of all things that he saw.

Date

Around 95 A.C, during the reign of Domitian (81-96). Some say during the reign of Nero (54-68). During the reign of Domitian emperor worship spread. Domitian was the custom to banish their enemies, while Nero did not; their persecution was local, in Rome. Domitian's policy was legal and widespread. John was released from Patmos to die Domitian. He tells us that he was on Patmos, suffering for the word of God and the testimony of Jesus (1:9). It should be noted that John was told to write what he had seen and to send it to the seven churches (1:11 cf 1:19). So I wrote this book in Patmos and sent it to the seven churches, presumably before being released.

On that Ephesus had lost their first love and Sardis was dead are facts that point both to a late date.

Revelation was written clearly in a time of persecution (Morris):

1. Antipas had been killed (2:13).

2. John was exiled to Patmos for his faith (1:9).

3. The church of Smyrna was about to be incarcerated (2:10).

4. There are more dead souls by the word of God and their testimony (6:9).

5. The woman is drunk with the blood of the saints (17:6).

What is also clear is that most of the New Testament must have been written when Revelation was written.
Both Paul and Peter died during the reign of Nero. John uses Old Testament sources simultaneously and New Testament in Revelation.

Compare the time Revelation was written with the dates they were written other books of the Bible:

Romans A.C. 57.

2nd Timothy, during the reign of Nero (54-68). Paul was martyred after the great fire of Rome in 64.

2nd Peter, Peter was martyred during the reign of Nero. (Before 68 A.C.).

Hebrews 50's or 60A.C.

Acts 63 A.C.

Lucas 59-63 or 70's or 80 A.C.

Mark 50's or 60 before A.C. 70 A.C.

Matthew 50 to 70's A.C.

John at the end of the first century.

As indicated Lenski, Revelation itself shows that John wrote the book while he was receiving visions. While repeated order "Write" at 1:19, 14:13, 19:9; would leave open the question of when exactly John should put it in writing , the very statement of John 10:4 informs us that he was about to write, but was prevented by the angel of write what the seven thunders said.

John must write "in a book" in 22:6-19 we see "this book" completed except the last few sentences.
The angel (22:7-15) and Jesus (22:18-19) speak of "the book" as one that has already been written (see 22:19). It is, therefore, wrong to think that John wrote in Patmos time after seeing these visions or had waited until he returned to Ephesus. Lenski also notes that it is presented to John as writing under "excitement" because it was in the spirit (1:10, 4:2 , 17:3 , 21:10), but rather that John's mental faculties were not altered in any way, on the contrary, were stimulated, exalted and worked perfectly.

Cf = Contrast

Taylor, R. A. (1998) Revelation: Authorship and Date, **www.apocalipsis.org**

THE WRATH OF SATAN

"Therefore, rejoice O heavens, and ye that dwell in them. Woe to the inhabitants of the earth and of the sea! For the devil is come down unto you, having great wrath, knowing that time is short. And when the dragon saw that he was cast unto the earth, he persecuted the woman which brought forth the man child". (Revelation 12:12-13).

The biggest confusion when reading the book of Revelations is the relation to the seventieth week of Daniel.

<u>The seven years of the reign of Satan in this world are divided into:</u>

* Three and a half years of great tribulation for the gentile Church: (The Wrath of Satan).

* Three and a half years of the tribulation of Jacob, to the Jewish and those who have not wanted to accept the gospel: (God's wrath).

During the wrath of Satan, the souls of the Gentile church will be protected by the seal of God; in the same way, the souls of the Jewish church will be protected by the same label, during God's wrath.

It is necessary to clarify that in the initial three and half years the gentile church will be persecuted for preaching that the antichrist is a messiah imposter, do not mark a change of power, joy and well-being because the True Messiah came and died on the cross of Calvary; also resurrected and will come again to raise all those overcoming saints from every tribe, people, tongue and nation that we are born of water and the Spirit, having lived in holiness of life and persevered in the doctrine of Christ.

The antichrist will say that these people are heretics, rebels who do not want the common good; and then persecute the gentile church: Tortured, mutilate, expropriate and murder with the blessing of the world and even from family and friends.

At this point, it should be noted that the whole world will be deceived by the kindness, intelligence, charisma and power of the false messiah, and signs and wonders of the false prophet. Only the gentile church will hinder and it will be persecuted.

When the Antichrist sits in the temple claiming to be God and be made known as the wicked is (since in the initial three and half years will be released as the Messiah, the Saviour, the Pacifist), is when will open your eyes to the people of Israel, the dead in Christ shall rise first and the Lord Jesus will raise the gentile church to meet Him in the clouds.

Therefore begins the persecution of the people of Israel (the abomination of desolation). The two witnesses and the 144,000 seals begin to preach the gospel of the Name of Jesus Christ.

These will be the final three and half years of the wrath of God in which He will pour out the vials of his wrath. At this stage, the gentile church will be in the third heaven or paradise of the resurrected. (Paul was caught up into the third heaven or paradise: 2nd Corinthians 12:2-4). According to 1st Thessalonians 5:9 God has not put the church to go through his anger.

There is a paradise for the <u>dead saved</u>, which is located in the place that was the bosom of Abraham and which the prophets and saints of the Old Testament are; also the dead in Christ throughout the period of grace that goes from the ministry of Jesus Christ until the end of the millennium. Jesus told the thief: "Today you will be with me in paradise"; but actually Jesus Christ ascended to the third heaven only until 40 days after his resurrection. What he did just his spirit and soul were separated from the body by death, it was down to Abraham bosom, to proclaim victory from the summit of now called paradise, to those who were there, including the thief; and to those who were in hell listening. This paradise will be destroyed along with the earth and the first heaven, in The War of the End of the World. (Luke 16: 19-31; Luke 23: 39-43; Ephesians 4: 8-10; 1st Peter 3: 18-20, 4: 6; Rev 21:1).

This paradise you can see in the Garden of Eden, where God placed as sovereign Adam and Eve. Satan was also in Eden. **Where is that Eden or Paradise?** according to the Bible it is in the midst of the land in the Middle East. We know that Israel is the center of the earth and that Jesus was three days when he died there. But when Adam, Eve and Satan were released this paradise; God took control of the garden and placed cherubim to guard the tree of life, which Jesus offered his followers who overcome enduring to the end of his life. **So where is this paradise?** Obviously where it has always been; but now deeply hidden. This is called Abraham's bosom or **paradise of the saved dead;** where is also separated and below the hell.
(Gen 2: 8-15 and 23-24; Ezekiel 5: 5,28: 13 and 38:12; Mt 12:40; Jn 20:17; Romans 10: 6-7; Eph 4: 9; Revelation 2: 7).

Another indubitable proof that the <u>dead saved</u> paradise is down and not in heaven is 1st Thessalonians 4: 16-17.

1. The Lord Jesus Christ will descent, come down from heaven; he alone.

2. Those who live **will be caught, raised; together, in conjunction** with the <u>dead saved</u>.

3. We receive Jesus Christ into the air; neither the <u>dead saved</u>, nor alive saved were in the same place with Christ.

There is another paradise by the resurrected saved; remaining in the third heaven where they go the resurrected saved including the Church of the Gentiles, after the judgment seat of Christ that will be in the air; the church of Jews and the saved to die during the millennium, will also be in this paradise; when they leave the earth at the end of the millennium.

The dead saved after the final judgment will not come into the third heaven; they will come to salvation, living in the New Jerusalem as servants to those who deserve this honour; and /or outside the New Jerusalem with the nations that will be saved, after The War of the End of the World.

The others dead that go out to condemnation will be cast into the lake of fire, in big and varied compartments according his punishment. This is the second death.

Recall that in the initial three and half years of great tribulation, Satan's wrath turns against the gentile church of Jesus Christ, who will be preaching to people that should not be put the mark and to not believe the antichrist, the gateway to the kingdom of heaven to the Gentiles is about to close. At the same time , there will be happiness to the world because the antichrist will be providing loans , will be giving away cars, homes, health care will be free, will be safe streets and every kind of earthly delight, all this, in exchange for which leave install a microchip in the right hand or forehead.

At this time anyone who wants to buy or sell will need a microchip containing all the details of each person: age, sex, blood type, address, workplace, health and more.

Each one will carry a personal computer and when he need to buy, will put his right hand or his forehead on the seller's computer; and they will put it in his personal computer the right hand when they would like to buy.

The amount - Quantity of money for the purchase or sale - will leave one account and move on to another , without any money handling; the entire transaction is done electronically; in this way who ever does not have the microchip, may not purchase or sell anything insomuch as money not will handled.

Here are some scientific predictions for the future: In 2020 it will be able to copy the mind and people will have nano chips in the brain to abolish serious diseases. In 2040, with the cloning; you will not know which is the copy and which is the original. The copy will have the ability to imitate all the senses: taste, touch, hearing, sight. Since 2008 there chips so they can see the blind and the deaf hear. All the flavours and smells or what we see is artificial, just a product of our mind and what she felt or seen orders.

Microchip The process has been done in several stages since many years ago, now we have reached the stage preceding the commitment whit the antichrist. How long this phase will last? Do not know, maybe 10, 20, 30 years or older. For now, it is announced the new health reform law that took effect in the United States in the year 2013: They implanted a voluntary chip in the right hand or forehead of every person who needs access to social security. Undoubtedly, then will spread to Europe and finally, the whole world. Weird? In no way, because even now we are using the mark of the beast (barcode), we are using the number of the beast (666). We only need us to use the name of the beast, which will occur at the time of signing the peace treaty between Israel and the world. Initially will be voluntary for after the gentile church is lifted, implemented mandatory on pain of death. Probably world government organizers already know the name of the beast. (Revelation 13:18).

This stage, we would say that is a test, a proof to see how people react, and how the chip does already implanted in people. Want to health? Implanters the chip. Want loans? Implanters the chip. Want to economic, political, and social? The solution is the chip.

For now, even we Christians, we can flee to the underdeveloped or developing where they do not have the technology, or the budget to carry out this implant in general, and so we avoided that mark.

In the next phase will already have possessed the Antichrist as president of the European Common Market and as saviour of the world; then the chip will be officially introduced, starting with the armed forces, continuing state worker, and finally with all those who want it voluntarily do change, yes, great advantages and benefits. Secretly begin pursuing those who are against that chip, and publicly expressed.

There will be some brothers who implanted the chip and will continue congregate in the church; other people will enter covertly posing as "brothers" these will be the ones later betray and denounce what place are gathering secretly the heretics; in the end, will be like in the persecution of the early church.

Matthew 10:16-22: "Behold, I send you out as sheep among wolves: be ye therefore wise as serpents, and harmless as doves. But beware of men they will deliver you up to councils and scourge you in their synagogues and before governors and kings will be brought for my sake, for a testimony against them and the Gentiles. But when they deliver you up, take no thought how or what to speak: for at that time shall be given you what ye shall speak. It is not ye that speak, but the Spirit of your Father which speak in you. Brother will betray brother to death, and the father the child: and the children shall rise up against parents, and cause them to die. And ye shall be hated of all men for my name's sake: but he that endures to the end shall be saved".

They will deliver you up to councils and scourge you in their synagogues, and before governors and kings will be brought for my sake, for a testimony against them and the Gentiles. But when they deliver you up, take no thought how or what to speak: for at that time shall be given you what ye shall speak. It is not ye that speak, but the Spirit of your Father which speak in you. Brother will betray brother to death, and the father the child: and the children shall rise up against parents, and cause them to die. And ye shall be hated of all men for my name's sake: but he that endures to the end shall be saved".

Matthew 10:34-39: "Think not that I am come to send peace on earth: I came not to send peace, but a sword. For I came to set a man at variance against his father, a daughter against her mother , and the daughter against her mother , and a man's foes shall be they of his house . He who loves father or mother more than me is not worthy of me: and he that love son or daughter more than me is not worthy of me: and he that take not his cross, and follow after me, not worthy of me. Whoever finds his life will lose it, and whoever loses his life for my sake shall find it".

And what will you do? Let you dial in exchange for health and welfare? What will the pastors and missionaries who are in these countries? What happens when you get sick or your loved ones from getting sick?

Sooner or later you'll have to make one of three decisions:

1. Make you mark the Beast.
2. Search naturopathy.
3. Pray for healing and if necessary, die for the gospel.

It's time to start thinking about what to do when we have to decide on our health, economy, purchases and sales. Perhaps we have not heard the gravity of the news of recent times, and what is in accordance with Biblical prophecy.

In the final phase, when the Antichrist is made known as it is: As the wicked, as the son of perdition and as the evil; the gentile church will be raised and then the mark of the beast will be fully binding, upon all who inhabit the planet land at that time.

The Arabs are expecting a Messiah called Mahdi, which they eradicate all tyranny and oppression bringing harmony and total peace; rule the world for 2555 days, the same period of the 70th week of Daniel.

The Hindus are expecting a Messiah in the reincarnation of Krishna. According to Hindu belief Krishna means "The Supreme Attractive" and can be called Allah, Jehovah, Buddha, Rama, etc. According to their belief, God has unlimited names, but is one.

Buddhists expect a Messiah called Buddha Maitreya. According to this belief this is the Messiah awaited by all religions, who will soon make his appearance to the world as "The instructor of the World". It is also believed that Maitreya incarnated 2000 years ago as Jesus Christ of Nazareth. This man will bring peace, security and equality to the world.

The Jews await the Messiah, who, according to them, brings peace and security to the whole world is a humanly born Jewish king, and it is unthinkable to believe that divinely born. Well what Christ said speaking by the Apostle John: "He came unto his own and did not receive him. I am come in my Father's name, and ye receive me not: if another shall come in his own name, him you will receive". (John 1:11 and 5:43).

The false messiah promised mankind that will be considered as one family; establishment of a new world order based on equality, sharing, economic justice, social, and global cooperation. This false Messiah promise too that the food, education, health and the roof will be universal rights, the above, plus the promise of peace and security, form a perfect world government plan.

In conclusion, we all expect a Messiah, why the world will be ready to receive it; pity that they do not investigate in the Bible are left confused by the false Messiah .

However, the gentile church is not in darkness, for today, we know the time when things will happen, do not know the day nor the hour, but the time. The Lord Jesus Christ has left signs and therefore when you come to raise their church, it will not be surprised, his coming will not be hidden for the gentile church. It is therefore necessary to be diligent and negligent about our salvation.

The purpose of the microchip is in total control of humanity, in the economic, political, social, labour and health. Also, people will be located 24 hours. The excuse for using such microchip is health, economic, and security. Implants have been made in animals show that after a period of use, they have developed cancer. You can read more specifically Internet on microchip and control of mind and body, and on the use of directed energy weapons and neuropsicotronics with micro and nanotechnology. There are many well-documented information.

WHY MUST THE CHURCH GO THROUGH THE WRATH OF SATAN, BUT NEVER BY THE WRATH OF GOD?

A. BY PREACH THE TRUTH

* **If the church does not suffer tribulation means Satan is happy with it and so is troubling not, leave her in peace.**

* **A preacher when he preaches** and does not hurt the enemy, this is unfazed is happy because he does not require any change.

* **IF the church is not troubled is because it is in the world,** and the world is happy with the church. A church that will accommodate the world and the world settles into the church.

* **From Genesis to Revelation,** those who wanted to follow or serve God have had to suffer persecutions and tribulations. Since original sin, man has had to suffer, if you want to follow God. We see the case of the prophets, Jesus, the apostles, the church. It stands to reason that before the church to be raised, also must suffer, be shaken, troubled, so yes you know, really, who is who ... as in the early church.

* **Requires tribulation the church to expand the gospel and, at the same time, so you know who they are in Christ and those who do not, or you confess with your mouth, or deny it.**

* **On love:** Love is patient, if not suffer or suffer, not really love.

Love is measured by the suffering you know when you love only those problems.

It is necessary to love the enemy, and not only that loves us and does well, otherwise this would be a little love worked.

* **Why so much fear of death or dying in tribulation, the reward will be greater? Makes sense:** Not the same one death from heart attack, that torture.

* **We must preach the two sides of the coin** even if it costs us repudiation of denominations, the mediocre Christians and the world.

* **The Lord Jesus was preaching to souls that God is love but it is also a consuming fire; This same message was preached by the apostles, the early church, a few of us are preaching now and certainly will be preached in the future. This is why Jesus was left almost alone, the early church was persecuted, we are today rejected and in the future will be killed for preaching the gospel truth.**

B. <u>MESSAGE TO PHILADELPHIA</u>

The Bible does not mention that we will be delivered from trouble; there is no verse that supports such a theory. On the contrary, it says that just as the Lord Jesus Christ suffered tribulation and great tribulation, also us as the faithful followers for the Name of Jesus Christ have to suffer tribulation, because "the servant is not greater than his Lord". To no one is hidden that today we are living an easy and flattering gospel, to be a Christian today is a great advantage as well as to die in Christ, without suffering by cause of of Jesus Christ.

One of the verses that teach that apparently the church apparently will be delivered from the Apocalypse, is Revelation 3:10; which says: God keep you from the hour of temptation, which shall come upon the entire world to those who have kept the word of the God's patience. **However, now let's learn some truths about it.**

Revelation 3:7-13

The message to Philadelphia

7 And to the angel of the church in Philadelphia it writes: He who is holy and true, who holds the key of David, who opens and no one shuts, and shuts and no one opens:
8 I know thy works: behold, I have set before you an open door, and no man can shut it: for thou hast a little strength, and hast kept my word, and hast not denied my name. 9 Behold , I give of the synagogue of Satan, which say they are Jews and are not, but lie- behold, I will make them come and fall down at your feet and acknowledge that I have loved. 10 Because thou hast kept the word of my patience, I also will keep thee from the hour of trial [peirasmos], which

shall come upon all the world, to try them that dwell upon the earth. 11 Behold, I come quickly: hold that fast which thou hast, that no man takes thy crown. 12 He who overcomes will I make a pillar in the temple of my God , and there never will write upon him the name of my God and the name of the city of my God, the new Jerusalem, which cometh down of heaven from my God, and my new Name. 13 He who has an ear let him hear what the Spirit says to the churches.

With certainty and confidence of the believers in a secret rapture, say proof that the Church will not go through tribulation, is based on the promise that he made to the Church of Philadelphia at the beginning of the book of Revelation. Interestingly (and very sadly) it is the custom of many modern Christians including pre - tribulationist to repeat what they hear and what they say to one another without taking the time to investigate for themselves whether such things are true. As it often happens a look at 'test text ' of the "pre - tribulationist " does not confirm anything such interpreters so confidently preach, unlike refutes! Here is a brief analysis of the phrase **"I also will keep thee from the hour of trial"** and as we shall see God is not promising the Church of Philadelphia what pre-tribulationists say.

The Pre-tribulationist make their emphasis to a secret rapture 'before' the Second Coming of Christ based on the meaning of the word [**ek**] in Greek is "**taking off**". Although this is not the only meaning for that preposition, for starters, that same definition clearly implies that what is "**taken out**" must come first "**inside**". The word would be better defined **"out from"** as used in **Revelation 7:14** to refer to the large crowd that **came out of** [ek] the great tribulation.

Revelation 7:14

I said, Lord, thou know. And he said, these are they which **came out of [ek] the great tribulation,** and have washed their robes and made them white in the blood of the Lamb

The word [**ek**] is used in other verses in the same chapter 3 of Revelation which clearly demonstrates its meaning (see Revelation 3:5,9,10,12,16 and18) **at all times what is 'ek' (left) is required to be first inside.**

Revelation 3

5 He who overcomes shall be clothed in white garments, and I will not erase his name **from [ek]** book of life, but will acknowledge his name before my Father and before his angels.

9 Behold , I give **of [ek]** the synagogue of Satan, which say they are Jews and are not, but lie- behold, I will make them come and fall down at your feet and acknowledge that I have loved.

10 Because thou hast kept the word of my patience, I also will keep thee **from [ek]** the hour of trial which shall come upon all the world , to try them that dwell upon the earth.

12 He who overcomes will I make a pillar in the temple of my God , and there never will write upon him the name of my God and the name of the city of my God, the new Jerusalem , which cometh down **of [ek]** heaven from My God , and My new name.

16 So then because thou art lukewarm, and neither cold nor hot, I will spew you out **of [ek]** my mouth.

18 Therefore I counsel you to buy from me gold refined **in**

[ek] the fire, that thou majesty be rich, and white clothes to wear, and that the shame of thy nakedness, and anoint your eyes with eye salve, that see it.

Fortunately the very Word of God gives us light on this verse. Although this text is used to "prove" pre -tribulation rapture, the original words used there do not. Those words **are the same as those used in John 17:15 to refer to those who are "saved in" the world, not "taken out" of the world as Jesus prayed. Consider the literal translation from Greek into Spanish of John 17:15:**

John 17:15 Erotao (I pray) **ou** (no) **hina** (that) **airo** (serves) **cars** (they) **ek** (from) **kosmos** (world) **alla** (but) **hina** (that) **tereo** (keep) **cars** (they) **ek** (to) **put you** (evil).

We see how it is that in **Revelation 3:10** promises to the church of Philadelphia the same thing in John 17:15 Jesus prayed, not be removed from the world, but saved in the world. Consider the original Greek Revelation 3:10:

Revelation 3:10 Kago (me too) **tereo** (keep) **you** (you) **ek** (from) **hour** (the time) **peirasmos** (temptation).

What we have is that **Revelation 3:10** does not prove in any way a secret rapture to rid the church of the time of the test but does confirm that God cares for his people in times of temptation. The statement means "**get out**" is [**airo ek**] literally "**take**", but that is NOT the phrase used in **Revelation 3:10**. It says [**tereo ek**] which means "**to watch for**". We see then that the phrase [**airos ek**] **means "out of"** while the phrase [**tereo ek**] means to "**watch for**". In **Revelation 3:10** is not used "**airos ek**" but used "**tereo ek**". So this tells us very clearly that what God has in mind is not what the pre - tributationist has in mind. The second part in John 17:15 says "*but you to watch (keep) of evil*" which is the Greek [tereo cars hina ek] means that are **cared by God NOT being removed from the world** as Christ said.

When we look at the meaning of the words "airos" and "tereo" we find the following definitions in Strong's lexicon:

Airos:

1) Lift up, raise, upload.

  a) Lift off the ground, collect: stones.

  b) Lift up, raise, rise: the hand.

  c) Remove: a fish.

2) take upon himself and charge what has been raised, carry.

3) Take what is up, upload.

  a) Move your site.

  b) Remove or move what is attached to something.

  c) Remove.

Tereo:

1) Attend carefully, take care of.

  a) Save.

  b) Metaphorically - save one in the state that is.

  c) Watch (watch, guard).

  d) Reserve: suffer something (preserve).

It is clear that the promise of Revelation 3:10 does not say in any way that the Church will be raptured before the tribulation but says it will be "saved" from the hour of trial.

Jesus repeated the same words in his prayer in John 17:11 when He said, *"And now I am in the world, but these are in the world, and I come to thee. Holy Father, who hast given me, keep them [tereo] in your name, that they may be one as we are"*.

God promises to 'save' his people. As we saw in the reading of the Gospel of John, Christ asked the father to not take us out of the [ek airos] world, but that we should be saved from the[tereo ek] world.

2nd Peter 2:9-10:

The Lord knoweth how tempting [peirasmos] the pious, and to reserve the unjust under punishment for the day of judgment, 10 and especially those who, following the flesh in the lust of uncleanness, and despise government.

1st Corinthians 10:

13 There hath no temptation [peirasmos] than man: but God is faithful, who will not suffer you to **be tempted beyond what you are able,** but will with the temptation [peirasmos] **output, so you can bear.**

James 1:

2 My brethren, count it all joy when you fall into various trials [peirasmos], 3 knowing that **the testing of your faith produces patience.** 4 But let patience have her perfect work, that ye may be perfect and complete, not lacking anything. 12 Blessed is the man that **endureth temptation:** for when **he is tried, he shall receive the crown of life** that God has promised to those who love him.

That's what God does, "pound of temptation [peirasmos] the pious". But how does he do it, abducting us? No! He Does it by 'taking care of them' in the world. Taking care of them in the temptation to have "**way out**" as he told the Church of Philadelphia which also gives you *a way out* of the hour of trial : **"Behold , I have set before you an open door , which no one can shut**"(verse 8) , but not flying to heaven but **"resist"** the test (1st Corinthians 10:13, James 1:2 and 12). James makes it very clear, will receive the crown of life **"when he has stood the test".** Having stood the test.

If we look at the context of the passage of the letter written to the church of Philadelphia we realize it. God says to the church of Philadelphia that he "saved from the hour of trial [peirasmos]" (verse 10), but also tells him to "hold what you have" (verse 11). What has the church of Philadelphia is:

Revelation 3:

8 Thou hast a little strength, and **hast kept my word (Of my patience), and have not denied my name.**

And I keep saying **" He who overcomes, I will make a pillar in the temple of my God "** (verse 12). This means that it expires with patience and keeps the Word of Christ in the midst of **"the hour of trial [peirasmos]"** will be made a pillar in the temple of God. When John wrote Revelation letter referred to himself as one who takes part in "the tribulation and kingdom and patience of Jesus Christ". The same thing happens with the Church of Philadelphia which is "partner" with him.

Revelation 1:

9 I John, **your brother and fellow partaker in the tribulation and kingdom and patience in Jesus,** was on the island called Patmos **because of the word of God and the testimony of Jesus.**

Throughout the book of Revelation are identified in the same way believers. (Revelation 2:2-3, 19; 13:10; 14:12):

Revelation 14:

9 And the third angel followed them, saying with a loud voice, If any man worship the beast and his image and receives his mark on his forehead or on his hand, 10 The same shall drink of the wine of the wrath of God, which has been poured full strength into the cup of his anger, and he shall be tormented with fire and brimstone before the holy angels and of the Lamb: 11 And the smoke of their torment goes up forever and ever. And they have no rest day or night, who worship the beast and his image, and whoever receives the mark of his name. **12 Here is the patience of the saints who keep the commandments of God and the faith of Jesus.**

How is it possible that the church showing the test expires faith and patience _**"keeping the Word of God without denying His name"**_ (Rev. 3:8) has been kidnapped and "out of the world" in the hour of trial? It is not possible! The text shows two Bible truths are in all the Bible, God's Sovereign Grace keeping their children on their mercy and man's responsibility in fidelity to God in the midst of trial (peirasmos). God rewards the faithful that he himself has facilitated resulting in future blessings as saying to the Church of Philadelphia. The Church on earth will be "saved" **[tereo]** (John 17:5, Rev. 3:10) until the day of the Lord (2nd Thess. 2:1) at his Second Coming.

(Hebrews 9:28), that day and not before is when we will be "caught up" to meet the Lord in the air (1st Thess 4:17) to be delivered from the fire of the wrath of God. (2nd Thess. 1: 5-11) which will be shed on the earth.

Trujillo, Jorge Luis, _"I'll save you the time of Proof"_ _What does that mean?_ - Eschatology Amillennial.

_http://www.vidaeterna.org/esp/profecia/te_guardare.htm_

Another indubitable proof that the gentile Church will be saved within the wrath of Satan, is presents Revelation 9:1-4, which states that when the fifth angel sounded, and there came a judgment on the inhabitants of the land, but were <u>delivered those who had the seal of God</u> on their foreheads. Who do you think is speaking in these verses? Do not you see that, just as when the judgment of God is poured into Egypt on wicked men and preserved the lives of those who pleased him, just as He knows to keep those who live according to his word? No matter the persecution and tribulation that suffers the church by the Antichrist and his followers, in the end, this will be victorious.

In 2nd Timothy 2:19 Paul tells us that <u>God knows</u> his own with the <u>seal</u> and depart from iniquity.

The apostle also speaks concerning this seal on 1st Corinthians 1:20-22 saying that <u>God has sealed us</u> with the Holy Spirit and Revelation 9:1-6 when the fifth trumpet sounds God commands locusts that torment to men which have not the seal of God on their foreheads.

As we can see this also confirms that the fifth trumpet, the gentile Church is still here on earth by God to be saved in the Great Tribulation, and hoping that the seventh trumpet sounds to be lifted to heaven.

In Revelation 7:2 speaks of an angel who <u>had the seal of the living God,</u> with which seal the 144,000 Jews of all the tribes of Israel. In Revelation 9: 4 tells us that when the fifth trumpet sounds; God commanded the demons that tormented not the men who have the seal of God on their foreheads. In Revelation 9: 4 tells us that when the fifth trumpet sounds; God commanded the demons that tormented not the men who have the seal of God on their foreheads. This shows us that the wrath of Satan, the gentile Church is sealed, so that their souls are not touched (Rev 9:4); and during the wrath of God will be sealed 144,000 Israel village, which will be saved (Rev 7:2). Both the gentile Church, as the 144,000 Jews, will be saved by God here on earth, within the respective stage, during the 70th week of Daniel.

The gentile Church goes through the wrath of Satan, but shall be delivered from the wrath of God. The Israel people live in peace for the wrath of Satan, but those who not are sealed by God, will suffer the wrath of God.

Satan wants to <u>mark</u> on their foreheads men so that God does not put his stamp saviour on them, and many be deceived and occupy his forehead with the brand, thus preventing the seal God, but in the end only be marked those without the name written in the book of life (Rev 13:8). <u>The Bible is clear in stating that those made mark on his forehead, these drink of the fierce wrath of God.</u> (Rev 14:9-10).

<u>Conclusion:</u> The Church of the Gentiles will be saved from the wrath of Satan; just as the church of Jews will be saved from the wrath of God; but living it from the inside, with courage, not to deny their faith even if it costs the death. Never, and read well, never the church will be delivered from their respective wrath; as the wrath of Satan, for the church of gentiles, or the wrath of God for the church of Jews; as never Job was delivered from evil that caused the devil even though the end, it resulted in a great blessing ... "because those who love God all things work together for good. "

47

C. <u>THE TRIBULATION IN THE CONCORDANCE</u>

Analyzing the texts that appears in Scripture of the tribulation we realize we have to go through the tribulation; if Christ suffered, who are we to be free from it? If we suffer with Him, we shall also reign with Him.

Just read and see for yourself: The true Gospel is the same as saying "Tribulation":

2nd Chronicles 15:4: "... in their distress they turned to the Lord God ...".

20:9: "... and because of our troubles cry unto thee ...".

Nehemiah 9:27 "...in the time of their trouble they cried to you...".

Job 5:19: "deliver thee in six troubles and in the seventh ...

15:24: " Tribulation and anguish make him afraid, and ... against him ...".

27:9: "Will God hear his cry when trouble cometh upon him?

Psalm 10:1: "... And you hide yourself in times of trouble?

46:1: "God ... a very present help in trouble".

78:33: "... their days in ... and their years in trouble".

Proverbs 1:27 "... come on you distress and anguish".

11:8: "The righteous is delivered out of trouble, more the wicked...

12:13: " The wicked ... but the just shall come out of trouble".

Isaiah 5:30: "... look at ... behold darkness and sorrow ..."

8:22: " ... and behold trouble and darkness, dimness of ..."

26:16: "... in trouble thee, they poured out a prayer ...".

30:6: "... the land of trouble and anguish, from whence ..."

33:2: "... our salvation also in the time of trouble".

46:7: " ... and not answer, nor of his trouble".

Zechariah 10:11 "And he shall pass through the sea, and hurt...

Matthew 24:9: "... deliver you to tribulation, and shall kill you: and ye shall ...".

24:21: "For then shall be great tribulation, no ...".

24:29: "... after the tribulation of those days ...".

Mark 4:17: "... when tribulation or ... then they stumble".

13:19: " ... those days shall be affliction, never ..." .

13:24: "... in those days, after that tribulation ...".

Acts 7:10: "*And delivered him out of all his afflictions, and gave him ...*".

7:11: "*And there came a famine in the ... and great affliction....*".

14:22: "*... that through many tribulations enter ...*".

20:23: "*... saying that bonds and afflictions wait for me*".

Romans 2:9 "*tribulation and distress for every human being ...*

5:3: "*... we glory in tribulations ... tribulation worketh patience ...*".

8:35: "*... Shall tribulation, or distress, or persecution, or famine ...*".

12:12: "*... patient in tribulation, be constant in prayer*".

2 Corinthians 1:4: "*who comforts us in all our tribulation ... comfort them which are in any trouble ...?*"

1:8: "*... you ignorant of our trouble we ...*".

2:4: "*For out of much affliction ... wrote with many ...*".

4:17: "*... light affliction is producing for us ...*".

6:4: "*... in much patience, in tribulation, in necessities ...*" .

7:4: "*... exceeding joyful in all our tribulation*".

8:2: "*Large trial of affliction the abundance of ...*".

Ephesians 3:13 "... ask you not to lose heart at my tribulations...".

Philippians 4:14 "Good of you to share ... in my tribulation".

1st Thessalonians 1:6: "... received the word in the middle of ... tribulation ...".

3:3: "... so that no one be moved by these afflictions ...".

3:4: "... we were going to spend tribulation, such as has occurred ...".

2nd Thessalonians 1:4: "... endure persecution and tribulation....".

1:6: "Because it is right ... pay back trouble to those who ...".

1:7: "... you who are troubled ...".

Hebrews 10:33: "... with ... trials were made a spectacle; ...".

James 1:27: "... visit ... and widows in their affliction ...".

Revelation 1:9: "... and fellow partaker in the tribulation...".

2:9: "I know ... your tribulation and your poverty ...".

2:10 "... to test you, and ye shall have tribulation ...".

2:22: "... in great tribulation to them that commit adultery with her".

7:14: "... are they which came out of great tribulation".

D. <u>THE CHURCH PROVEN AS GOLD</u>

The idea that the church should not go through the great tribulation is of pagan origin; there are many interested in spreading this false doctrine, teaching that the church will not go through the great tribulation. According to them, a so good and merciful God would not allow their children to be troubled.

The reality, of what is written in the Bible, is that the church of Jesus Christ needs to be tested like gold and the gold is tested by fire. "That the trial of your faith, being much more precious than gold which though it be tried with fire, might be found unto praise and glory and honour at the revelation of Jesus Christ". (1st Peter 1:7).

"And I will bring the fire to the third party, and will refine them as silver is refined, and test them as gold is tested. They will call on my name, and I will hear, and tell my people: and they shall say, The Lord is my God". (Zechariah 13:9).

"O Lord of hosts, THAT TESTS THE RIGHTEOUS, and sees the reins and the heart, ...". (Jeremiah 20:12).

"Therefore thus saith the Lord of hosts: Behold, I will refine and test them, for what else can I do for the daughter of my people?". (Jeremiah 9:7).

" ... Every man's work shall be made manifest: for the day shall declare it, because it shall be revealed by fire, and the work of each man's, the fire shall try". (1st Corinthians 3:13).

"Examine yourselves, whether ye be in the faith: prove your own selves. Do you not know yourselves, that Jesus Christ is in you, except ye be reprobates?". (2nd Corinthians 13:5).

"…as we were allowed of God to which we are given the gospel, so we speak, not as pleasing men, but God, who tests our hearts". (1st Thessalonians 2:4).

"Do not fear what is going to suffer. Behold, the devil shall cast some of you into prison to test you, and ye shall have tribulation ten days. Be faithful until death, and I will give thee a crown of life". (Revelation 2:10).

E. <u>MYSTERY OF MATTHEW 24:14</u>

The Bible tells us in Matthew 24:14 that the gospel will be preached in the whole world and then the end will come. But, what end is the Bible speaking of?

Matthew 24:14 "And this gospel of the kingdom in the entire world for a witness unto all nations and then shall the end come".

It is also necessary to address a series of words and then know what purpose the Lord Jesus Christ is concerned.

Gospel of the Kingdom: (Matthew 4:23, Matthew 9:35, Matthew 24:14, Mark 1:14, Luke 4:43, Luke 8:1 Acts 8:12). All these scriptures tell us that Jesus and his disciples preached the gospel everywhere the kingdom of God, and told them: "Repent and believe the gospel". In which gospel? The gospel of the name of Jesus Christ of course: (Acts 8:12; Acts 4:11-12).

Whole world:
(Job 34:13; Matthew 16:26 ; Matthew 24:14; Mark 16:15; Luke 2:1; Acts 24:5; Romans 1:8; Romans 3:19; Colossians 1:5-6; 1st Peter 5:9; 1st John 2:2; Revelation 16:14).

"Go into all the world and preach the gospel to every creature". In this verse summarizes (Mark 16:15).

All nations : (Psalm 72:11; Psalm 67:2 ; Psalm 86:9; Isaiah 2:2; Isaiah 52:10; Isaiah 61:11; Isaiah 66:18; Revelation 15:4; Romans 1:5; Mark 13:10; Matthew 28:19; Luke 24:47):

"... will be preached in his name repentance and forgiveness of sins to all nations , beginning at Jerusalem".

What end will come?
What end speak us the Lord Jesus Christ?

The end of the time of the preaching of the gospel to the Gentiles.

(Romans 11:25-32; Revelation 10:6-7 and 11:15 and 18; 1st Corinthians 15:51-52, 1st Thessalonians 4:15-17).

When the time preaching the gospel to the Gentiles is fulfilled, then will be out of the way "The Due Time" and will be manifest the Antichrist as wicked; because in the beginning of his reign, had only appeared as the "saviour of the world". (2nd Thessalonians 2:1-8).

F. THE LAST TRUMPET

1st Corinthians 15:51-52 tells us that the rapture of the gentile church will be "in the blink of an eye, at the last trump: for the trumpet shall sound, and the dead shall be raised incorruptible, and we shall be changed".

In Revelation 10:7: " ... in the days of the voice of the seventh angel , when he shall begin to sound , the mystery of God is finished , how he hath declared to his servants the prophets"

It tells of a mighty angel come down from heaven and swore by Him who lives forever and ever who created heaven and the things that therein are, and the earth and the things that therein are, and the sea and the things that are in it, THAT WOULD BE NO MORE TIME , but in the days of the voice of the seventh angel, when he shall begin to sound, the mystery of God should be finished , as he hath declared to his servants the prophets.

"What will be the remaining mystery finished?
Obviously, we are talking about the mystery of the gospel, which is being announced completion. This mighty angel is the VOICE CONTROL, THE VOICE OF THE ARCHANGEL, announcing that when sounding the seventh trumpet, will close the door to the Gentiles.

1st Thessalonians 4:16 declares that the Lord Jesus Christ "... WITH VOICE CONTROL, VOICE OF THE ARCHANGEL, AND WITH TRUMPET OF GOD, descend from heaven ...".
This trumpet of God we hear sound in Revelation 11 : 15: "And the seventh angel sounded: And there were loud voices in heaven , saying, The kingdoms of this world are becoming

to our Lord and of His Christ, and He shall reign forever and ever". **This will not happen without first gospel has been preached to the inhabitants of the earth , as we read in Revelation 14:6.** "I saw flying through the midst of heaven, another angel , having the everlasting gospel to preach to the inhabitants of the earth , to every nation, kindred, tongue". **This is precisely what we are talking about Matthew 24:14.**

We can conclude , then, that the gentile church will not be lifted until THE LAST TRUMPET sound that announced as we saw in Revelation 10:7 and shall sound in Revelation 11:15; this will be after the 7 seals are opened and the first 6 trumpets sound, and the play of the 7th trumpet, at the beginning of his sound, the gentile church is going with Jesus Christ.

The kingdoms of this world will become of Jesus Christ, and Satan will have only partial control over the planet. It's the time of commencement of the wrath of God upon the inhabitants of the earth. (Revelation 11:15).

G. <u>WHEN WILL THE CHURCH BE LIFTED?</u>

1. 1st Thessalonians 5:3 "<u>... when they shall say, Peace and safety</u>, then sudden destruction cometh upon them, as travail upon a woman with child, and they shall not escape". When they say peace and safety come the day of the Lord is speaking as the apostle, in the preceding verses, it is the rapture of the church.

2. 1st Thessalonians 4:13-18: "But we would not, brethren, concerning them which are asleep, lest you sorrow as others who have no hope. For if we believe that Jesus died and rose again, even so God will bring with Him those who sleep in Jesus. For this we say unto you in the words of the Lord, that we who are alive, who are left until the coming of the Lord shall not prevent them which are asleep. For the Lord himself with a shout, with the voice of an angel, and with God's trumpet, will descend from heaven and the dead in Christ shall rise first. Then we who are alive, who are left, shall be caught up together with them in the clouds to meet the Lord in the air: and so shall we ever be with the Lord. Therefore comfort one another with these words".

• Now we know perfectly well that Israel start peace when signing the peace treaty that the Antichrist will offer between Israel and the world. This peace treaty will be broken after three and a half years of being signed when the antichrist sits in the temple.

• Israel peace will last three and a half years and, during this period, they will be saying: "We are in peace and security " "We live in peace and safety".

• **This is the first clue that this time,** the Lord Jesus will raise the gentile church.

• **As it says in 1st Thessalonians 5:4, we are not in darkness, that that day should overtake us as a thief.**

3. 1st Thessalonians 5:9: "For God hath not appointed us to wrath, but to obtain salvation through our Lord Jesus Christ". For God did not appoint us to wrath, **this is the second clue.** The wrath of God begins when the Antichrist sits in the temple to end the seventh bowl of wrath. (Daniel 11:36). **Then, before the start of the wrath of God, the gentile church will be raised,** that is, in the middle of the 70th week of Daniel.

4. 2nd Thessalonians 2: 1-3

2:1 "Now concerning the coming of our Lord Jesus Christ and our being gathered to him, we beseech you, brethren, 2:2 that you not be quickly shaken from your composure or be troubled, neither by spirit, nor by word, nor by letter as from us, in the sense that the day of the Lord is near. 2:3 Let no man deceive you by any means: for that day shall not come, except there come a falling away first, and that man of sin revealed, the son of perdition".

There is a false teaching theory that what will come when they show the man of sin and apostasy is: The Lord's Day. This belief is contrary to the Bible for several reasons:

A. The Bible says in **1st Thessalonians 4:13-17** that the Lord Jesus will raise up the gentile church, and according to **1st Thessalonians 5:2,** this will happen on the day of the Lord. Now, **1st Thessalonians 5:3** tells us that when they say peace and safety, is when the Lord's Day will. We know that in the first three and half years, the people of Israel are saying, "We are finally at peace and we have safety". The key of the exact moment of the beginning of the day of the Lord is when sudden destruction comes upon them. When will this happen? According to **Matthew 24:15, Daniel 9:27, 11:31 and 12:11,** this will happen in the middle of the 70th week of Daniel.

B. In a very clear way, **2nd Thessalonians 2:1-3** tells us that the coming of the Lord Jesus Christ to raise the gentile church will be on the Lord's day and this will not happen until it manifests as the wicked antichrist.

C. The day of the Lord will be conducted in three phases: in the middle of the 70th week of Daniel, at the end of the 70th week of Daniel and after the millennium.
(There is a deeper study of the Day of the Lord later in this book).

D. According to **1st Thessalonians 4:13-18 and 5:1-4; 2nd Thessalonians 2:1-3,** the Lord's day begins with the rising of the gentile church, and meeting the Lord Jesus Christ in the clouds.

2nd Thessalonians 2:2: " ... the day of the Lord is near"; 2:3 : " ... will not come in there come a falling away first ..."

(what apostasy? : Matthew 24:9-10 , Matthew 10: 16-25). Also must be manifested before or coming to know the man of sin, the son of perdition.

When will be the antichrist revealed as a man of sin, and as a son of perdition? When he sit in the temple of God will be known as a man of sin and son of perdition; also that is the one which is lost or predestined for this position. (John 17:12).

But when exactly will the lifting of the gentile church be? The key verse in 2nd Thessalonians 2:3.

The Bible clearly tells us that when he is known to be the false Messiah as wicked then the gentile church will be lifted. (2nd Thessalonians 2:1-3). This will happen in the middle of the 70th week of Daniel.

At the beginning of the three and half years of the seventieth week of Daniel when signing the peace treaty, the wicked will be revealed as the Messiah, the Redeemer, the man of peace, The saviour in the world. (Daniel 11:21 And in his estate shall stand as vile they shall not give the honour of the kingdom. He shall come without warning and obtain the kingdom by flatteries).

In the second half, he will be known as the evil one and will remove the mask of kindness and display it as it is: The Wicked. This will happen when he sits in the temple that the Jews have built in Jerusalem to sacrifice and worship God, with the permission and approval of the antichrist.

SUMMARY : 1st Thessalonians 5:1-3 The Day of the Lord will come when they say peace and safety , which will be during the 70th week of Daniel, in that day will come sudden destruction, better known as: "The Desolating Abomination". (Daniel 9: 27, 11:31, 12:11 and Matthew 24:15).

Now, The Lord's Day will not come BEFORE the man of sin is shown, the son of perdition and come falling away (2nd Thessalonians 2:1-3), this leads us to conclude that the Day of the Lord , will be the beginning of Wrath of God, which we all know is half of the 70th week of Daniel.

It is also necessary to clarify that the gentile church cannot be the one that stops the expression of the wicked, because the Bible clearly teaches that 1st the wicked is shown and 2nd the gentile church is lifted.
(2nd Thessalonians 2:1-3 and 7-8).

THE SIGNAL THAT COMMENCES THE DAY OF THE LORD WILL BE THE LIFTING OF THE GENTILE CHURCH.

WHY? "The Bible is clear when it says that God has not put the gentile church to go through his wrath, by referring to the 7 bowls of God's wrath that will be poured in the middle of the 70th week of Daniel".
(1st Thessalonians 5:9, Revelation Chapters 15 and 16).

H. THE COMING OF THE LORD JESUS CHRIST TO LIFT THE CHURCH

As it is so important to make clear this issue of lifting the church, and since there are so many erroneous theories based purely on feelings, emotions, senses and reasoning, that followed concepts and traditions, but have left aside the word of God and his profound teachings contained in each of the passages of the Bible, that all perfectly clear to us concerning this matter. We then delve into the subject.

Many do not want to go through the part of the great tribulation called Satan's wrath; based on deductions, trepidation and fears of being trampled, abused, tortured and killed by the Antichrist and his followers. Then make guesses as: Noah was warned and escaped the flood; Lot was warned and escaped death in the destruction of Sodom and Gomorrah; likewise the church will be alerted and rid of the great tribulation. **They think:** What husband would like his wife to receive abuse and harm before marriage? Whose parents want their children to fail? **Imagine:** That John saw from above the vision underneath because he was not suffering. They wonder how is it that such a good God will allow his beloved church go through such suffering?.
(As if the brothers of the early church had not been abused, beaten, tortured and killed under horrible conditions).

We can think this way, but the Bible is not based on traditions, emotions, conjecture, or is influenced by feelings or senses. The word of God teaches us that we must be tested like gold; that before death or torture it will be known who is the real Christian; that there is nothing new under the sun, what once was, it will be later. This good God has commanded to kill children, pregnant women and babies in the past. Not because God be evil; but because he knew that those people were bad and would continue being bad and doing bad things; and even their children would grow up and would become bad. (1st Samuel 15:2-3, 1st Peter 1:7, Matthew 24:9, 1st Thessalonians 1:6, Revelation 7:14 and 20:4, Matthew 24:13, Ecclesiastes 1:9).

15:2-3 Thus saith the LORD of hosts: 'I will punish what Amalek did to Israel in opposing them on the way when he came up from Egypt. 3 Go and smite Amalek, and utterly destroy all that they have, and not spare them, but kill man and woman, infant and suckling, ox and sheep, camel and ass.

1:7 Because faith is like gold: their quality must be tested by fire. The faith that stands the test worth more than gold, which can be destroyed. So your faith, being well proven, merit praise, glory and honour when Jesus Christ appears.

24:9 Then they will deliver you up to abuse them, and kill them, and everyone will hate you because of me.

1:6 You became imitators of us and of the Lord, having received the word in much affliction, with joy of the Holy Spirit.

7:14 And I said: Lord, thou knowest. And he said these are they which came out of great tribulation, and have washed their robes and made them white in the blood of the Lamb.

20:4 And I saw thrones, and they sat upon them, and judgment was given, and I saw the souls of them that were beheaded for the witness of Jesus and for the word of God, and which had not worshiped the beast or his image and had not received his mark on their foreheads or their hands: and they lived and reigned with Christ a thousand years.

24:13 But he who endures to the end shall be saved.

1:9 What was it? The same will be. What has been done?
The same will be done, and there is nothing new under the
sun.

**There is a stream that has risen lately, it seems very
reasonable, but which lacks the truth. I must clarify then,
this theory, which can be confusing to readers of the
Bible.**
2nd Thessalonians 2:1-8: Now concerning the coming of
our Lord Jesus Christ and our being gathered to him, we
implore you, brothers,
2 that you not be quickly shaken from your composure or be
disturbed either by a spirit, nor by word, nor by letter as
from us, in the sense that the day of the Lord is near.
3 Let no man deceive you by any means: for that day shall
not come, except there come a falling away first, and that
man of sin revealed, the son of perdition,
4 who opposes and exalts himself above all that is called
God or that is worship, so that he sitteth in the temple of
God, proclaiming himself to be God.
5 Do you not remember that when I was still with you I told
you this?
6 And now ye know what restrains him, so that in due time
manifest.
7 For already the mystery of iniquity, only he who now
restrains will do so until he is taken out of the way.
8 And then shall that Wicked be revealed, whom the Lord
shall consume with the spirit of his mouth, and shall destroy
with the brightness of his coming.

**According to this thesis, when speaking in 2nd
Thessalonians 2:1 of the coming of our Lord Jesus Christ**

and our being gathered to him, these would be two completely different events. We also conclude that verses 2 and 3 explain that the day of the Lord is the one who will not come until the apostasy comes first and the man of sin revealed , the son of perdition; They discuss that in no way do these verses refer to the coming the Lord Jesus Christ to raise the church.

To support this theory rely on Titus 2:13 where it says: Looking for that blessed hope, and the glorious appearing of our great God and Saviour Jesus Christ. **According to believes blessed hope is one thing, and glorious is another.** Then the blessed hope is equal to our meeting with the Lord Jesus Christ, and the glorious, is equal to the coming of the Lord Jesus Christ or the Lord's day.

Another situation to consider is that as you coach them; the coming of the Lord Jesus Christ spoken of here is not to raise the church; because the parousia that the Bible says it's early, expect it soon, it may be right now; whereas here the verse says that the coming of the Lord Jesus Christ is not close.

They teach that the Lord's day have signs, but our meeting with him, are NOT signals.

Moreover he said in verse 7, what prevents the manifestation of the wicked or antichrist is the Holy Spirit working in the church, but that when the time is out of the way the Holy Spirit and the church along with it.

<u>Given all these theories, we then put things in order; broken down one by one all the points, so that everything is clear:</u>

1. To have a correct view of this text we will take a more accurate translation, for the King James translation is very inaccurate as we all know.

2nd Thessalonians 2:1-8: Now, brethren, concerning the coming of our Lord Jesus Christ and our being gathered to him, we ask you easily change that way of thinking nor be frightened by **anyone who claims to have had a revelation of Spirit, or received a teaching given by word or by letter, according to which we would have <u>said that the day of the return of the Lord is here.</u>**
3 Do not be misled in any way. Well before that day must come rebellion against God, when will the evil man, who is doomed to destruction.
4 This is the enemy that stands against everything that bears the name of God or deserves to be worshiped, and he even set his throne in the temple of God, showing himself that he is God.
5 Do you not remember that I told them about this when I was still with you?
6 And now you know what restrains from appearing before their due time.
7 For the mystery of lawlessness plan is already in place, just need to be out of the way which is stopping now.
8 And will that wicked, whom the Lord Jesus will destroy with the breath of his mouth and reduced to impotence when he returns in all its glory.

We can clearly see in this translation, the apostle was exhorting regarding the coming of the Lord Jesus Christ, do not be deceived by those who said that the Lord's coming had already occurred . This is very different from the King James Version, which translates to the Lord's coming is near.

The confusion was presented by those in Thessalonica thought that the coming of Christ had already occurred and that they had been left. This is due to the large number of fraudulent letters and books abounded at that time due to be forming the New Testament books. Another great deal said that the coming of the Lord Jesus Christ had already occurred because when the resurrected, the graves were opened and many of the saints resurrected, then that meant he and the dead in Christ had risen and as a result this was the coming of Lord Jesus Christ for the church, and he was still on earth, it was because he had run.

Matthew 27:52-53 And the graves were opened, and to many holy people who had died, came back to life. 53 They went out of their tombs after Jesus' resurrection, and went into the holy city of Jerusalem, where many people saw them.

2. The Bible speaks of the coming of the Lord Jesus Christ in three ways:

A. When it comes to raising the gentile church.
(1st Corinthians 5:5 and 15:22-24; 2nd Corinthians 1:14; Philippians 1:6; 1st Thessalonians 4:15 and 5:23; 2nd Thessalonians 2:1; 2nd Timothy 4 8; James 5:7-8; 2nd Peter 1:10-16).

5:5 that man shall be delivered unto Satan, that his body be destroyed and his spirit may be saved when the Lord comes.
15:22 And as in Adam all die, so in Christ all will have life.
23 But each one in the order that applies to you: God first, then when Christ returns, those who are his.
24 Then comes the end, when Christ defeats all dominions, authorities and powers, and delivered up the kingdom to God the Father.

1:14 as part of what we have understood, that when our Lord Jesus returns you will be proud of us, as we will be proud of you.

1:6 I am sure that God who began this good work in you will carry it on to completion until the day of Christ Jesus.

4:15 For this we say to you by the word of the Lord, that we, who are left alive until the coming of the Lord shall not precede those who have died.

5:23 May God himself, the God of peace, sanctify you entirely holy, and they may your whole spirit and soul and body blameless at the coming of our Lord Jesus Christ.

2:1 Now, brethren, concerning the coming of our Lord Jesus Christ and our being gathered to him, please.

4:8 Now for me the crown of righteousness which the Lord, the righteous judge, shall give me at that day. And I do not give only to me but also to all who lovingly await his coming in glory.

5:7 But you, brothers, be patient until the Lord comes. The farmer who hopes to collect the precious harvest, you have to wait patiently for the rainy season. 8 You also be patient and stand firm, because the Lord will return soon.

1:10 Therefore, brethren, since God has called and chosen, see that this root in you, because doing so will never fall. 11 Thus will be opened wide the gates of the eternal kingdom of our Lord and Saviour is why I continue Jesus Christ. 12 always remembering all this, even if you already know and stand firm in the truth that they have been taught. 13 While I live, I think I'm on duty to call your attention to these tips. 14 Our Lord Jesus Christ has told me that soon I will have to leave this life, 15 but I will do everything so that even after my death you will agree these things. 16 education we gave you the power and coming of our Lord Jesus Christ, was to cleverly invented stories, as with our own eyes we saw the Lord in his greatness.

B) When you return to the gentile church in the battle of Armageddon: (Malachi 3:2; 1st Thessalonians 3:13).

3:2 But who can endure the day of His coming? Who will then remain standing? Well come like a fire, to purify, will be like a soap that will remove our stains.
3:13 That made firm their hearts, holy and blameless before our God and Father when our Lord Jesus returns with all his holy people. Amen.

There are verses that speak of the two events at once: (Matthew 24:3, 2nd Thessalonians 2:8, 1st John 2:28).

24:3 Then they went to the Mount of Olives. Sitting down, Jesus and the disciples came to him to ask him privately, want you to tell us when it will happen this. What will signal your return and the end of the world?
2:8 And then shall appear that wicked, whom the Lord Jesus will destroy with the breath of his mouth and reduced to impotence when he returns in all its glory.
2:28 Now, little children, abide in Christ, so that when he appears we may have confidence and not feel ashamed in front of him when he comes.

C) When conducting the doomsday war after the millennium: (2nd Peter 3:10).

3:10 But the day of the Lord will come like a thief. Then the heavens will be undone with a loud noise, the elements will be destroyed by fire, and earth, with all that is therein, shall be subject to God's judgment.

3. Titus 2:13 Looking for that blessed hope, and the glorious appearing of our great God and Saviour Jesus Christ. (King James translation).

2:13 while we wait for the happy fulfilment of our hope: the glorious return of our great God and Saviour Jesus Christ. (New Living Translation).

Apart from Titus 2:13 The verses that speak of the manifestation or appearance of the Lord Jesus Christ, are: (Luke 17:29-30, 1st Corinthians 1:7-8, 2nd Timothy 4:1, 2nd Thessalonians 1:7, 1st Peter 1:7 and 13; 1st John 2:28, 1st John 3:2).

17:29-30 but when Lot went out of Sodom it rained fire and brimstone, and all died. 30 This is the day when the Son of man appears.
1:7 Thus do not lack any spiritual gift of God while waiting for the day when our Lord Jesus Christ appears. 8 God will keep you strong to the end, so no one can blame them nothing when our Lord Jesus Christ returns.
4:1 Before God and Christ Jesus, who will come as King Glory to judge the living and the dead, I charge a lot.
1:7 and to you, the suffering, give them rest as well as to us. This will be in the day when the Lord Jesus appears with his mighty angels, coming from heaven in blazing fire.
1:7 Because faith is like gold: their quality must be tested by fire. The faith that stands the test worth more than gold, which can be destroyed. So your faith, being well proven, merit praise, glory and honour when Jesus Christ appears.
1:13 So be prepared and use your good judgment. Put all your hope in what God in his kindness to them will bring you when he is revealed.
2:28 Now, little children, abide in Christ, so that when he appears we may have confidence and not feel ashamed in front of him when he comes.
3:2 Beloved, we are God's children. And although it is not yet what we shall then know that when Christ appears we shall be like him, for we shall see him as he is.

We can clearly see in these texts speaks of the manifestation or appearance of the Lord Jesus Christ in three stages: When you come to raise the gentile church, when he comes with the angels and the gentile church to fight the battle of Armageddon and when it comes to war end of the world . In these verses we see that the glorious, also takes place when the Lord Jesus Christ comes to raise the gentile church, **therefore the glorious and blessed hope are part of a single event and in no way are two separate events.**

On the other side in that the coming of the Lord Jesus Christ and our being gathered to him, would also be two separate events, we can see that the Bible specifically teaches that these verses are part of a single event. <u>We conclude therefore that Titus 2:13 and 1st Thessalonians 2:1 is the same situation/event.</u>

Analyzing grammatically Titus 2:13 and 1st Thessalonians 2:1, we can realize that the two sentences to which we refer in these verses, carry a **(and),** which comes from the Greek, this **(and)** is a connective element and serves to adding, not to separate. But the followers of **this theory seek to use the (and) as a separator.** According to them "the blessed hope is an event, (and) the glorious is another event, perhaps because they have a **(and)** in the middle. Then by the same rule we conclude that, "Our great God is one **(and)** Our Saviour Jesus Christ is another" because they also separated by a **(and).** Accordingly the apostle Paul was waiting for these two events, even if they were to happen at the same time, as the verse says: <u>Looking for that blessed hope, and the glorious.</u>

Similarly, when the Bible says, "Now concerning the coming of our Lord Jesus Christ **(and)** our meeting with him" the two phrases are separated by one **(and)** this **(and)** does not separate , but on the contrary serves to unite otherwise when 2nd Thessalonians says, "And the same Jesus Christ our Lord, **(and)** God our Father , who loved us and gave us eternal comfort ... "then this would be referring to two" "Father and the son", when in fact one is talking about , as it not says: "and they loved us , and gave us life", but rather the **(and)** tells us that Jesus Christ is God our father. In this text St. Paul holds everything in one event or happening: "The Lord's Day", it suggests that in the two letters to the Thessalonians. **(See 1st Thessalonians 4:13-18 and 5:1; 2nd Thessalonians chapter 2).** The apostle was hoping it was the lifting of the church in his time, as we also hope it is in ours, and as we await those who come after us if the Lord has not yet come.

If we grammatically clarify these texts, we also come to the same conclusion: Titus 2:13 and 1st Thessalonians 2:1 refer to one and the same event, the coming of the Lord Jesus Christ to raise the gentile church.

4. We are used to hearing the preachers say: Today, in this moment the Lord Jesus Christ can come for his church, but the Bible doesn't say that anywhere. **The Lord Jesus Christ said:** Behold I come quickly, come quickly come and not say at this moment. Now if the Lord Jesus Christ were to come today, **this today on our watch, would be 1000 years in God's time**, if said to come within 12 hours, would be 500 years in God's clock, if said to come and , in this moment, this would be 5 days, 11 hours, 45 minutes and 7.5

seconds. (2nd Peter 3:8 Again, dear friends, do not forget that with the Lord one day is as a thousand years and a thousand years as one day). (Hosea 6:2 He will revive us after two days, on the third day rise again we may live before him). (Psalm 90:4 For a thousand years in your sight are like yesterday when it is past, and like a watch in the night).

When the Lord Jesus Christ comes now and at this moment, is when the person dies. Why? Because today we have life, we wake up dead tomorrow, now we are alive, then we do not know, because no one has purchased life. (Luke 12:19-20 Then I say: Dude, you have many goods laid up for many years, rest, eat, drink, be merry. 20 But God said: Thou fool, this night loses your life, and you have saved, who will own).

5. The Lord Jesus Christ left signs for the gentile church, so they wouldn't complained that they had not been warned, because if you notify yours before trial, for his coming as a thief not surprise us, so his arrival won't surprise us unaware, unnoticed. **No one knows the day or the hour, but we know the year and month, for the Bible declares and teaches.** (1st Thessalonians 4:15-17 and 5:1-4, 2nd Thessalonians 2:1-3, Matthew 24:32-33).

4:15-17 For this we say to you by the word of the Lord, that we, who are left alive until the coming of the Lord shall not precede those who have died. 16 For you will hear a shout, the voice of an archangel and the sound of the trumpet of God, and the Lord Himself will descend from heaven. And those who have died believing in Christ will rise first 17 then who are left alive will be caught up together with them in the clouds to meet the Lord in the air: and so we will be with the Lord forever.

5:1-4 **For dates and times, brethren, do not need to write**. 2 For you know very well that the day of the Lord's return will come when you least expect it, like a thief that comes in the night. 3 **When people say**, "Everything is peaceful and quiet", **then come suddenly upon them the destruction**, as they are the birth pangs of a woman who is pregnant, and cannot escape. 4 **But you, brethren, are not in darkness**, that the day of the return of the Lord overtakes you as a thief. 2:1-3 Now, brethren, concerning the coming of our Lord Jesus Christ and our being gathered to him, we ask two easily change that way of thinking nor be frightened by anyone who claims to have had a revelation of the Spirit, or have received a teaching given by word or by letter, according to which we would have said that the day of the return of the Lord is here. 3 Do not be misled in any way. **Well before that day must come rebellion against God**, when will the evil man, who is doomed to destruction. Learn 24:32-33 **this teaching of the fig tree:** When its branch becomes tender and puts forth its leaves, you realize that summer is already near. 33 In the same way, **when you see this, know that the Son of man is already at the door.**

At the time of the Great Tribulation possibly be one hour be a month, one day be a week and one hour, be one day. Why? Because time passes quickly. The anguish, distress and suffering will be so great, that a second will be crucial in life. We see this when we are going through great suffering great pain, a serious illness, time seems to be eternal, and a second seems like a day.

(Matthew 24:22 And except those days should be shortened, no flesh is saved: but for the elect's sake those days shall be shortened).

6. Do not get confused because the Bible speaks of the Lord's day as I explained that was carried out in three stages, and that begins with the lifting of the gentile church, it continues with the battle of Armageddon and ends with the War of the End the world. <u>**This day the Lord has signs and to start with the lifting of the church; therefore our meeting with him, also have signs, which are the same as the Lord's day.**</u>

furthermore the word of God exhorts us to watch out and be ready for our meeting with the Lord Jesus Christ, for if we are not watchful, if we are not careful, the Lord Jesus will also come as a thief and stay the gentile's church lifting. We see this in the parable of the 10 virgins in Matthew 25:1-13, and also more clearly in Revelation 3:2-3. (Wake up and strengthen the things that remain, but they are already about to die, for I have seen that you do not do perfect before my God. 3 Remember therefore the education you received, follow it and turn to God. If you do not wake up, will come to you like a thief, when you least expect it).

What does not have signs is the coming of the son of man, that will take place during the battle of Armageddon, when the Lord Jesus stands on the Mount of Olives and divides Israel into two. **This coming will be as a thief for the people of Israel, and let those who are passing this final stage of the great tribulation.** In this coming every eye will see him, but when this already here on earth.

(Matthew 24:30, 37 and 42-44; Revelation 1:7 and 16:14-16).

24:30 Then you will see in heaven the sign of the Son of man, and full of terror all peoples of the world will mourn, and they shall see the Son of man coming in the clouds of heaven with power and great glory. 37 As in the days of Noah, so shall it be also when the Son of Man returns. 42-44 Keep you awake, they do not know what day your Lord will come. 43 But know this, that if the master of the house had known at what time of night when the thief was coming, would have kept watch and would not let anyone get into your house to steal. 44 Therefore you also be ready, for the Son of Man will come when least expected. 1:7 Christ comes in the clouds! Everyone will see, even those who pierced him; and all the peoples of the world will mourn for him. Yes, amen. 16:14-16 They were spirits of devils, working miracles and made out to gather all the kings of the world for the battle of the great day of God almighty. 15 Look, I come as a thief. Blessed is he who stays awake and keeps his clothes, lest he walks naked and they see the shame of their nakedness. "16 And the kings together to the place that in Hebrew is called Armageddon".

Neither has signs the Lord's day in its third phase, during the war of the end of the world.
(Matthew 24:29 and 42-44, 2nd Peter 3:10-13).

24:29 As soon as you spend those days of suffering, the sun will be darkened, the moon will not give its light, the stars will fall from heaven and the heavenly forces tremble.

42-44 Keep you awake, they do not know what day your Lord will come.

43 But know this, that if the master of the house had known at what time of night when the thief was coming, would have kept watch and would not let anyone get into your house to steal.

44 Therefore you also be ready, for the Son of Man will come when least expected.

3:10-13 But the day of the Lord will come like a thief. Then the heavens will be undone with a loud noise, the elements will be destroyed by fire, and earth, with all that is therein, shall be subject to the judgment of God.

11 Since everything will be destroyed in this way, with holiness and devotion how you should live.

12 Wait for the arrival of the day of God and to endeavour to hasten it. That day the heavens will be destroyed by fire, and the elements will melt in the flames;

13 but we hope the new heaven and the new earth which God has promised, in which everything will be just and good.

7. With respect to who it is that prevents the manifestation   of the Antichrist as wicked , for the Bible we learn that it prevents is the Due Time. In other words that the manifestation of the antichrist stops as wicked , is the order of events that since God in his infinite omniscience is pre -set.

This point is clearly explained in the chapter: DUE TIME.

I. DUE TIME

The Bible clearly teaches in 2nd Thessalonians, chapter two, before the coming of the Lord Jesus Christ to raise the gentile church, it must come a falling away first, and has to manifest the Antichrist as wicked. Today, we are using the brand of antichrist (bar codes), we know the number of the Antichrist (666), we can say that is the mystery of iniquity, but the antichrist itself has not appeared, has not been revealed, we do not know his name, and he will manifest when signing the peace treaty with Israel for a period of seven years, from then on, will begin his reign.

Look at 2nd Thessalonians 2: 6-8:

6 And now you know what restrains him, so that in **Due Time** manifest.

7 Because it is the mystery of iniquity, only he who now restrains will do so until he is taken out of the way.

8 "And then shall that Wicked be revealed, whom the Lord shall consume with the spirit of His mouth and destroy with the brightness of his coming ..."

Most interpreters have imagined that when the Bible tells us: "And now you know what restrains him, so that in due time be revealed", this means that the gentile church is what is preventing manifest the Antichrist, others say the Holy Spirit working in the gentile church prevents it. But really is not the gentile church, nor the Holy Spirit which prevent it. He who prevents the wicked manifestation of the antichrist is the DUE TIME, in other words, the order of events that God has prescribed.

Let's analyze this passage in the light of other texts of the Bible:

* Revelation 10:6 : "And sware by him that liveth forever and ever , who created heaven and the things that therein are, and the earth and the things that therein are, and the sea and the things that are in it , that time would be no more".

* Revelation 6:11: "And they were given a white robe and told to rest a little time, while until they complete the number of their fellow servants and brothers who were to be killed as they".

* Revelation 1:3: "Blessed is he who reads and those who hear the words of this prophecy, and keep those things which are written therein: for the time is near".

* 1st John 2:18: "Little children, it is the last time: and as ye have heard that antichrist shall come, even now are there many antichrists, whereby we know that is the last time".

* 1st Peter 1:11: "Searching what , or what manner of time the Spirit of Christ which was in them , when it testified beforehand the sufferings of Christ and the glories that would follow".

* 1st Peter 1:5: "Who are kept by the power of God through faith for a salvation ready to be revealed in the last time".

* 1st Thessalonians 5:1: "But of the times and the seasons, you need not, brethren, that I write unto you".

* 2nd Timothy 1:9 "Who hath saved us and called us with an holy calling , not according to our works, but according to

his own purpose and grace which was given us in Christ Jesus before time began".

* 2nd Timothy 3:1: "But know this, that in the last days perilous times shall come".

* Titus 3:3: "For we ourselves also were sometimes foolish, disobedient, deceived, enslaved to various lusts and pleasures, living in malice and envy, hateful, and hating one another".

* Hebrews 9:9: "Which was a figure for the time then present, in which were offered both gifts and sacrifices can not perfect, in terms of consciousness, the worshiper".

* Hebrews 9:10: "but deal only with food and drink, various washings, regulations for the body imposed until the time of reformation".

* 1st Peter 1:5: "Who are kept by the power of God through faith for a salvation ready to be revealed in the last time".

* 1st Peter 1:17 "And if you invoke as Father the one who without partiality judges according to each one's work, conduct yourselves in fear during the time of your exile".

* 1st Peter 2:10: "At one time you were not God's people, but now you are his people; at one time you did not know God's mercy, but now you have received his mercy".

* 1st Peter 3:5: "For this is the manner in the old time the holy women who trusted in God, being submissive to their husbands".

* 1st Peter 3:20 "Which sometime were disobedient, when once the longsuffering of God waited in the days of Noah ...

* 1st Peter 4:2: "not to live the remaining time in the flesh to the lusts of men, but according to the will of God".

* 1st Peter 4:3: "For the time past suffice for doing what the Gentiles living in debauchery, lust, drunkenness, orgies, carousing and detestable idolatry".

* 2nd Peter 3:5: But they deliberately forget that in ancient times were made by the word of God the heavens existed and the earth was formed out of water and in the water:

* 1st John 2:18 : "Little children, it is the last time: and as ye have heard that antichrist is coming, even now many antichrists have come, by this we know that is the last time".

* Revelation 11:18: "... and the time to judge the dead, and for rewarding your servants the prophets and your saints and those who reverence your name, both small and great, and to destroy the which destroy the earth".

* Ephesians 1:10: "to unite all things in Christ, in the dispensation of the fullness of times, both which are in heaven, and which are on earth".

* Ephesians 2:13: "But now in Christ Jesus you who once time were far off have been brought near by the blood of Christ".

* Ephesians 5:8: "For you were once time darkness, but now I am   light in the Lord: walk as children of light".

* Ephesians 2:11 "Wherefore remember, that ye being in time past Gentiles in the flesh, ye were called uncircumcised by the hand called the Circumcision made in the flesh".

* Galatians 6:9: "So let us not become tired in doing good; for it we do not give up, the time will come when we will reap the harvest".

* Galatians 4:4 "But when the fullness of time, God sent his Son, born of woman, born under the law".

* 2nd Corinthians 6:2: "For he saith in acceptable time I heard you, and in the day of salvation I helped you. Now is the acceptable time, behold now is the day of salvation".

* Romans 16:25: "And that you according to my gospel and the preaching of Jesus Christ according to the revelation of the mystery, which was hidden for long ages in the past".

* Romans 5:6: "For Christ, while we were yet without strength, in due time Christ died for the ungodly".

* Acts 17:30: "But God, having overlooked the times of ignorance, now he commands all men everywhere to repent"

* Acts 7:17: "But when the time approaches for the promise, which God had sworn to Abraham, the people grew and multiplied in Egypt".

* Acts 3:19 "Repent therefore and be converted, that your sins may be blotted out, that they come from the presence of the Lord times of refreshing".

* Luke 21:24: "And they shall fall by the sword, and shall be led away captive into all nations: and Jerusalem shall be trodden down of the Gentiles, until the times of the Gentiles are fulfilled. The "times of the Gentiles" are the three years in which the Gentiles will trample the Holy City.

* Titus 1:2-3: "in hope of eternal life, which God, that cannot lie, promised before the world began, and in due times manifested his word through the preaching with which I was entrusted by command of God our Saviour".

REFLEXIONS, DUE TIME:

He who gave himself to liberate all, of which was to be testified in due time. (1st Timothy 2:6). But when the time had fully come, God sent his Son, born of woman, born under the law.(Galatians 4:4).

**Thus we see that everything has its Due Time:
The testimony of the sacrifice of Jesus, the word of the gospel and of course, the revelation of the lawless.**

Everything has its Time. Ecclesiastes 3:11 says, "He has made everything beautiful in its time, and has put eternity in their heart, yet so that man can find out the work that God makes from the beginning to the end".

* **2nd Thessalonians 2:6-7:** "To be revealed at the proper time the mystery of iniquity must be out of the way: "what is restraining"; "...who now restrains will do so until he in turn is out of the way".

You know what stops him in results of the due time to manifest.

"What stops you" = What is holding him back?
The Due Time.

"Who stops him now in the present?
The Due Time has not come.

"Who is who is to be taken out of the way?"
The Due Time should be out of the way.

When is the proper Time?
When the Fullness of the Gentiles enter to the Church.
When the mystery of God is consummated; when
apostasy is revealed and made known the antichrist as
wicked; It is then and only then arrived, "Due Time".

* 2nd Thessalonians 2:7: "doth already work the mystery of
iniquity, only that now dominates, dominate until he be
taken". (From the midst = "Gone in between"); him be
removed from in between (the one or he who is hindering).

2nd Thessalonians 2:6 Due Time= Kairos = Time God.
Kairos = "time of opportunity". An opportunity for
what? For Salvation of the gentile church.

The time of the gentile church will be out of the way:
(Revelation 12:6-7 and Matthew 24:14).

Only until they show the man of chaos is to be lifted the
gentile church. When is this? In the initial three and half
years of great tribulation he will manifest as "Christ",
"Messiah", "Saviour", in the final three and half years, it
will be as it really is: The son of perdition and sin man .
When you discover the face and sit in the temple claiming to
be God, is when it will be released as wicked.
(2nd Thessalonians 2:8).

85

1) The Holy Spirit cannot be the one that prevents the manifestation of antichrist.

2nd Thessalonians 2:7-8 For the mystery of lawlessness plan is already in place and only needs to be out of the way which is stopping now. 8 And will that wicked, whom the Lord Jesus will destroy with the breath of his mouth and reduced to impotence when he returns in all its glory.

Many have speculated on who it is that prevents the wicked from being revealed, among all views is this that is preventing the Holy Spirit working in the church, but this is out of the way, and goes along with the church. They also comment that the Holy Spirit within the believer now, but it was not always so, and before grace in the believer operated momentarily, when he was acting on it. (David, Samson, Gideon, etc).

According to this reasoning and when it will be out of the way the Holy Spirit and go along with the church, you are acting on again believer.

This hypothesis seems reasonable, but it is not the truth, and it is not truth for the following Biblical objections:

A. According to the Bible for the Holy Spirit to come to the believer, it first had to go the Lord Jesus.
John 16:7 But I tell you the truth: It is better for you that I go away. Because if I do not go, the supporter will not come to be with you, but if I go, I will send him.

In the same way that the Holy Spirit could not come until the Lord Jesus goes to Heaven, then the Holy Spirit cannot go to heaven, until the Lord Jesus comes to earth again.

Why? Because a manifestation must be present on the ground to operate, guide and teach the believer.
The Bible tells us that when the Lord Jesus Christ comes to raise the gentile church, He will only come to the air (possibly a part of the atmosphere called the ionosphere), but his feet will not touch the ground. The second time that the Lord Jesus will be here on the planet his feet will land on the Mount of Olives and split the land in two, and this will happen at the beginning of the battle of Armageddon , during the pouring of the seventh bowl of the wrath of God at the end of the 70th week of Daniel .

Zechariah 14:4 On that day the Lord will place His feet on the Mount of Olives, which is before Jerusalem, to the eastern side on a large valley, which will run from east to west, will be divided into two Mount of Olives. One half of the mountain shall move toward the north and the other half southward. (See also Revelation chapter 19).

The Lord Jesus will be with the Jewish/Gentle church ruling for 1000 years here on earth, and in that time the Holy Spirit will be in heaven.

After the millennium, Satan will spend many years convincing nations to destroy Israel.

Here invasion of Gog and Magog and his followers will also occur, the destruction of Damascus and the war of the end of the world.

Revelation 20:7-10 When the thousand years have passed , Satan shall be loosed out of his prison, 8 And shall go out to deceive the nations in the four corners of the earth , Gog and Magog, whose armies are as numerous as the sand of the sea, gather for battle. 9 and they ascended by the breadth of the earth and surrounded the camp of the saints, and the city he loves. But fire came down from heaven and devoured them completely. 10 And the devil, who deceived them, was thrown into the lake of fire and brimstone where the monster had been dumped and the false prophet. They will be tormented day and night forever and ever.

In this time of course the Lord Jesus and the gentile church will be in heaven again, while the Holy Spirit is on earth guiding all unto truth the nations who shall be saved in this terrible war.

2nd Peter 3:10-13 But the day of the Lord will come like a thief. Then the heavens will be undone with a loud noise, the elements will be destroyed by fire, and earth, with all that is therein, shall be subject to the judgment of God. 11 Since everything will be destroyed in this way, with holiness and devotion how you should live 12 Wait for the arrival of the day of God and to endeavour to hasten it. That day the heavens will be destroyed by fire , and the elements will melt in the flames; 13 but we hope the new heaven and the new earth which God has promised, in which everything will be just and good.

Revelation 21:24 And the nations shall walk by its light, and the kings of the earth bring their glory and honour into it.

B. The Holy Spirit is the one who leads all truth and is picked up along with the gentile church, who will lead the truth of the gospel to the Jews? If it only comes temporarily to the believer, these will go from fall to fall as the people of Israel in ancient times, as the Holy Spirit took them only on special occasions and will not be for everyone, but for a few, as in the cases in the old Testament.

C. The Holy Spirit is the one who gives the power to not deny the Lord Jesus Christ even in persecution, torture or death. If the Holy Spirit is going along with the gentile church in the rapture and it is only for the believer, for a short time, temporary and on a selected few, then 90% of the world's population who stays in the great tribulation will not have entry into the kingdom of God, will receive the mark of the beast and refuse Jesus, **why?** Because they are cowards, they will fear, panic, have terror of losing their lives or those of their loved ones for the testimony of Jesus Christ.

The Bible on the other hand claims that many will give their lives for the gospel, at this time.

Revelation 20:4 And I saw thrones, and they sat upon them, and judgment was given, and I saw the souls of them that were beheaded for the testimony of Jesus and for the word of God, and which had not worshiped the beast or its image and had not received his mark on their foreheads or their hands: and they lived and reigned with Christ a thousand years.
2nd Timothy 1:7 For God has not given us a spirit of fear, but of power and of love and of a sound mind.

Finally, the Lord Jesus Christ promised to be with His followers every day until the end of the world, which will occur after the millennium; obviously not be in flesh but in the Spirit.

Matthew 28:20 Teaching them to observe all things whatsoever I have commanded you: and lo, I am with you

always, even unto the end of the world. Amen.
John 14:16-17 And I will pray the Father, and he shall give you another Comforter, that he may abide with you forever. 17 the Spirit of truth, whom the world cannot receive, because it seeth him not, neither knoweth him: But you know Him because He abides with you and will be in you.

2) The church cannot be what stops it either because it would be contrary to the Bible and the Apostle Paul. Why? 2nd Thessalonians 2:3 says that the church will be lifted until the wicked one will be revealed.

2nd Thessalonians 2:7 says that when it stops only be lifted or removed until then the wicked one will be revealed.

So how is it? Is the church taken from earth so the wicked manifests or the unrighteous one emerges first and is then the gentile church is lifted?

Logically, it is as the Bible says: **The wicked is manifested and disclosed as a son of perdition or man of sin and then the gentile church is lifted.**

When is the gentile church lifted, or somewhat, when will the time of salvation for the Gentiles end?
When you have entered the fullness of the Gentiles (Romans 11:25) and they have been added to the gentile church those who are determined to be saved. (Acts 2:47).

Conclusion: **The time of opportunity is removed for salvation for the gentile church. But also, the man of sin manifested and the church is lifted.
(2nd Thessalonians 2:3, 7, 8).**

J. <u>MULTITUDE IN WHITE ROBES</u>

* **Revelation 6:9** tells us that when he had opened the fifth seal, the apostle John saw under the altar the souls of them that were slain for the word of God and for the testimony which they held. After the four judgments on the earth and the four initial seals saints showed clamouring for his resurrection. In this cry, they were told that they should rest until all the numbers of their fellow servants and brothers who were to be killed as they were completed.

* **Revelation 7:9** on forward tells us about a multitude of white robes, of all nations and tribes and peoples and tongues. When asked: Who are they, and where did they come from? He answered: *"**These are they which came out of great tribulation**, and have washed their robes and made them white in the blood of the Lamb"*. Some claim that the correct translation is: "Which came out **of great tribulation**; explaining that this verse refers only to those who through the ages have suffered great tribulation. So where they are shown to have not suffered great tribulation? Are these not part of the church?. Thank God that the original translates, "have come out **of The Great Tribulation**".

* **Revelation 15:2 tells us:** *"I saw something like a sea of glass mingled with fire: and them that had gotten the victory over the beast and his image, his mark and the number of his name, stand on the sea of glass, having the harps of God"*. **This will take place in the interval between the sounding of the seventh trumpet and the beginning of the WRATH**

OF GOD. (Revelation 15:7 and 19:1-10).

* Who then is this multitude in white robes? The Bible clearly says in Revelation 7:14, Revelation 6:9 and Revelation 15:2.

1. These are those who came out of the Great Tribulation.

2. They have washed their robes and made them white in the blood of the Lamb. (Revelation 22: 14).

3. They are those who had been slain because of the word of God and for the testimony which they held.

4. They had to rest until the full number of their fellow servants and brothers who were to be killed as they were complete.

The reward for the one who endured till the end, without denying the gospel, those who were killed for their testimony of Jesus Christ and did not received the mark of the beast; these are finally standing on the sea of glass, having the harps of God. By this great victory over the beast, they are before the throne of God and also serve him day and night. (Revelations 3:4-5).

Conclusion: This crowd are the martyrs of the great tribulation, during the wrath of Satan (initial three and a half years of the 70th week of Daniel); They gave their lives for the sake of preaching the gospel of the name, which will form part of the Gentile church of Jesus Christ.

K. ALL FOR PEACE

The rise of idolatry began with a statue and ends with an image. (Daniel 2 and Revelation 13). History repeats itself. Previously this regime of seven years was given to the dictator of the world over every tribe, people, language and nation (Revelation 13:7). They named three things that are specifically placed in their hands: Christians, time and laws. (For a time, times and half a time, total three and a half years).

The Antichrist, in the first half of the 70th week of Daniel:

1. Made war with the saints and prevailed. (Daniel 7:21 and Revelation 13:7).

2. Shall wear out the saints of the Most High (Daniel 7:25).

3. (Daniel 11:33) *"And the wise men of the people shall instruct many, though for a time they will fall by sword and flame, by captivity and plundering"*.

4. (Daniel 11:35) And some of them of understanding shall fall, to refine and cleansed and made white, until the time of, because it is yet for a time appointed. This absolute power is given to the antichrist during the initial three and half years of the seventieth week of Daniel. Meanwhile, the world will enjoy peace and security; eating, drinking, buying, selling, planting, building. (Luke 17:26-30).
By contrast true Christians will be forced to live a secret life; tortured, stripped of their property, their family, and hunted like wild animals, all this happens when the gospel expand

throughout the world.

* The story chronicles the years 117 to 180 A. C. as the most peaceful period the world has experienced. Yet millions of Christians were being killed, after stripping them of their property, after mistreating them, after torturing them and being killed in the most horrific possible ways by the Roman Empire, ALL IN THE NAME OF PEACE . This new Caesar, presented by the renewed Roman Empire, destroyed many by surprise. (Daniel 8:25).
(Some translations say, **"For peace"**).

* **A U.S. president once said:**
"Sometimes war is justified to achieve peace".

* **Eduardo Galeano said:** "Wars always invoke noble motives , kill in the name of peace , in the name of God , in the name of civilization , in the name of progress , in the name of democracy and, in case, if such lie not reach , there are the mainstream media willing to invent imaginary enemies to justify the conversion of the world in a large mental hospital and an immense slaughter".

* *I wonder how long? How long the peace of the world will be in the hands of those who do the business of war?*

Conclusion: A powerful world leader said: "We are expecting a great leader who will bring world peace, and no matter if it comes from God or the devil, we are ready to receive it". What do these words suggest? Everything is ready for his possession, the only thing missing is ....the establishment. **When will that be? Only God knows.**

WHY IS THE CHURCH ERECTED IN MIDDLE OF THE SEVENTIETH WEEK OF DANIEL?

The 70th week of Daniel is divided into three and half years of the wrath of Satan and in three and half years of the wrath of God. Now, we must take into account certain significant aspects:

* God has promised to get rid of his anger.

* God never promised that we will be delivered from the wrath of Satan, on the other hand remember the holy Job suffered the full force of the wrath of the devil.

* Satan can touch the body of Christ, but can never touch their souls.

* Jesus always tells us that as He suffered, we too must and we have to suffer, if we preach like He preached.

* Satan afflicted the prophets, patriarchs, apostles, the early church and Jesus himself. How then, can we even consider that we will not be troubled?

* **There is not one verse in the Bible that tells me that the church will not be troubled.**

2nd Thessalonians 2:1-7: "Now concerning the avenue of our Lord Jesus Christ and our being gathered to him , we beseech you brethren, do not be quickly shaken from your composure or be troubled, neither by spirit, nor by word, nor by letter as from us, in the sense that the day of the Lord is near. Let no man deceive you by any means, it will not come, except there come a falling away first, and that man of sin revealed, the son of perdition, who opposes and exalts himself against all that is called God or that is worshiped; so that he sitteth in the temple of God, proclaiming himself to be God . Do you not remember that when I was still with you I told you this? And now you know what restrains him, so that in due time manifest. Because it is the mystery of iniquity, only he who now restrains will do so until he is taken out of the way".

* **The Apostle Paul suggests that the gentile church will be raised when the Jews say there is peace and security,** they are confident, they are relaxed, so sudden destruction cometh upon them, when you least expect it. **When will that be?** In the middle of the 70th week of Daniel, they had three and a half years living in peace. It is understandable that when you sign the peace treaty between Israel and the rest of the world, the Jews will not be confident, have misgivings, have your eyes open for any strange movement; but when they see that its real peace, who lasts weeks, months, years and no hostilities, strife, and rumours of wars, then and only then will they be confident.
(1st Thessalonians 4:13-18 and 5:1-3).

* **In 2nd Thessalonians 2:1-3, St. Paul confirms in a more solid way that the lifting of the gentile church will be in the middle of the 70th week of Daniel.** Here we are told HE WILL NOT COME until the Antichrist is pacifist remove the mask and be made known as wicked. This will happen when this man of sin sits in the temple rebuilt by the people of Israel and ask to be worshiped as God. As the

people of Israel refuses to worship, the antichrist begins a cruel persecution against them, which is known as the abomination of desolation and anguish of Jacob.
According to Daniel 9:27, Jeremiah 30:1-10 and Matthew 24:15-28; this will happen in the middle of the 70th week of Daniel.

 * The time of grace to the Gentiles ends and for the people of Israel, the time of grace begins.

* The opportunity of saving time ends for the Gentiles, and begins the time of opportunity for the people of Israel.

* The door closes to the revelation of the gospel to the Gentiles when his church is lifted, and opened for the people of Israel.

Let's look now a little about the government of the Antichrist:

The extreme wickedness of this world dictator will not be released until the inhabitants of the earth are in the middle of this period of seven years, when the Federation of the ten European nations, who hates the apostate world church; It has been formed by seven nations and himself Antichrist who will be the eighth. (Revelation 17:16).

In the first three years and a half the world dictator:

A. For the first time will receive a specific kingdom. He had risen from the ten European nations, but it is another, an eleventh king horn. These ten nations will give their power to him and becomes their leader.

(Revelation 17:11, 17; Daniel 7:8).

B. Destroy three of the 10 European Nations.
(Daniel 7: 7-8 and 19-20).

C. He is mortally wounded and miraculously healed by the false prophet. (Revelation 13: 3).

D. Delivers its power to the false prophet.
(Revelation. 13: 11-12).

E. This man makes war on the Gentile church and overcomes them. (Revelation 13: 5-7).

In the second three and a half years the world dictator:

A. Moves his capital to Jerusalem.
(Daniel 11:45, 2nd Thessalonians 2:4).

B. Invalidates the seven-year treaty to protect Israel.
(Daniel 9:27, 11:31).

C. He sits in the temple of Jerusalem and declares himself as God. (2nd Thessalonians 2:4).

D. Forbids Jews to sacrifice and deliver offerings to God.
(Daniel 9:27, 11:31).

E. Requires worship of the Jews, who were the only people on earth to that during the first three years and a half were not required to worship the beast or his image; but, under the treaty had been allowed to continue worshiping and sacrificing their God. **(Actually, this was part of the treaty that led them to sign it and convinced them that he was the messiah).**

When the great world dictator allied with the West, the other powers of the world are outraged. Southern contends with him, (Daniel 11:40). Observe how we are given specific time, "the time of the end, the king of the south". (The last, in Hebrew, means end of the order). The end, or over time, referring to the last three and half years where wars starts. **Daniel 11:32-35 tells us that the Jews will suffer severe persecution.**

Yes; they will through troubles, sword, captivity and plundering. **What for?** To test them, to purify, to whiten "until the end of times". (Exactly the same time in Hebrew). The tribulation of Jacob will last the first three and a half years thereafter, the wrath of God begins.

As North Federation and allies are against Israel in the middle of the week, the Jewish will experience in the last three and half years what Christians suffered in the first three years and a half: **Purification.** In the first period the Antichrist will be trying to destroy the gentile church (but only purify, because then will be known the true Christian). When Jesus Christ comes to raise the gentile church it will be without stain or wrinkle or no such thing, those who have lived in holiness to expose everything they have, including their lives for the gospel. In the last three and half years the Antichrist will make a last attempt to exterminate the Jews.

There will also be news that will cause this disorder. **The abomination in the middle of the week,** (This is the desecration of the temple in Jerusalem, speaking Daniel and Jesus in Daniel 9:27 and 11:28; Matthew 24:15; Ezekiel 7-10). Jews flee to a place that will have been provided in advance for them.

There are photographs of houses in caves dug in the mountain regions provided with food and everything for this occasion. Seems that only half of one third of the Jews living in Israel that escape from death. (Zechariah 13:8, 14:2).

What makes tribulation for Christians in the first three years and a half is preparing them to be lifted up to meet the Lord in the air. Jacob's affliction in the final three and a half will do the same for the few remaining Jews, preparing them to meet their true Messiah. (Zechariah 14:4-5).

In the last three and half years will be the wrath of God. The buying and selling will continue until the coming of our Lord Jesus Christ (Luke 17:26-30).
In the middle of the week, silver and gold will no longer have a value. (Zephaniah 1:18 confirms Ezekiel 7:19). Neither their silver nor gold can deliver them in the day of wrath of God.

In Ezekiel Chapters 7 and 8 God speaks and suggests that the end will come to the Jews and they will be punished for their abominations and wrong doings as well as their wrong ways. Although they cry out loudly, they will not be heard. Will begin the mandatory marking of the beast, or death by torture.

* **Romans 11:26, Acts 2:14-22** Peter told the Jews that every Israelite shall call upon the name of Jesus Christ in the time of Jacob's trouble will be saved.

* **Ezekiel 9:3-6** Speaks of a sign that will be placed on the foreheads of the men that sigh and cry for all the abominations that be done in the midst of Jerusalem, this signal corresponds to the seal or mark of the **144,000** of

Revelation 7:3, which takes place immediately after the gentile church is raised. Wars and the wrath of God begins. **The Lord Jesus Christ will come to the world as a thief in the night,** they will be buying, selling, giving into marriage, drinking and enjoying life according to them. But the gentile church will be summoned, will be announced and, for this will be prepared and ready, not living in the delights and pleasures that the world offers to go to meet the Lord Jesus Christ. (Lk 17:26-29; Mt 24:7; 1st Thess 5:1-4).

CONCLUSION:

1) **2nd Thessalonians 2: 1-3 confirms that the gentile church has to be on earth until the antichrist is revealed as a man of sin, as lawless one; what will happen when the Antichrist sits in the temple and ask to be worshiped as if was God.**

2) **2 Thessalonians 2: 7-8 clearly state that the Antichrist will not be manifest as lawless one, if not until when be out of the way, what restrain his manifestation.**

3) **First, it is out of the way which restrain the manifestation of the Antichrist as lawless one.**

Second, the Antichrist is manifested as lawless one.

Third, the gentile church is raised.

The gentile church will be erected in the middle of the 70th week of Daniel, as the prophets, evangelists and apostles confirm.

THE RESURRECTIONS

With regard to this issue it is necessary to clarify that there are five resurrections ranging from the ministry of Jesus, to trial before the great white throne. These five resurrections are divided into two groups called the first and the second resurrections.

First resurrection: This will take place in three phases.
A) First Phase: Here resurrect all the dead in Christ from the resurrection of Jesus, to complete the wrath of Satan.
B) Second Phase: Here resurrect all the dead since the lifting of the Gentile church, to complete the wrath of God.
C) Phase Three: Here they resurrect all the dead who lived in the millennium and were faithful to Jesus Christ and his doctrine; but obviously they had not risen in the previous two resurrections.

Second Resurrection: This will take place in two phases.
A) First Phase: Here resurrect all the dead from Adam to The War of the End of the World; but they had not been raised in the previous three resurrections. These will resurrected and will judged according to their works and according to them will be saved or condemned.
B) Second Phase: Here resurrect all the dead from Adam to The War of the End of the World; but they had not been raised in the four previous resurrections. These resurrected and judged according to whether or not his name was written in the book of life. Whoever was not found written is convicted.

As we can see, and as confirmed by the Bible, in each of

these resurrections will be saved. I also want to clarify that there was already a resurrection when Jesus was resurrected; but not taken into account within the two large groups of resurrections. Why? Simply because these died again and will have to return to resurrect in one of the five phases of future resurrections.

Now we are going to see them separately:

We could call this the **"Pre-Resurrection."**
Here resurrected many saints who had died probably during the ministry of Jesus and we can assumed this due to the words: "They appeared to many" this suggest that the people of that time knew them when they were alive; otherwise when the people saw them, people would not recognize them.

These saints died again; because the Bible does not record that they ascended to heaven with Jesus or at any other time. It shouldn't' surprised us that they died again as we see in the Bible many cases of people that were resurrected and then died again.

Elijah resurrected the widow's son; Elisha resurrected and even when they threw a dead man into his grave, this man resurrected; Jesus resurrected Lazarus; Paul resurrected Eutychus; Pedro resurrected Dorcas). All of these were resurrected, but died again, to be able to resurrect in their respective resurrection.
When the Lord Jesus was resurrected, the bible says that the tombs were opened and many saints were resurrected; **but this is neither part of the first, nor the second resurrection.** (Matthew 27:52-53).

52 and the graves were opened; and many bodies of the saints who had fallen asleep were raised; 53 and coming out of the graves after His resurrection, they went into the holy city and appeared to many.

According to Revelation 20: 4-6 the first resurrection is carried out in three phases:

1. First phase of the first resurrection: The resurrection of the "first fruits"; when the Lord Jesus comes to raise the church; here the dead in Christ will be resurrected and only the dead in Christ either by normal death or by killed, from the ministry of Jesus, until the lifting up of the church; that, as we already know, will be at the end of the wrath of Satan or in the middle of the seventieth week of Daniel. (1st Co 15:51-52; 1st Thess 4:13-17; Rev 6:9-11).

51 Behold, I tell you a mystery: We shall not all sleep, but we shall all be changed 52 in a moment, in the twinkling of an eye, at the last trumpet. For the trumpet will sound, and the dead will be raised incorruptible, and we shall be changed. 13 But I do not want you to be ignorant, brethren, concerning those who have fallen asleep, lest you sorrow as others who have no hope. 14 For if we believe that Jesus died and rose again, even so God will bring with Him those who sleep in Jesus. 15 For this we say to you by the word of the Lord, that we who are alive and remain until the coming of the Lord will by no means precede those who are asleep. 16 For the Lord Himself will descend from heaven with a shout, with the voice of an archangel, and with the trumpet of God. And the dead in Christ will rise first. 17 Then we who are alive and remain shall be caught up together with them in the clouds to meet the Lord in the air. And thus we shall always be with the Lord.

9 When He opened the fifth seal, I saw under the altar the souls of those who had been slain for the word of God and for the testimony which they held. 10 And they cried with a loud voice, saying, "How long, O Lord, holy and true, until you judge and avenge our blood on those who dwell on the earth?" 11 Then a white robe was given to each of them; and it was said to them that they should rest a little while longer, until both the number of their fellow servants and their brethren, who would be killed as they were, was completed.

2. Second phase of the first resurrection: takes place at the end of the seventieth week of Daniel and the beginning of the millennium. Here the people will resurrected from the lifting of the church, to the judgment to the nations. This covers the wrath of God or the three and a half final years of the seventieth week of Daniel. **This Jewish church will share with Jesus Christ and the Gentile church for the reign of a thousand years. will also participate the remnant alive, after the battle of Armageddon.**

* **In Revelation 20:4** John saw thrones, and they sat on them, and judgment was committed to them. Who are them and who will they judge? The Bible teaches that these are the Apostles and the Church; the ones that will judge the twelve tribes of Israel and the whole world during the millennium. (Mt 19:28 and 25:31; Ac 3:21; 1st Co 6:2-3; Rev 3:21).

*__John also saw__ the souls of those who were beheaded for the cause of the testimony of Jesus. Here will resurrect all of those that have died beheaded or because they gave testimony of Jesus during the wrath of God.
(Rev 11:7; 12:10-11 and 17; 19:10).

* __Others that saw John__ were beheaded for the cause of the word of God. These are the ones that preaching the gospel were killed during the wrath of God. (Rev 14:9-13 y 16:5-7).

* __We also found__ in this group, the ones that had not worshiped the beast or his image. Let's remember that during the wrath of God; the antichrist asks to be worship, and the false prophet command to worship the image of the false messiah. This will happen when this man of sin sits in the temple of God and will asks to be worship.
(2nd Thess 2:3-4; Rev 13:4,8 and 12-17).

* __Finally__ those who didn't receive the mark of the beast on their foreheads or in their hands will be resurrected. At the beginning of the great tribulation the mark of the beast was voluntary in exchange for power, wealth, welfare, etc. So that in this way deny voluntarily the Lord Jesus Christ; but in the final three and a half years, the mark will be mandatory; so either they will be marked or they will die, and this will not necessarily be a very pleasant death. (Rev 13:15-17 and 15:2).

* __Revelation 11:3 and 7-12__ show us the two witnesses __Enoch__ and __Elijah__ preaching the gospel throughout the period of the wrath of God, and at the end of this period are killed by the Antichrist, the one that together with the pagan nations don't allow the people to buried them; but after three and a half days God resurrected them and they ascend to heaven in a cloud. **We could say that this is a special resurrection.**

3. Third phase of the first resurrection: This is found in Revelation 20: 5 which will take place at the end of the millennium. The Bible identifies this as **"The Other Dead."** Who are these dead? These are those who came and lived in the millennium and they believed Jesus Christ obeying his precepts.

This can be deduced by the following reasons:

1] The verse says: "The rest of the dead live not again"; we know from the Bible that many of the dead of the judgment before the great white throne will not live again; but rise to die again; that's why it is called the second death. (Rev 20:5-6 y 14).

2] The resurrection from the judgment before the great white throne, takes place until after the war of the end of the world and this is many years after the millennium. (Rev 20:7-11).

* At this second phase of the first resurrection there will be no baptisms neither in water nor in spirit because the Lord Jesus Christ will be present in body, soul and spirit; meanwhile the Holy Spirit will be in heaven. (John 16:7 and 13).

The ones of this resurrection will obviously not take part in the government of the millennium.

<u>Finally we come to the last resurrection, the one about the judgment before the great white throne</u>.

Contrary to what they have taught us; in this last resurrection there will be saved individually and collectively.

(Dn 12:2; Jn 5:28-29; Rom 2:5-11).

As individuals the ones that are preaching the everlasting gospel at that time. As a nation will be salvation for those nations that didn't agree with Satan, the demons and other nations to destroy Israel. (Rev 14:6-7 and 21:24).

The Bible teaches that in this resurrection the dead and only the dead will be judge as follows:

1. First phase of the second resurrection:
According to their works: It is here where the nations that were not associated with this pagan trinity and also abstained from taking part in this war; these nations that possibly helped Israel in one or another way in the most critical moments; by this act, for such works; the judgment is favourable for them and that's why they are allowed to attend as guests to the wedding of the Lamb; although they will never live inside the new Jerusalem, but outside of it. These nations will have to come back once a year to worship Jesus Christ in the new Jerusalem or they will be punish. (Rev 20:11-13; 21:24 and 26; 22:2).

2. Second phase of the second resurrection: The name is sought in the book of life; and who is not enrolled in this book you will be cast into the lake of fire and brimstone, which is the second death. (Revelation 20:15).

* 1 Corinthians 15:22-24 summarized as follows the resurrections:

1] **Christ:** With the nice consequence of his resurrection, and that there were many saints who benefited from this event and also resurrected. (Mt 27:52-53).

2] **The first fruits:** This will be the ones that were resurrected in the lifting of the church. (Jas 1:18; 1st Thess 4:13-17).

3] **Those who are Christ's at his coming**: As we already saw these are divided into two groups: Those who rose immediately before the millennium and those who are resurrect once the millennium is finish. {When the Lord Jesus comes for the second time, and every eye will see him this will be to stay ruling the earth until the end of the millennium; his presence on earth will of course bring many benefits to both believers and unbelievers; in the same way for both alive or dead believers}. (Rom 20:4-6).

* **Then the end:** This one will be the true end of the entire ministry of Jesus Christ and will be when he judges at the great white throne pious and impious according to their works and only to the pious according if their name is inscribe in the book of life or not. This judgment will include every human being who has not risen in the previous resurrections. (1st Cor 15:22-28; Rev 20:11-15).

11 Then I saw a great white throne and Him who sat on it, from whose face the earth and the heaven fled away. And there was found no place for them. 12 And I saw the dead, small and great, standing before God, and books were opened. And another book was opened, which is the Book of Life. And the dead were judged according to their works, by the things which were written in the books. 13 The sea gave up the dead who were in it, and Death and Hades delivered up the dead who were in them. And they were judged, each one according to his works. 14 Then Death and Hades were cast into the lake of fire. This is the second death. ¹⁵And anyone not found written in the Book of Life was cast into the lake of fire.

* God in his infinite mercy, not willing that any should perish but that all should come to repentance; waiting until the last moment to judge the world with righteousness. Now we can see in the Bible that this final judgment will take place immediately after they heaven and earth are destroyed. (Ac 17:31; 2ª Pet 3:7, 9 and 15; Rev 20:11).

This is a summary of the resurrected in the previous five resurrections:

1) The first fruits or dead in Christ. This is the church that will be raised from the resurrection of Jesus Christ until his coming for his church. {Evangelists, pastors, teachers, faithful believers, etc}. They are not dead in Christ some patriarchs, nor the prophets of the old covenant, neither Adam nor Eve; because they did not even know the name of the gospel; the Bible even says that this mystery was hidden at that time. (Rom 16:25-26; Eph 6:19; Col 1:26-27).

2) The ones of the first resurrection immediately before the millennium, named in Revelation 20:4. {Dead in Christ since the lifting of the church until the judgment to the nations and those who did not mark for the beast, and didn't worship the beast neither. Here will also be resurrected those who were given authority to judge between the twelve patriarchs and the twelve apostles; Adam, Eve, Noah, Prophets, Jews Kings obedient to God, saints and those who pleased God from Adam to the resurrection}. (Dn 12:1; Ez 37:12-14; Lk 13:28-30, 20:37-38 and 22:28-30; Rev 3:21).

3) The ones from the first resurrection immediately ended the millennium; called **"the other dead"** {They Believers in Jesus Christ will be resurrected during the millennium}. (Rev 20:5).

4) The resurrection of the white throne divided into two phases: (The resurrected according to their works and the resurrected according to whether or not his name was written in the book of life). Here will be resurrected those who did not rise before from Adam to the war of the end of the world.

* It is necessary to emphasized that in this judgment will be saved people; yes my dear reader, contrary to what we have learned and what we have heard; the Bible specifies in several verses that in this judgment many will resurrected for salvation.

Where will resurrect those who will be saved between the end of the millennium, until the final word war?

God will not save people in this time period?

There will not be a remnant of saved people although it is very small?

Absolutely all mankind will be deceived by Satan at that time?

We are going to develop this issue with the help of the Bible:

1] **Revelation 20:12-13** tells us that all those that are resurrected in this judgment; those who were in the sea, those who were in the tombs and those who were in hell; all of them were judged by the works which were written in the books, according to their works.

* The dead who are in hell will be entirely excluded of salvation. These will only resurrect to be condemned and to be cast into the lake of fire. (Mt 10:28 y 23:33; Lk 16:19-31; 2nd Pet 2:4-6 y 17; Rev 20:13-14).

We can realize that there are some books of works, and that each one was judged by the things which were written in these books. What are these books? Are there two or more books? Who are written in those books? What is recorded in these books? Are there only bad works or are there good works also written? **To answer these questions, it is necessary to study the word of God:**

A) **These books are** where the works of every human being are written since they have knowledge to know what is good and what is wrong, which is when they can be judged by their works. It also includes the works of the ones who pertain to the church, for we must all appear before the judgment seat of Christ to be judged by our works; although this judgment will not be for condemnation, but as we already saw earlier in the chapter "the judgment seat of Christ"; will be to receive more, less or no reward and likewise regarding the crowns. (Rev 20:12-13; 2nd Cor 5:10).

B) **Possibly** there will be four books for each person: Two to write the good works; one of them to what was said and the other one for what was done while the person was alive. Two to write the bad works; likewise one for what was said and the other one for what the person spoke when the person was alive. (Mt 12:36-37; 16:27; Rom 2:6, 2:16, 3:4, 14:12; 1st Tim 5:24-25; Jas 2:25-26; 1st Pet 1:17, 4:3-6; 1st Jn 3:12; Jud 12; Rev 2:23, 3:2; Prov 13:3; Lk 19:22; 1st Pet 2:22; Rev 14:5).

C) **God does NOT take into account what we think even if it is good or bad,** because for God what counts are the works and words, as this is the only evidence that the angels see and hear, the demons and Satan himself; as they cannot know what we think, only God knows. Although the Bible affirms categorically that our thoughts lead us to the works, that what we think is what we are and that God hates and

takes our evil thoughts as sin; but even with all of these we will not be judged by what we think.
(Prov 6:18; 15:26,28; 21:4; 23:7; 24:8-9; Mk 7:21; Lk 2:35; Acts 8:22; Rom 10:8-10; Eph 2:3; Heb 4:12; Rev 20:12-13).

D) **Daniel 12:2; John 5:28-29; Romans 2:5-16 and 1ˢᵗ Corinthians 15:24-28,** are talking about the same event and it is the one who will take place in the judgment before the great white throne. These verses are clear in manifesting that on that day mankind will be judged according to their works. There is no other time in which the Bible speaks of a resurrection in which it is judge on **the same day** the good and bad that has been done and during **the same day** the person is saved and then condemned. **This is more than a biblical reason to hold that even during the final judgment there will be people who will be saved.**

12:2 And many of those who sleep in the dust of the earth shall awake, Some to everlasting life, Some to shame and everlasting contempt.
5:28 Do not marvel at this; for the hour is coming in which all who are in the graves will hear His voice 29 and come forth those who have done good, to the resurrection of life, and those who have done evil, to the resurrection of condemnation.
2:5 But in accordance with your hardness and your impenitent heart you are treasuring up for yourself wrath in the day of wrath and revelation of the righteous judgment of God, 6 who "will render to each one according to his deeds": 7 eternal life to those who by patient continuance in doing good seek for glory, honor, and immortality; 8 but to those who are self-seeking and do not obey the truth, but obey unrighteousness—indignation and wrath, 9 tribulation and anguish, on every soul of man who does evil, of the Jew first and also of the Greek ;10 but glory, honor, and peace to

everyone who works what is good, to the Jew first and also to the Greek. ¹¹ For there is no partiality with God. ¹² For as many as have sinned without law will also perish without law, and as many as have sinned in the law will be judged by the law ¹³ (for not the hearers of the law arejust in the sight of God, but the doers of the law will be justified; ¹⁴ for when Gentiles, who do not have the law, by nature do the things in the law, these, although not having the law, are a law to themselves, ¹⁵ who show the work of the law written in their hearts, their conscience also bearing witness, and between themselves theirthoughts accusing or else excusing them) ¹⁶ in the day when God will judge the secrets of men by Jesus Christ, according to my gospel.

¹⁵:²⁴ Then comes the end, when He delivers the kingdom to God the Father, when He puts an end to all rule and all authority and power. ²⁵ For He must reign till He has put all enemies under His feet. ²⁶ The last enemy that will be destroyed is death. ²⁷ For "He has put all things under His feet." But when He says "all things are put under Him," it is evident that He who put all things under Him is excepted. ²⁸ Now when all things are made subject to Him, then the Son Himself will also be subject to Him who put all things under Him, that God may be all in all.

* We cannot confuse the resurrections of the judgment before the great white throne, with the resurrections of the last day. To make everything more clearly, we can go and study in this book the chapter called **"The Last Day"**. (Isa 30:8; John 6:39-40, 11:24 and 12:48).

2] **Revelation 20:12 and 15** tells us about the book of life and it is clarified that anyone that was not found written in this book, was cast into the lake of fire which is the second death. And we come here with the following questions: **What is the book life? Who are enrolled in the book of** life? How do we register our name in this book? When are the registrations close for this book?

A) **The book of life** is a book that God has and where are registered all of those that are going to be saved and that are going to live in the New Jerusalem. This book is independent of the books of the works. It is important to note that only until this moment they will realise if their names were or were not registered in this book, which shows that it is at that moment when they will be sent to their final dwelling to those who had not risen before. (Rev 20:15).

Why was the book of life not opened and was reviewed in the previous resurrections? Why it is clearly specified that only the one that was **NOT** enrolled was cast into the lake of fire? Simply because there were those who had their name inscribed in this book, but had not yet risen.
(Heb 12:22-23; Rev 22:19).

B) **How did they know if they were inscribed or not?** Because they had to look for their name. **Why only until the final judgment were they looking if they were enrolled or not?** Because God in his mercy waited patiently until the death of the last man to close the inscriptions in this book. They had not bothered to look up the names in the book of life if they knew they were not registered, or if this book had been closed during the millennium or before the millennium. Simply they had said there is no need to look for your name as the inscriptions were closed many years ago, in dispensations or past resurrections. (Rev 13:8 y 17:8).

C) **The book of life** existed since the foundation of the world and some are specifically enrolled.
(Dn 12:1, Eph 1:4-5, Rev 13:8 and 17:8).

D) **For others** it is necessary that through actions of faith, their name is inscribed in this book. (Phil 4:3, Heb 12:23-29).

E) **Having written the name in the book of life,** in many occasions it is not forever; because this can be erased. We have the example of Balaam, some kings of Israel and Judas himself. (Ex 32:32-33 Rev 3:5 and 22:19).

F) **To the New Jerusalem** those that are written in the book of life will only enter. (Rev 21:27).

G) **All members of the church** have their names written in the book of life. (Heb 12:22-23).

H) **The seventy** that Jesus sent out to preach the gospel also have their name inscribed in this book. (Luke 10:1 and 17-20).

I) **God himself enrolled into the book of life, names** of people that he wanted to saved: {Adam and Eve, Noah, Abraham, patriarchs, Moses, prophets, some kings of Israel, apostles, ect}. (Heb 32:32-33, Phil 4:3, Lk 10:20).

J) **In every dispensation there are different ways to enrol the name in the book of life; there are different men who preached about salvation and there are different ways to be saved.** This salvation was mostly, and will be by works. Only in the dispensation of grace, the salvation is by grace. I will prove this biblically, so that there is no doubt that after the millennium people can and be saved and according to the Bible it will be by works. **Let's then look at what the Bible says about it:**

1} **INNOCENCE:** (Gen 1:28 to 2:25). It covers the period of Adam and Eve in the Garden of Eden. **Adam and Eve are** the only logically people written in the book of life, in this dispensation.

* **Salvation or condemnation** was preached in this period by God. (Gen 1:27-30, 2:15-25, 3: 9-24).

* In this dispensation **salvation** was for Adam and Eve for obedience to God. (Gen 1:27-31 and 2:15-25).

2} **AWARENESS:** (Gen 3:24 to 8:22). It begins from the expulsion of Adam and Eve from paradise, until the flood. It lasted about 1,656 years. **Inscribed in the book of life are those decided to do what is right.**

* In this dispensation salvation or condemnation was **preached** by Adam, Eve, Seth, Enosh, Noah, Shem, Ham and Japheth, among others. (Gn. 4:1-7 and 25-26; Gn 5:32,8,18; 8:20-21; 9:8-11; Heb 11:7).

* In the consciousness **salvation** was by obedience and the works of Noah, the ones that were counted as faith.
(Gn. 6:5-8 and 11-13; Gn 6:18-20 and 22; Gn 8:21; Heb 11:7).

3} **HUMAN GOVERNMENT**: (Gn 8 to Gn 11:9). God destroyed the earth with a flood, to restart only with Noah and his family the human race. In the year 325 after the flood people started to build the tower of Babel.
Registered in the book of life are Noah and part of his family.

*Salvation or condemnation was **preached** by Noah, Shem and his family, Japheth and his family, among others.
(Gn 10:2-5; 10:21-31; Heb 11:7).

* **Ham and his family were excluded** from preaching the gospel because Noah cursed him and since then they decided to do evil before the sight of God. (Gn 9:22-25, 10:6-20, 10:10 and 11:1-9).

* **In the human government salvation** was also due to the work of obedience that Noah did before God; therefore God promised not destroy man with water, although man was continually doing evil before his eyes. (Gn 9:8-17).

4} **PROMISE:** (Gn 12 to Ex 19:25). It lasted 430 years. It began with the call of Abraham, it continued with the lives of the patriarchs and ended with the exodus of the Jewish people from Egypt.
Registry in the book: Abraham, Isaac, Jacob, his twelve sons and the other patriarchs, kings obedient to God and others. (Heb 11:9-10 and 11:13-16).

* Here **preached** Abraham, Isaac, Jacob and his family, among others.

* **In the promise;** Abraham's works were counted to him by faith; as works without faith and faith without works is dead. (Jas 2:21-26, Rom 4:3,9; Gal 3:6, Heb 11:8).

5} **THE LAW:** (Ex 20 to Mt 27:54). It lasted for almost 1,500 years. It began when God gave the law to Israel through Moses and it ended with the death of Jesus on the cross of Calvary.
Enrolled their names in the book: Moses, Prophets and those who obeyed the laws, decrees and precepts of God. (Rom 7:4 and 10:4).

* **The preachers were:** Moses, the prophets, Jews kings obedient to God, Judges followers of God, Jesus, among others.

* At this time of the law **salvation** was also by works of obedience to the law which God gave to Moses to be put into practice. (Rom 2:12-13,27; Rom 3:19; 7:12-14; 10:4-5; 13:8-10; Gal 3:23-24).

* The law *is* good if one uses it lawfully; the law is not made for a righteous person, but for the impious and those who is contrary to sound doctrine. (1st Tim 1:8-11).

* **What purpose then *does* the law *serve?***
The law was our tutor *to bring us* to Christ, that we might be justified by faith in Christ Jesus. (Gal 3:19-29).

* Christ *is* the end of the law for righteousness to everyone who believes. (Rom 10:4).

6} **GRACE:** (Mk 16:1-20 to Rev 20:6). This is the dispensation in which we live. Contrary to what we belief; **it covers from the resurrection of Jesus until the millennium.**
Inscribed in the book here: The church composed of Jews and Gentiles borned of water and of the Spirit and who persevered to the end; also those who lived during the millennium and that did the will of the Lord Jesus Christ in this his millennial ministry.

* **The evangelists** from the resurrection of Jesus until the rise of the church at the end of Satan's wrath, were and we will: Jesus, the apostles, the Gentile church and some Jews converted to the gospel. (Acts 1:1 and Rev 10:7).

* **After** the removal of the church that takes place throughout the Wrath of God, the 144,000 sealed and the two witnesses will preach. (Rev 7:1-8 and 11:3).

* **During the millennium** the Lord Jesus Christ and the church compose of Jews and Gentiles will be in charge. (Mt 19:27-29, Rev 2:26-27; 5:10 and 20:4).

* **During the period of grace** in which we live and as we already know stars from the resurrection of Jesus until the end of the millennium; salvation is by grace and not by works, lest anyone should boast.
(Ro 3:28; Ro 6:14; 7:6; 10:4 and 11:5-6, Eph 2:8-9).

* **The apostle James** shows us something about the faith and the works. He says that just as the body without the spirit is dead, so in the same way faith without works is dead. Therefore we need faith, but we also need works to be saved. (Jam 2:14-26, Heb 10:38-39).

* **The Apostle Paul** tells us in his epistle to the Galatians in chapter 2:16 he tells us clearly that no man in the age of grace can be justified by works of the law; only through the faith in Jesus Christ.

7} **FINAL JUDGMENT:** This is the last dispensation and not the millennium as many teach; because human life does not end with the millennium, but with the war of the end of the world; which takes places many years after the millennium. It goes from the end of the millennium, until the war of the end of the world. In this period the Holy Spirit will be on earth again; as the Lord Jesus Christ and the church will go to heaven. (1st Cor 15:22-28; Rev 20:1-3 and 7-9).

* Guided by the Holy Spirit many Jews and Gentiles will be preaching the everlasting gospel to the nations. **These will be the ones that enrol their names in the book of life.** There will be nations that will be saved in this period as they didn't gang up with Satan to destroy Israel, but these nations will not live in the New Jerusalem. (Rom 2:5-11, Rev 14:6-7; 21:24 and 26).

* For the judgment before the great white throne, **salvation will also be by work.** (Rev 20:11-12; 21:24 and 26; 22:2).

K) **Revelation 20:6** gives a blessing for those that will be resurrected in the first resurrection before the millennium; as they will reign with Christ for a thousand years.

L) **Is not the same** the resurrection of a believer by natural causes or by accident, by a murder, torment or torture. (Heb 11:35; 1st Cor 3:8 and 14-15).

M) **The gospel** consists in the birth, death and resurrection of the Lord Jesus from the dead. (Acts 4:2; 17:18 and 26:23).

N) **From Adam until the last human being lives, both, the gospel of salvation and damnation will be preached.**
It started with a man and it will end with a man. Whenever there is human life, there will be preaching. In the New Jerusalem there will be no preaching of the gospel, because God himself will be present as a living temple. Besides all that are inside will be saved and that's why there will be no need to preach salvation.
(1st Tim 2:3-4, 2nd Pet 3:9-10, Rev 14:6 and 21:22).

O) We need to clarify that in **Matthew 24:14** the gospel that must be preached so that the end comes is the gospel of the kingdom; which will take place during the millennium. The end that is here spoken about is the end of the preaching of the gospel to the gentiles; as it will be preached later to the Jews by the Jews. (Rom 11:25-31, Rev 7:3-4 and 11:3).

P) **The angel that had the everlasting gospel** to preach to the people of the earth; is doesn't mean that he was going to preach it; because the angels are not sent to preach the gospel; this work is only for humans. This angel had the everlasting gospel, but the Bible doesn't mention that he preached it. The only thing that he did was to proclaim that the judgment of God had come and that they have to worship the creator of the universe. (Heb 1:14; 2nd Cor 5:18; 1st Pet 1:12; Rom 10:15; Tit 1:3; Rev 14:6-7).

Q) **The Bible clearly says** that in the New Jerusalem there will not enter anything unclean or corruptible; that's why all of those that will be in this beautiful place will have new, powerful and immortal bodies.
(1st Cor 15:42-44,50 and 53-54; Rev 21:8, 27).

R) **Those that will be in the New Jerusalem,** will enjoy the presence of the Lord Jesus Christ at all times.
(Rev 7:9 and 15-17).

S) The ones from the **second death** will be excluded from the presence of God, which will bring disastrous moral and physical consequences. (2nd Thess 1:7-10).

T) The ones from the **lake of fire and brimstone** will have their corruptible bodies and that's why they will suffer eternally in their flesh the rigors of evil in which they died. (Lk 13:27-29; 1st Cor 15:50).

V) **The wicked** will coexist in the lake of fire and brimstone with Satan, the antichrist, the false prophet, with the death and with those who will be in hell for the time of the final judgment. (Rev 19:20; 20:10 and 14).

W) **The only people who are living in hell right now are:** Korah, Dathan, Abiram and their families. Also possibly the intimates of King David, who offered him guidance and were also members of his family and walked with him in the house of God. (Num 16:24-33; Ps 55:12-15).

X) **The only ones alive in the lake of fire and brimstone will be:** The antichrist, the false prophet and the devil. (Rev 19:20; 20:10).

Y) **Many** that will be in the lake of fire and brimstone after the final judgment are already named in the Bible. (Jud 3-6 and 12-13; Rev 21:8 and 27; Rev 22:15).

Z) The only ones alive that are now in the heaven are **Elijah** and **Enoch.** (2nd R 2:11-12; Gn 5:24, Heb 11:5).

* **Cain had a son which he called Enoch** and who builded a city called Enoch; but this was not the one that God carried alive to heaven. The one that is alive in heaven was the son of Jared, who descends from the genealogy of Seth. (Gn 4:17 and 5:18-24).

LAST MINUTE

* **We can clearly see that in the final judgment there are two judgments:** one for works and the other one according to whether or not their name was written in the book of life. If we were only judged by the book of life, then for what do we open the other books?

If they are already condemned in advance it would not be necessary to make them a trial; **because the trial is to determine if the person is guilty or innocent;** that's why it is called trial, otherwise it would be called sentence. **Then it will not be called the judgment before the great white throne, but "the condemnation of the great white throne."**

***John 3:18** says that the one who does not believe in Jesus is already condemned; which will mean that these people have already been tried and have been found guilty. **But how could this be?** Although the ones that do not believe in Jesus are declared wicked; only in the final judgment the wicked are judged, and only the ones from hell have already been condemned, as we know that from there they will go to the lake of fire and brimstone; they will only resurrected to receive the judgment of guilt.

The explanation is that there is an universal law which specifies: All of those who do not believe in Jesus, all of those who deny him with their deeds or words, all of those who deny the faith of Jesus, those who deny his name; all of those automatically are already condemned.
(Mt 10:33; 2nd Tim 2:12; Tit 1:16; Jud 4; Rev 2:13 and 3:8).

* **The only exception to the rule is:** If that person being in life gives himself to the Lord Jesus Christ as Lord recognizing him as Lord and Savior; and having the opportunity is born of water and of the Spirit, enduring to the end of his life, in order to be saved. (Jn 3:5; Rom 10:9-13; Fhil 2:5-11; 1st Jn 2:22-23 and 4:2-3; Mt 24:13).

* **At the time of grace** that goes from the resurrection of the Lord Jesus Christ until the end of the millennium; in this period of time it is quite clear that none can be saved by the works of the law. This salvation is only through the grace by the faith in Jesus Christ; but often **in many occasions is not enough just to have faith;** we must demonstrate that we have faith, we must give evidences of our faith; which is tested and it is shows only by our works, because **faith is perfected with the works**. As faith without works is dead. We have to do works worthy of repentance. (Acts 9:36 and 26:20; Jam 2:22-26; 1st Jn 3:12; Rev 2:26; 3:8; 14:13).

* **Works of faith, works of law, works of grace**: The works are divided into this three main groups; considering that each one of the groups has several subdivisions.

1] **The works of faith**: From the beginning of mankind until the end of it, we read in the Bible that everything is done by faith and for faith. In Hebrews chapter 11, the apostle Paul reminds us how in the Old Testament all things were made by faith. With regard to the New Testament from Matthew to Revelation we see that faith is always present. We are told that the just shall live by faith, that we need to have faith in order to preserve the soul and that the end of our faith is the salvation of the soul. (Heb 10:38-39 and chapter 11; 1st Pet 1:7-9; Rev 2:13 and 19, Rev 14:12).

2] **The works of law**: we found them in Exodus 20:1-17; these works also cover the statutes, precepts and decrees that God gave to Israel and that are specified in the Pentateuch, so that this people may be guided by them and so they could be saved; because in that dispensation salvation was carried out fulfilling the law. Although no one except Jesus Christ could completely fulfil the law. (Ex 20:1-17; Lv 26:1-46; Dt 28:1-68)

3] **Works of grace**: These works are condensed in the Gospels, the Pauline Epistles, the letters of Peter, James and John. All of these saints agree in that the works of the grace are mainly to obey the commandments of the Lord Jesus Christ as these are not burdensome and bring salvation. (Mt 5:17-20 and 22:36-40; Rom 8:1-9 and 12-13; 2nd Pet 2:21 and 3:1-2; 1st Jn 2:3-4; 3:23-24 and 5:2-3).

* We should **not** be confused with the commandments imposed by men and that they even make a doctrine of them; as these ones lead to eternal death. (Mt 15:1-6; Mk 7:6-8; Col 2:8; 1st Tim4:1; 2nd Tim 3:1-7; 1st Jn 4:1-6; 2nd Jn 7-11).

* We need to clarify that all the commandments, works, faith and grace; the Lord Jesus Christ summed it up in a single expression: **LOVE**. Because if there is not **LOVE**, it is useless to try to keep the commandments, our works are worthless, it is useless to have grace and faith. (Mt 22:36-40; Jn 13:34-35; 1st Jn 2:7-11 and 15-17; 1st Cor chapter 13).

* **In hell** there are different compartments or patios; which will also be in the lake of fire and brimstone. This is to differentiate prisoners.

Hell: Prisons where angels who didn't keep their dignity and the wicked are waiting for the sentence of guilt. Let's remember that according to 2nd Peter 2:4 and Jude 6; the angels who did not keep their dignity were thrown into eternal **PRISONS** of darkness. **Prisons** in plural, this means that there were several.

Lake of fire and brimstone: Place of torment where many will be passed their sentence including: Satan, the demons, the angels that didn't keep their dignity, the antichrist, the false prophet, the ones that were not found written in the book of life and the wicked.
The compartment that corresponds in hell and the punishment in the lake of fire and brimstone will be according to their works that he will have done while he was alive.
(Mt 13:40-43 and 47-50; Mt 22:13, Lk 16:19-31; 1st Pet 3:18-20; 2nd Pet 2:4; Jud 6; Rev 20:7 and 11-15).

* **The book of 1st Enoch** 1:9, 1st Enoch 6:8, 1st Enoch 7:3-6 and 1st Enoch 8:1-4; seems to be an explanation of Genesis 6:1-7, Deuteronomy 33:2, 2nd Peter 2:4 and Jude 6, 14 and 15. This is an intertestamental book {period of silence between the Old and New Testament book. Between Malachi and John the Baptist. Approximately 450 years}, it is consists of three volumes. It is said that it was very valuable for the first Christians; besides that references to the book of Enoch are found in multiple bible scriptures. {You can find out more about this book in Wikipedia}. The book of 1st Enoch in his Chapters 21, 22, 23 and 27 speaks about the divisions or compartments that are in hell, for the sinners according to their sin.

* **In Revelation 20:2-3** the Bible says that an an angel **CAUGHT** the devil, put a **STAMP** on him and chained him for a thousand years; then **THREW** him into the abyss until the thousand years were fulfilled; then he **MUST** be loosed for a little time. In verse 8 says that when he will let him go; Satan **WILL GO** to deceive the nations.

I am going to try to explain this better:

The angel **IMMOBILIZED** and **SILENCED** the devil, chaining him and **THROWING HIM** {the angel didn't leave him in some compartment of hell}; there he will be unable to communicate with anyone so he will not be able to do bad things, for a thousand years. Then for the scripture to be fulfilled, he **MUST** be released and he **WILL GO** on his own will to deceive the nations and prepare them for the war of the end of the world.

* **We know that hell is a place of temporary torment** for the story or teaching of the rich men and Lazarus.
{This is not a parable because the Lord Jesus was talking to his disciples in Luke 16:1, 17:1 and 5. He had said in Mark 4:10-13 and 33-34, that he spoke to the disciples without using parables so that they could understand the whole mystery of the kingdom of God}.
Even the demons that possessed the Gadarene begged Jesus not to be send to hell so that they wouldn't be tormented before time. (Luke 16:23-5 and 28; Luke 8:28 and 31).
The lake of fire and brimstone is a permanent place of torment, according to the Bible. (Rev 14:10-11 and 20:10).

* **The devil and the demons know perfectly the Bible** and therefore know the terrible punishment and torment for which they are intended. The devil deceived Eve with the word of God and tempted the Lord Jesus with the promises of the Bible. The demons also know that God is one and tremble when they know that they are deceiving mankind regarding the deity of God. (Gn 3:13; Lk 4:1-13; 2nd Cor 11:3; Jas 2:19; Rev. 12:9).

* In the trial before the great white throne the Bible says, that the dead will be judged **ACCORDING** to their works; This **ACCORDING** indicates **CLASSIFICATION**; the dead were classified by their works and thus they were thrown into the lake of fire in a compartment **BY THE CLASSIFICATION OF THEIR SINS.** This shouldn't surprise us because in life God himself classifies the sins **ACCORDING** whether they be death or not. **There are sins against the Spirit, against our own body and the sins committed outside the body**; called general or least. **It cannot be** the same punishment for a blasphemer, idolatrous, sorcerer, witch, satanist; that for a parricide, rapist or murderer; in the same manner it is not the same punishment for an homosexual, fornicator or adulterer; that for a liar, greedy or cursing. (Rev 20:12-13; 1st John 5:16-17; Mt 12:31-32; 1st Cor 6:18-20; Mt 18:21-22; Lk 17:3-4).

* **In the lake of fire and brimstone will be ranges**: The Devil; the demons each one depending on their current status; the angels that didn't keep their dignity; the antichrist, the false prophet; and the ones that are named in Galatians 5:19-21 and Revelation 20:12-15, 21:8 and 22:15. (Rev 20:10; Mt 8:28-29; Jud 6; Rev 19:20).

* **God has established ranges in heaven:** The four beasts full of eyes inside and outside that are in the corners of the throne of God permanently. There are also cherubims, seraphims, archangels and angels. (Ez chapter 1; Rev 4:6-8; Isa 37:16 and 6:1-3; Ju 9; Heb 1:6-7)

* **The Devil is an imitator;** he also divided his armies, according to what he learned from God when he was in heaven serving God as a cherub. **He divided them into:** principalities, powers, rulers of darkness, spiritual wickedness, and demons. (Ez 28:13-19; Eph 6:11-12; Jas 2:19).

* **In the New Jerusalem there will be ranges**: (1stCor 15:35-41). We know from Hebrews 8:5 and 9:1-7; that in the tabernacle, the one which typify the throne of God

in heaven; there was no "abodes". In John 14:1-4 the Lord Jesus said that in the house of his father there were many abodes and that he was going to prepare a place for the church. The house of the father is a type of the temple and of the new Jerusalem. (Jn 2:16; Heb 8:5; Lk 19:46; Isa 56:7).

Certainly in the temple of God there were many abodes and were occupied hierarchically for officials and/or servants of the temple depending if they were the temple keeper, priest, high priest, prince, ect.
(Jer 35:2 and 36:10; 1st Ki 6:5; Ezr 8:29).

The Bible tells us that in the New Jerusalem there will be no temple; but affirms that Jesus Christ is preparing two special places: one in the kingdom of God on earth during the millennium; and another in the New Jerusalem were there will be new heavens and new earth.
(Rev 21:2-3 and 22; Mt 25:34; Lk 22:28-30).

The Temple of Jerusalem that existed in the time of Jesus; was a type of the temple of God and of the new Jerusalem. So what the Lord Jesus is preparing also is the position that we are going to occupy both in the kingdom of God and in the new Jerusalem; this will depend on what we do in life with the gifts that have been given to us.
(2nd Cor 5:1 and 10-11).

Let's remember that during the tribunal of Christ we will receive more or less crowns; more or less awards and likewise it will be assign to us the position that we will occupy in the reign of the new Jerusalem.
(Lk 6:23 and 35; 2nd Jn 8; Rev 3:11 and 22:12).

Now we are going to see a possible hierarchy order: Jesus Christ himself like the husband; wife; the apostles and patriarchs who were given the right to be judges of fallen angels and disobedient, and also judges of the pagan world; those who sit on the right or left on the throne; those who sit on the throne with Jesus which are the conquerors; those who will be pillars in the temple of God, which it is understood to be the New Jerusalem; among others. (1st Co 6:2-3; Rev 20:4; Mt 20:20-23; Rev 3:12 and 21; Rev 4:4; Mt 5:19-20 and 11:11).

* **In the same church there are currently ranges established by Jesus and others established by man.**
The Lord Jesus established: Apostles, prophets, evangelists, pastors and teachers.
Men established: Bishops, deacons, youth committees, ladies, evangelism, social support, prayer, prison and hospital labour, ect. (Eph 4:7-13; 1st Tim 3:1; 2nd Tm 2:15, Phil 1:1).

THE DAY OF THE LORD

There are many theories about the rapture of the church and resurrections. Also about the "day", some say one thing and others say another. But what does the Bible say? That is the transcendental part because the Bible has always the first and last word.

We analyze everything about the "day" to leave once and for all any doubts that may arise with respect to that "day".

* Joel 2:31: "The sun shall be turned into darkness and the moon into blood, before the coming of the great and terrible day of the Lord".

* Acts 2:20: "The sun shall be turned into darkness, and the moon into blood, before the coming of the day of the Lord, great and glorious".

* 1st Thessalonians 5:2: "For yourselves know perfectly that the day of the Lord so cometh as a thief in the night".

* 2nd Thessalonians 2:2: "... do not be quickly shaken from your composure or be troubled, neither by spirit, nor by word, nor by letter as from us, to the effect that the day of Christ is at hand".

* 2nd Peter 3:10 "But the day of the Lord will come like a thief in the night, in which the heavens will pass away with a roar and the elements will be dissolved, and the earth and the works that are therein shall be burned up".

* 2nd Peter 3:12 "waiting for and hastening the coming of

the day of God , wherein the heavens being on fire shall be dissolved, and the elements being on fire , will melt".

* Revelation 1:10: "I was in the Spirit on the Lord's day and heard behind me a loud voice like a trumpet".

REFLECTION

* In Joel 2:31 we have a translation problem because we can clearly see that Acts 2:20 translates the Lord's day in the words of the prophet Joel who translates it as the day of the Lord, according to the context and pretext we know who really is talking about the day of the Lord when He brings together all nations in the battle of Armageddon.

* In 2nd Peter 3:10 the apostle speaks of the Lord's day, referring to the moment when the earth will be destroyed.

* 2nd Peter 3:12 This biblical quote makes the same reference to when the earth will be destroyed, but speaks of the day of God.

* In 2nd Peter 3:7,10 and 12 the heaven and the earth will be destroyed in the day of judgment of ungodly men. **This is called the Lord's day too.**

But the church waiting for new heaven and new earth. (2nd Peter 3:13).

We also know from Revelation 20:9-10, that the heaven and earth will be destroyed in the final war that takes place after the millennium.

* In 1st Thessalonians 5:2 and 2nd Thessalonians 2:2 refers to the time when the Lord Jesus lifts the gentile church. We know this from the context and pretext, as it happens in the middle of the 70th week of Daniel.

How long will it last? A moment? How long until the dead in Christ rise? How long till the gentile church is lifted? How long to reunite them?

Conclusion

The day of the Lord encompasses three major events:

1. The lifting of the gentile church.
2. The trial for the battle of Armageddon.
3. The judgment of the final war.

THE DAY OF WRATH

* Job 21:30: "That the wicked is reserved to the day of destruction? Saved will be in the day of wrath".

* Proverbs 11:4: "Riches profit not in the day of wrath, but righteousness delivers from death".

* Zephaniah 1:18, "Neither their silver nor their gold shall be able to deliver them in the day of Jehovah's anger, but the whole land shall be devoured by the fire of his jealousy: for he will certainly hasty destruction of all the inhabitants of the earth".

* Romans 2:5-10: "But after thy hardness and impenitent heart you are treasuring up for yourself wrath in the day of wrath and revelation of the righteous judgment of God , who will render to every man according to his works: eternal life to those who by persistence in doing good seek glory, honour and immortality , but wrath and anger to those who are factious and do not obey the truth , but obey unrighteousness, tribulation and distress for every human being who does evil, the Jew first and also the Greek".

 * 1st Thessalonians 5:9: "For God hath not appointed us to wrath, but to obtain salvation through our Lord Jesus Christ".

 * Matthew 3:7: "Seeing that many of the Pharisees and Sadducees come to his baptism, he said unto them brood of vipers! Who warned you to flee from the wrath to come"?.

* Romans 5:9 "Much more then, being now justified by his blood, we shall be saved from wrath".

* 1st Thessalonians 1:10 "And to wait for his Son from heaven, whom he raised from the dead, <u>even Jesus, which delivered us from the wrath to come</u>".

REFLECTIONS

From the context and pretext we can analyze that the day of Jehovah's anger is revealed when God's judgment on the wicked, as Zephaniah 1:18 "Neither their silver nor their gold shall be able to deliver them in the day of wrath of the LORD, all the earth shall be devoured with the fire of his jealousy: For he will certainly hasty destruction of all the inhabitants of the earth".

* 1st Thessalonians 5:9 "For God hath not appointed us to wrath, but to obtain salvation through our Lord Jesus Christ".

* Revelation 19:15: "Out of his mouth comes a sharp sword with which to strike down the nations, and he shall rule them with a rod of iron: and he treads the winepress of the fierceness and wrath of Almighty God".

Matthew 3:7 "but when he saw many of the Pharisees and Sadducees come to his baptism, he said unto them brood of vipers! Who warned you to flee from the wrath to come"?.

* Romans 5:9 "Much more then, being now justified by his blood, we shall be saved from wrath".

* 1st Thessalonians 1:10 "And to wait for his Son from heaven, whom he raised from the dead, even Jesus, which delivered us from the wrath to come".

* Revelation 6:16 "And said to the mountains and rocks, fall on us, and hide us from the face of him that sitteth on the throne and from the wrath of the Lamb".

* Revelation 14:10: "The same shall drink of the wine of the wrath of God, which is poured out without mixture into the cup of his anger, and he shall be tormented with fire and brimstone before the holy angels and of the Lamb".

* Revelation 14:19: "And the angel thrust in his sickle into the earth, and gathered the vine of the earth, and cast it into the great winepress grapes of the wrath of God".

* Revelation 15:1: "And I saw another sign in heaven, great and marvellous, seven angels having the seven last plagues, for in them is filled up the wrath of God".

<u>Conclusion</u>: This day will take three and a half years, in other words, the time it takes the seven bowls of the wrath of God.

THE DAY OF JEHOVAH

* Isaiah 13: 6: "Howl ye is the day of the Lord will come like destruction from the Almighty".

* Isaiah 13:9: "Behold, the day of the Lord cometh, cruel both with wrath and fierce anger, to make the land desolation and to destroy its sinners from it".

* Ezekiel 13: 5: "Ye have not gone up into the gaps, neither made up the hedge for the house of Israel to stand in the battle in the day of Jehovah".

* Ezekiel 30: 3: "For the day is near, nearby is the day of the Lord, a day of clouds, a time of punishment of the nations will be".

* Joel 1:15: "There is the day For near is the day of the Lord will come like destruction from the Almighty"?.

* Joel 2:1 "Blow the trumpet in Zion, and sound an alarm in my holy mountain: let all the inhabitants of the earth, because the day of the LORD is near".

* Joel 2:11: "And the Lord shall utter his voice before his army: for his camp is very great: he is strong that executes his word: for great is the day of the Lord, and very terrible; who can endure it"?.

* Joel 2:31: "The sun shall be turned into darkness and the moon into blood, before the coming of the great and terrible day of the Lord".

* Joel 3:14-16 "Multitudes, multitudes in the valley of decision: for near is the day of the Lord in the valley of

decision. The sun and the moon are darkened, and the stars withdraw their shining. And Jehovah will roar from Zion, and utter his voice from Jerusalem, and shake the heavens and the earth, the LORD will be the hope of his people, and the strength of the children of Israel".

* Amos 5:18: "Woe unto you that desire the day of Jehovah! What purpose will the day of the Lord? It is darkness, and not light".

* Amos 5:20, "Shall not the day of Jehovah and darkness, and not light, dark, and no brightness in it"?.

* Obadiah 1:15 "For near is the day of the Lord upon all the nations: as thou hast with thee shall thy reward shall return upon thine own head".

Zephaniah 1:7: "Be silent before the Lord GOD: for the day of Jehovah is at hand: for the LORD hath prepared a sacrifice, and has provided his guests".

* Zephaniah 1:14: "Near is the great day of the Lord, near and coming quickly, even the voice of the day of the LORD: the mighty man shall cry there".

* Zephaniah 14: 1: "Behold, the day of the Lord cometh, and amid your spoil will be divided".

* Malachi 4:5: "Behold, I send you Elijah the prophet before the coming of the day of Jehovah, great and terrible".

REFLECTIONS

The day of the Lord will be when all nations meet in the valley of Jehoshaphat (Joel 3:2), that is, when He brings them together in the battle of Armageddon, immediately before the millennium and when He comes in a cloud and every eye will see Him. (Revelation 19:11-21, Matthew 24:29-30). As God's Word says, before this terrible day comes send the prophet Elijah to preach repentance, and against the antichrist and false prophet. (Revelation 11:4-12). **Elijah will be a witness Enoch the other. Not Moses and Elijah as most think or speculate. Why? Because these two witnesses will be killed by the Antichrist, and Moses is dead, he cannot die twice, because only the wicked die twice.**

How long will the day of the Lord be? How long did God take to destroy Sodom and Gomorrah? Possibly, hours?. As the Bible tells us, once you have gathered all the nations in the battle of Armageddon. How long does an earthquake take? How much does it destroy? Possibly the day of Jehovah is 24 hours before the millennium. (Revelation 20:6).

THE LAST DAY

* Isaiah 30:8: "Go, now, write it on a table in front of them, and note it in a book, so it is the time to come forever and ever".

* John 6:39: "And this is the will of Him who sent me, that of all you give me, I should lose nothing, but raise it up at the last day".

* John 6:40: "And this is the will of him that sent me, that every one which seeth the Son, and believeth on him, may have everlasting life: and I will raise him up at the last day".

* John 6:44: "No man can come to me unless the Father who sent me draws him, and I will raise him up at the last day".

* John 6:54: "He who eats my flesh and drinks my blood has eternal life, and I will raise him up at the last day".

* John 11:24: "Marta said, I know he will rise again in the resurrection at the last day".

* John 12:48: "He who rejects me, and receiveth not my words, hath one that judgeth him: the word that I have spoken will judge him in the last day".

What is the last day?

The last day begins with the rapture of the gentile church "I will raise him up at the last day"; "The dead in Christ shall rise first" **and ends with the judgment before the great white throne.** (The word judges him in the last day).

Biblically, speaking of the word "day" it does not necessarily refer to a period of 24 hours.

Daniel speaks of days being a year, seven days = Seven years.

Paul speaks of 1000 years = One day with God.

John speaks of judgment day and we all know that does not take 24 hours.

In Genesis speaks of the days of creation, ect.

* Isaiah 30:8: "Go, now, write it on a table in front of them, and recorded in a book, so it is the time to come forever and ever". **If we read the context and pretext, we realize that vision extends to Isaiah 30:26:** "And the light of the moon shall be as the light of the sun, and the light of the sun shall be sevenfold, as the light of seven days, the day the LORD binds up the wounds of his people, and heals the wound that caused it". **This verse will be fulfilled in Revelation 16:8-9 which speaks of a quarter cup of the wrath of God.**

*Last day = Resurrection of the dead in Christ, in the rapture of the gentile church. (1st Thessalonians 4:13-17).

*Last day = Resurrection of pious and impious together, from Adam to the end of the world war; on the doomsday. (Revelation 20: 11-15).

For the Jewish people, the time duration was not the most important, but the reality of an event: If fully done or only the beginning or if it kept making, etc... In this base their verbal conjugation system in both Hebrew and Greek. No time is what matters most in their verbs, but the look.

Hence we understand some biblical things as they understood them at that time. Apparently, that was because the Lord had prepared man mentally to the idea of eternity, where things are not measured by its length but by the looks of its accomplishment as such.

The modern approach is different. Human thought has concentrated much more in time where things are made and the IMMEDIATE effects, and not on the quality of the events as such. Even fundamental aspects have been neglected as long-range effects of the acts they commit, especially how they affect subsequent generations. The Bible does not reflect this type of modern thinking. To God and his loyal servants, we try to act in ways which He approves, the quality of our actions are essential, even more than life itself. **We are able to lose our life for fear of displeasing God, we know that adoption is ensuring eternity in the future, even if it was after being resurrected.**

BAD DAY

* Psalm 41:1: "Blessed is he who considers the poor; <u>on the day the Lord delivers him wrong</u>".
* Proverbs 16:4: "Everything Jehovah has made for himself, <u>and even the wicked for the evil day</u>".
* Jeremiah 17: 17: "Do not be a terror to you; <u>you are my refuge in the day of evil</u>".
* Amos 6:3: "<u>O ye that put far away the evil day</u>, and cause the seat of violence".
* Ephesians 6:13: "<u>Wherefore take unto you the whole armour of God, so that you can with stand in the evil day</u>, and having done all, to stand".

REFLECTIONS

In all these verses the only passage that sheds light on the evil day is Ephesians 6:13, when he says: " ... why can withstand in the evil day, and having done all to stand"

1st Thessalonians 5:8-9 tells us about the armor of God, namely the hope of salvation as a helmet; the pretext and context we know that talking about stronger with armor to expect to be raised as a faithful church to meet the Lord Jesus Christ; this will take place before the wrath of God.

* Isaiah 59:17-18 Describes the same God we dressed in his armour, especially garment of righteousness, helmet of salvation, vengeance clothing and clothing of zeal to repay with wrath to his enemies.

Taking all this into account, we see that God does justice to save the man who has taken his armour, but that, equally, punish with his wrath the wicked.

THE DAY OF PUNISHMENT

* Exodus 32:34: "Go therefore now, lead the people to which I have spoken unto thee: behold, mine Angel shall go before thee: <u>nevertheless in the day of punishment, I will punish them for their sin</u>".

* Isaiah 10:3: "<u>And what will ye do in the day of visitation?</u> Who will you flee for help, when he comes by far the desolation? Where will you leave your glory"?.

* Hosea 5:9: "<u>Ephraim shall be desolate in the day of rebuke</u>: among the tribes of Israel have I made known the truth".

REFLECTIONS

The day of punishment is the day of wrath, like the day of the Lord, and confirms Isaiah 10:3 and its context in Isaiah 9:19: "And what will ye do in the day of visitation? Who will you flee for help, when he comes by far the desolation?" "For the wrath of the Lord of hosts the land is angry, and the people are like fuel for the fire. Moreover, no man shall spare his brother".

THE BIG DAY

* Revelation 6:17: "<u>For the great day of their wrath has come</u>, and who can stand"?.

* Revelation 16:14: "For they are the spirits of devils, working miracles, which go forth unto the kings of the earth around the world, <u>to gather them to the battle of that great day of God Almighty</u>".

* Jude 1:6: "<u>And the angels which kept not their first estate</u>, but left their own habitation, he hath reserved under darkness in everlasting chains <u>for judgment on the great day</u>". (NKJV).

"This happened also with the angels who refused and left the place of honour that God had given them. God is forever tied with chains, and are locked in a dark, <u>until the great day of judgment</u>". (Translation Current Language).

"Remember also the angels who did not keep their positions of authority but abandoned their own place. God kept in darkness, bound forever in chains, <u>waiting for the great day of judgment</u>". (New International Version).

"And I remind you of the angels who did not stay within the limits of authority God gave them but left the place where they belonged. God has been firmly chained in prisons of darkness, <u>waiting for the great day of judgment</u>". (New Living Translation).

* 2nd Peter 2:4: "For if God spared not the angels that sinned, but cast them down to hell and delivered them into

chains of darkness, <u>to be reserved unto judgment</u>".

As we can see, other versions we clarify that the angels who did not stay within the limits of authority that God gave them, but they refused and left the place of honour that God had given them; were locked and chained in prisons of darkness in hell or abyss , until the great day of judgment. When will be this judgment of the fallen angels?

* In Revelation 9:1-11 we describe the output of the demons or fallen angels that were reserved for the day of judgment.

*In Revelation 16:13-14 we see how some of these evil spirits are sent to deceive the nations to gather in the battle of Armageddon.

*In Revelation 20:2 we see how Satan and his hosts of evil logically, are bound for 1,000 years (It is only logical since Satan cannot do anything more, he cannot be everywhere at once).

*In Revelation 20:7 **we see how after the millennium, Satan and his hosts are loose from his prison and out to deceive the nations and prepare for the final battle.**

* **Finally, in Revelation 20:10 we realize that Satan and his forces are defeated, judged and sent to the lake of fire and brimstone.**

REFLECTIONS

Revelation 6:17 and Revelation 16:14 refers to the day of the Lord, speaking of the same great day.

Now, we have a completely different reference to that great day when Judas talking of the big day, but not the same great day for humans, this is the great day of judgment for the fallen angels, which takes place in a time completely different other than the great day of Jehovah.

Conclusion: **There is a great day to prosecute human and another great day to prosecute Satan and the fallen angels.**

JUDGMENT DAY

* Matthew 10:15: "<u>Verily I say unto you in the day of</u> <u>judgment</u>, it shall be more tolerable for the land of Sodom and Gomorrah than for that city".

* Matthew 11:22: "<u>Therefore I tell you the day of judgment</u> it will be more tolerable for Tyre and Sidon than for you".

* Matthew 11:24 "<u>Therefore I say that in the day of</u> <u>judgment</u> it will be more tolerable for the land of Sodom than for you".

* Matthew 12:36: "But I say unto you, that every idle word that men shall speak, <u>they shall give account on the Day of</u> <u>Judgment</u>".

* Mark 6:11: "And if any place will not receive you and hear you, when ye depart thence, shake off the dust under your feet for a testimony against them. <u>Verily I say unto you in</u> <u>the day of judgment</u> it will be more bearable for Sodom and Gomorrah than for that city".

* 2nd Peter 2:9: "The Lord knoweth how to deliver the godly out of temptations, <u>and to reserve the unjust under</u> <u>punishment for the Day of Judgment</u>".

* 2nd Peter 3:7: "But the heavens and the earth which are now are reserved by the same word, <u>reserved unto fire</u> <u>against the day of judgment and perdition of ungodly men</u>".

* 1st John 4:17: "In this is love perfected with us, <u>that we</u> <u>may have boldness in the day of judgment</u>: because as he is, so are we in this world".

We have here another translation problem; verses from Matthew 12:36 and 2 Peter 2:9 are translated as follows in other versions:

* 2nd Peter 2:9: "This shows us that God is to solve the problems and difficulties faced by those who obey Him, but must also punish those who do wrong, and will in the day to judge all". (Actual Translation Language).

* 2nd Peter 2:9: "You see the Lord knows how to rescue the tests to all who live in obedience to God, while the wicked punished maintained until doomsday" .
(New Living Translation).

* 2nd Peter 2:9: "This is a proof that God knows how to rescue the difficulties of those who dedicate their lives to the king, but also knows how to punish the wicked as they await the day of judgment". (Word of God to all).

* Matthew 12:36: "I tell you in the judgment day everyone will have to explain why they spoke, to harm others".
(Actual Translation Language).

As we can see, it is clearly talking about the day of judgement that has nothing to do with the day of the Lord.
* 1st John 4:17: "If you really love the brethren, and live as Jesus Christ lived in this world, we will not be afraid when Jesus comes to judge the whole world". In this case, the translation Actual Language gives us to understand that if we live as Jesus lived, we shall be saved from doomsday, because we all know that the Bible again and again assures us that we live as Jesus lived will be delivered from the wrath and not pass the final judgment.
(Romans 5:9-10; 1st John 2:6 and 4:17).

REFLECTIONS

The Jewish/Gentile church will go through the judgment seat of Christ, but never for the final judgment.

Judgement day is when God will judge the wicked. This will be after the millennium, after the final war and after the destruction of the heaven and the earth we see now.

THE DAY OF THE LORD JESUS

* 1st Corinthians 5:5: "the deliver such a one to Satan for the destruction of the flesh, that the spirit may be saved in the day of Christ Jesus".

* 2nd Corinthians 1:14 "partly as ye understood that we are your rejoicing, even as ye also are ours in the day of Jesus".

REFLECTIONS

* 1st Corinthians 5:5: "At the time, delivered to Satan who committed the sin. His sinful desire be destroyed, but his spirit will be saved in the day when the Lord comes". (Word of God to all).

* "And they should give it to Satan thus, though Satan destroy his body, his spirit will be saved when the Lord Jesus returns". (Actual Translation Language).

* 2nd Corinthians 1:14, "What now not well understood. Thus, when the Lord Jesus Christ returns ...". (Actual Translation Language).

* "... The day when our Lord Jesus returns". (Word of God to all).

* "... Then, on the day that the Lord Jesus returns...". (New Living Translation).

* "... When our Lord Jesus returns ...". (Good News).

Conclusion: The day of Jesus Christ, the day of Christ and the day of the Lord Jesus are the same and refer to the day when He returns to lift the gentile church.

THE DAY OF CHRIST

* Philippians 1:10 "That ye may approve things that are excellent; that ye may be sincere and without offence till the day of Christ".

* Philippians 2:16 "Holding forth the word of life; that I may rejoice in the day of Christ, that I have not run in vain, neither laboured in vain".

REFLECTIONS

* Philippians 1:10 "so that you may be able to discern what is best and may be pure and blameless for the day of Christ". (NIV).

* Philippians 2:16: "as you hold firmly to the word of life. And then I will be able to boast on the day of Christ that I did not run or labour in vain". (NIV).

* Philippians 1:10 and Philippians 2:16 are continuing Philippians 1:6 "Being confident of this , that he who began a good work in you will perfect it until the day of Jesus Christ". **This verses refers to the coming of Jesus Christ for His gentile church.**

THE DAY OF JESUS CHRIST

* Philippians 1:6 "Being confident of this, that he who began a good work in you, I will complete it until the day of Jesus Christ".

*1st Corinthians 1:8 "which also confirm you to the end, blameless in the day of our Lord Jesus Christ".

REFLECTIONS

* Actual Language Translation says: "God began a good work among you, and I am sure he will perform it until the day when Jesus Christ returns".

* Word of God for all: "I am convinced that God began a good work among you and will continue to completion in the day of Christ Jesus".

* New translation: "And I am sure that God who began a good work in you will continue until it is completely finished on the day when Christ Jesus returns".
* New International Version: "I am sure that God who began a good work in you will carry it to fruition until the day of Christ Jesus".

The key to knowing what he means when he says "the day of Jesus Christ" is in the words "start" and "to", which means that since the gentile church began the work, from his conversion to Christ, until the coming to lift, it will be perfected the work of the gospel.

* Philippians 2:16 and Philippians 1:10 are the continuing of Philippians 1:6 "Being confident of this, that he who began a good work in you will perfect it until the day of Jesus Christ". **This refers to the coming of Jesus Christ for His gentile church.**

* The day of Christ and the day of Jesus Christ are the same event, namely the coming of Jesus Christ for the gentile church.

THAT DAY

1. What happened that day (history):

Genesis 7:11, 15:18; 26:32, 30:35, 33:16, 48:20 / Exodus 8:22; 13:8, 14:30, 32:28, 27:23 / Numbers 6:11 , 9:6 / 7:6 Samuel / Ezekiel 20:6, 23:38, 24:27 / Deuteronomy 27:11, 31:22 / Joshua 4:14, 8:25; 9:27 / Judges 3:30; 4:23; 5:1, 6:32; 20:21; 20:26; 20:35; 20:46 / 1 Sam 6:15; 7:6, 7:10; 9:24; 10:9, 12 18, 14:23-24, 14:31; 14:37; 16:13, 18:2, 18:9, 20:26; 21:7, 21:10; 22:18, 22:22; 27 6, 28:20, 30:25, 31:6 / 2 Samuel 2:17, 3:37, 5:8, 6:9, 11:12; 18:7, 18:8, 19:2-3; 23:10; 24:18 / 1 Kings 13:11; 22:35 / 1 Chronicles 13:12; 16:7; 29:22 / 2 Chronicles 18:24; 18.34; 35:16 / Nehemiah 4:16, 8:17; 12:43-44, 13:1 / 5:9 Esther / Jeremiah 39:17 / Zephaniah 3:11 / Matthew 13:1, 22:23, 22:46 / Mark 4:35, 14:25 / Luke 6: 23; 21:34; 23:12 / John 1:39, 5:9, 11:53, 16:26; 19:31.

2. What happened all that day and all night? Exodus 10:13 / Numbers 11:32 / 10:35 Joshua / Judges: 9:45 / 1 Sam 19:24; 28:20.

3. What is prophesied for that day (already met). Deuteronomy 31:16-18 / Joshua 14:12 / 1 Sam 3:12; 8:18 / 1 Kings 22:25 / Esther 3:14, 8:13 / Job 3:4 / Isaiah 19:16; 19:21; 20 6, 22:8, 22:20; 22:25; 23:15; 28:5, 31:7 / Jeremiah 39:16, 48:41 / Ezekiel 38:10, 39:22, 45:22, 48 35 / Hosea 1:5 / Amos 2:16, 8:3 / Haggai 2:23 / Zechariah 6:10.

4. What is prophesied for the day of the Old and New Testament is fulfilled.

Isaiah 2:11, 2:17, 2:20, 3:7, 3:18, 5:30; 7:18; 7:20, 12:1, 12:4, 17:7, 17:9, 24 : 21, 25:9, 26:1, 27:1, 27:2 / Jeremiah 4:9, 25:33, 49:22, 49:26 / 38:10 Hezekiah; 39:22 / Obadiah 1:8 / Micah 5:10, 7:11 / Zephaniah 1:9-10 / Zechariah 2:11, 3:10; 17:2.

FINAL THOUGHTS

The theory of lifting the church at the beginning of the seven years; does not lead to the resurrection of the righteous gentiles, who gave their lives for the witness of Jesus Christ at the time of the great tribulation. (Revelation 15:2 and 7:13 and 14).

Scripture clearly shows us that the rise of the church will be at the last trumpet can be no later, as there is only one resurrection for the gentile church; it is here at the last trumpet. If the last trumpet sounds at the beginning of the seven years, and therefore, the only resurrection for the gentile church; how then can the supporters of this theory, raise the dead saints for the wrath of Satan ? The Bible teaches us that these will rise in the first phase of the first resurrection called "First Fruits", which was explained clearly it is in the middle of the 70th Week of Daniel. (1st Thessalonians 4:16 and 18, 1st Corinthians 15: 51-52).

Luke 21:25-36 exactly in verse 27 tells us: *"Then shall they see the Son of man coming in a cloud with power and great glory"*. Here in this scripture refers to the end of seven years, when our Lord Jesus Christ will come to the gentile church to rule with the Jews church the earth for 1000 years.

Lucas through the verses 28,31 and 36; He declares us through the Holy Spirit that the church composed by Jews; should be prevented when signs in sun and moon and stars, when there is confusion in the people because of the roaring of the sea and the waves and when they are shaken the powers of heaven. To prepare for the approaching battle of Armageddon; which it is a sign that the millennium approaches.

Daniel 9:26-27 and 11:31-39, talks about what will happen in the seventieth week of Daniel, dividing it into two periods of three and a half years. Daniel sums into a covenant that Israel signed with the antichrist for seven years. In the first three and a half years allows the people of Israel restored sacrifices to their God YHWH (Vs 26-27); meanwhile, is being persecuted church to be purified, cleaned and bleached. (Vs 33-35).

1) When the secret number of brothers belonging to the Universal Church of the Name of the Lord Jesus Christ is complete, this will be lifted, once it has been refined, whitened their robes and tested their faith.

2) When is it coming? When they say "peace and security" in the middle of the week; then will come upon the Jewish people sudden destruction or the wrath of God. (1st Thessalonians 5:3).

3) 2nd Thessalonians 2:3 **says that the church will not be lifted until the apostasy comes first** (deny Jesus Christ) and the antichrist is revealed (That is when we know what it really is: a man of sin and son of perdition), **When will this be?** When he sit in the temple of God and to impersonate God; there will be the kick off to see us with Jesus Christ in the air.

4) 1st Thessalonians 5:9 **states that God has not appointed us to wrath,** but to obtain salvation through our Lord Jesus Christ.

5) Remember that the seventieth week of Daniel is divided into two: three and a half years of great tribulation for the gentile church (the wrath of Satan) and three and a half years of great tribulation to Jacob -Israel- or God's wrath.

6) Remember also that everyone will be deceived with kindness, intelligence and charisma of antichrist, **only the gentile church will hinder and for that matter, the chase.**

7)When the hundred and forty four thousand sealed of Israel is complete, **then will begin the wrath of God.**

If we consider all the prophecies of the Bible that agree, we will realize **that THE GENTILE CHURCH WILL GO BY THE WRATH OF SATAN, BUT WILL NEVER BY THE WRATH OF GOD.**

THE WRATH OF GOD

Revelation 15:1: "And I saw another sign in heaven, great and marvellous, seven angels having the seven last plagues, for in them the wrath of God is complete".

Revelation 16:1: "And I heard a loud voice from the temple saying to the angels feel: Go and pour out on the earth the seven bowls of the wrath of God".

There are a lot of Scriptures that tell us about those who live righteously and godly will BE FREED FROM THE WRATH OF GOD. Maybe that's why some confuse it and interpret it as being delivered from the great tribulation, but we have already clarified that the wrath of God will come in the mid-week, which are, three and a half years of the week seventy of Daniel.

Luke 21: 34-36 says: *Take heed to yourselves, lest your hearts be weighed down with carousing, drunkenness, and cares of this life, and come upon you that day. 35 For as a snare shall it come on all them that dwell on the face of all the earth. 36 "Watch therefore, and pray always, that ye may be accounted worthy to escape all these things to come, and to stand before the Son of Man."*

The text and context clearly shows how Jesus warns his Gentile church; to escape the wrath of God and His Jewish church shows you how to behave during the wrath of God.

In this part of God's wrath I don't think there's much to explain, because I practically already explained in the previous pages where we said that God's wrath will be poured out on those who remain on earth after the

gentile church Lord Jesus Christ has been lifted.

Satan's wrath is to test the Gentile church; The mark of the beast will be voluntary. The wrath of God is to test the Church of Jews; The mark of the beast will be mandatory. For the wrath of God the gospel of the name will be preached by the church of Jews, engendered by 144,000; under the subject of Elijah and Enoch. Prohibited The sacrifices, entrance to the temple and all Israel fleeing by persecution of the Antichrist; only remain in Israel, The Church of Jews, the 144,000 sealed, Elijah and Enoch; these will be protected by the seal of God.

The order of events for the wrath of God is as follows:

1. Revelation 16: 2, the first cup is poured out upon the men who had the mark of the beast and were tortured with painful, evil, foul and horrible ulcers.

2. Revelation 16: 3, the second is poured out upon the sea which becomes blood, killing every living thing; which it is reference that ends the shekel of life that begins at sea, as we know it.

3. Revelation 16: 4, the third bowl is poured out upon the rivers and water sources and also becomes blood; thus ending with drinking water.

4. Revelation 16: 8-9, the fourth bowl is poured out upon the sun which according to Isaiah 30:26 heated 7 times more; therefore men who have not the seal of God on their foreheads, they burn because the sun will penetrate directly into the ground, through the gaping hole which by then will have the ozone layer.

5. Revelation 16:10 the fifth bowl is poured out upon the throne of the beast that is the Antichrist, the false prophet, the powerful, the great politicians, members of the government of the false messiah, those who control the world economy , among others powerful; which they suffer intense pain, without some medicine that can mitigate even a little.

6. Revelation 16: 12-14, the sixth bowl is poured out upon the Euphrates river, causing it to dry; which China and its allies fail to jump to invade Israel as confirmed Daniel 11:44. Out of the mouth of the dragon an evil spirit that deceives the powerful and the great politicians; Mouth antichrist comes another evil spirit which deceives those who control the economy and global finance; finally comes another evil spirit in the mouth of the false prophet who deceived the religious power of the planet. They meet in the valley of Armageddon; all these powers with nations deceived.

7. Revelation 16: 17-21, the seventh bowl is poured out into the air and occurs a great earthquake such as never has been, nor will occur; Rome and the islands are destroyed by atomic bombs, causing a shower of hail up to 40 kilos of weight. According to Revelation 19: 11-21 in that moment descends the Lord Jesus Christ together with the gentile church and angels to fighting against the antichrist, the false prophet and the nations deceived. begins trial to Israel, followed by the trial of the beast and the false prophet, who are cast alive into a lake of fire; and ending with the trial nations deceived.

In Revelation 6:16 "And said to the mountains and rocks, fall on us, and hide us from the face of him that sitteth on the throne and from the wrath of the Lam". **We are told of the coming of Wrath the Lamb,** but not immediately come to the wrath of the Lamb, or are experiencing the wrath of the Lamb opened only for the first six seals, subtract the opening of the seventh seal and the sound of the seven trumpets. **The completion of this Announcement we noted in Revelation 11:18:** "And the nations were angry, and thy wrath is they come, and the time for judging the dead, and for rewarding your servants the prophets and the saints, and them that fear thy name, small and great, and for destroying those who destroy the earth", **when the seventh angel SOUNDS THE LAST TRUMPET.**

Revelation 14:9-10 "And the third angel followed them, saying with a loud voice, If any man worship the beast and his image and receives his mark on his forehead or on his hand, 10 the same shall drink of the wine of the wrath of God, which is poured out without mixture into the cup of his wrath, and he shall be tormented with fire and brimstone before the holy angels and of the Lamb". **Speaks of those who will be tormented or those who are going to be poured by the anger of God, whom? On those who receive the mark of the beast.**

Revelation 14:14-20: "And I looked, and behold a white cloud, and upon the cloud one sat like unto the Son of man, having on his head a golden crown, and in his hand a sharp sickle.

163

15 And another angel came out of the temple, crying with a loud voice to him that sat on the cloud, Thrust in thy sickle and reap, for the hour to reap has come, for the harvest of the earth is ripe. 16 And he that sat on the cloud thrust in his sickle into the earth, and the earth was reaped. 17 Another angel came out of the temple which is in heaven, he also having a sharp sickle. 18 And another angel came out from the altar , which had power over fire, and cried with a loud voice to him who had the sharp sickle, saying, Thrust in thy sickle and sharp, and gather the clusters of the earth, because its grapes are ripe it . 19 And the angel thrust in his sickle into the earth and gathered the vine of the earth, and threw the grapes into the great winepress of the wrath of God. 20 And the winepress was trodden outside the city , and blood came out of the winepress up to the horses' bridles , for one thousand six hundred furlongs".

Joel 3:13 "Put in the sickle, for the harvest is ripe. Come, tread, for the winepress is full, the vats overflow, for their wickedness is great for them". **They corroborate us who are trampled in the winepress of the wrath of God.**

Finally, in Revelation Chapter 16, the seven bowls of God's wrath are poured. And in Revelation 19:11-21 we are told about the final battle between the Lord Jesus Christ and the church against Satan, the demons and all who have been living on the land and have been marked by the beast. CONCLUSION: THE GENTILE CHURCH WILL GO THROUGH THE GREAT TRIBULATION OR THE WRATH OF SATAN IN THE FIRST THREE YEARS; THE JEWS CHURCH GO THROUGH THE WRATH OF GOD IN THE LAST THREE YEARS AND THE FINAL OR TRIAL OF JACOB.

THE SEVENTIETH WEEK OF DANIEL IN VERSES

Great tribulation for the Gentile Church: First three and a half years	Great tribulation for the Jews Church: The last three and a half years
SEVENTIETH WEEK OF DANIEL	
Daniel 2:37-43	Daniel 2:44-45
Daniel 7:2-14	Daniel 7:2-14
Daniel 7:23-25	Daniel 7:26-27
Daniel 8:3-8	Daniel 8:9-12
Daniel 8:20-22	Daniel 8:23-25
Daniel 11:21-30	Daniel 11:31-45
Mathew 24:3-14	Daniel 12:1-13
Luke 21:7-19	Isaiah 4:1-6
1st Thessalonians 4:13-18	Isaiah 24:17-23
1st Thessalonians 5:1-9	Isaiah 26:19-21
2nd Thessalonians 2:1-12	Isaiah 28:14-22
1st Corinthians 15:51-52	Isaiah 30:25-28
2nd Thessalonians 2:8 A	Isaiah 63:1-6

Revelation 13	Mathew 24:15-44
Revelation 6:1-12 A	Luke 21:20-28
Revelation 21:5-8	2nd Thessalonians 2:8B Then shall that Wicked be revealed, whom the Lord shall consume with the spirit of his mouth, and shall destroy with the brightness of his coming.
Revelation 8	Revelation 12
Revelation 9	Revelation 7:1-8
Revelation 11:14	Revelation 11:1-13
Revelation 10:1-11	Revelation 14:1-20
Revelation 11:15-19	Revelation 15:1-8
Revelation 7:9-17	Revelation 17
	Revelation 16:1-16 Revelation 18 Revelation 16:17-21 Revelation 19:1-6 Rev 16:12B y 15-17 Revelation 19:11-21

WHY SHOULD THIS BE THE CORRECT ORDER OF THE REVELATIONS?

1) The first correction corresponds to chapter 6 verse 12: "And I beheld when he had opened the sixth seal, and, lo, there was a great earthquake and the sun became black as sackcloth of hair, and the moon became as blood". **This same description is found elsewhere in the Bible, such as:**

A. Joel 2:27-32 and 3:1-2: "And know that in the midst of Israel I am, and that I am the Lord your God, and none else: and my people shall never be ashamed. And I will pour out my Spirit upon all flesh, and your sons will prophesy and your daughters, your old men shall dream dreams, your young men shall see visions. And also upon the servants and upon the handmaids I will pour out my Spirit in those days. I will show wonders in heaven and on earth, blood, and fire, and pillars of smoke. The sun shall be turned into darkness, and the moon into blood, before the great and terrible day of the Lord. And everyone who calls on the name of the LORD shall be delivered: for in mount Zion and in Jerusalem shall be deliverance, as the LORD hath said, and in the remnant whom the LORD shall call".

"For behold, in those days, and at that time I will cause the captivity of Judah and Jerusalem, I will gather all nations and bring them down to the valley of Jehoshaphat, and will plead with them there for my people and for my heritage Israel , whom they have scattered among the nations, and parted my land".

Joel 3:14-15: "Many people in the valley of decision: for the day is near Jehovah in the valley of decision. The sun and moon are darkened, and the stars withdraw their shining".

* This clearly shows that these signals will happen when all nations are gathered in the Valley of Jehoshaphat, which will happen in the sixth bowl of God's wrath.

* Revelation 16:12,14,16: "The sixth angel poured out his bowl on the great river Euphrates, and its water was dried up to prepare the way for the kings from the east ... they are spirits of demons, miracles, which go forth unto the kings of the earth around the world, to gather them to the battle of that great day of God Almighty ... and they assembled them at the place that in Hebrew is called Armageddon".

B. Isaiah 4:3-6; 13:9-10: "And it shall be that is left in Zion, and he that remaineth in Jerusalem, shall be called holy, all who are in Jerusalem among the living when the Lord wash the filth of the daughters of Zion, and purged the blood of Jerusalem from the midst thereof by the spirit of judgment and a spirit of fire. And the Lord will create upon every dwelling place of Mount Zion and over her assemblies, a cloud and smoke by day, and evening glow of fire that throws flames for upon all the glory shall be a canopy, and will be a shelter to amaze against the heat of the day, and a refuge and for a covert from storm and from rain".

"Behold, the day of the Lord cometh, cruel both with wrath and fierce anger, to make the land desolation and to destroy out of it its fishermen. As the stars of heaven and their constellations will not give their light: the sun be darkened, and the moon shall not give her light".

* This will happen when God enters judgment and devastation from Jerusalem, and served in the seventh bowl of God's wrath.

C. Ezekiel 32:7-8: *"And when you have extinguished cover the heavens and make their stars dark; cover the sun with a cloud, and the moon shall not give her light. I will darken all the bright lights of heaven for you, and set darkness upon thy land, saith the Lord".*

* We must not be amused by both these signals of the moon and the sun because God used these same signals against the Pharaoh King of Egypt, and it was not the end of the world.

D. Revelation 8:12: "And the fourth angel sounded, and was wounded a third of the sun, and the third part of the moon, and the third part of the stars, so that the third part of them was darkened , and no not shine in the third part of the day and the night likewise".

* During the fourth trumpet happen as a indication of things to come in the sixth bowl of God's wrath so that the world becomes aware, but even so they apperceive.

E. Matthew 24:29-30: "Immediately after the tribulation of those days shall the sun be darkened, and the moon shall not give her light, and the stars shall fall from heaven, and the powers of heaven shall be shaken. Then the sign of the Son of man in heaven: and then shall all the tribes of the earth will see the Son of Man coming on the clouds of heaven with power and great glory".

* This passage tells us that if they have passed all the disasters of the seven seals, seven trumpets and seven bowls of wrath, only then will the signals of the sun and moon happen. Which predate the second coming of Jesus Christ to this earth to save the people of Israel from destruction imminent at the hands of all the nations gathered at Armageddon. **This is when every eye will see him in Revelation 1:7:** *"Behold, he* *cometh with clouds, and every eye will see Him, even those who pierced him: and all the tribes of the earth shall wail because of him. Yes, amen".*

* In short, the events of Revelation 6:12 will happen in the seventh bowl of God's wrath. That is why this text is incorrectly ordered according to the sequence of events that happen during the seven seals, seven trumpets and seven bowls of God's wrath.

2) The second correction is Chapter 6, verses 13 and 14: "And the stars of heaven fell unto the earth, as a fig tree casts its unripe figs when shaken by a strong wind. And the heaven departed as a scroll when it is rolled up, and every mountain and island was removed from its place".

* The last thing that will happen before the New Jerusalem descends is the destruction of the heaven and earth that now exist. It is impossible, after the destruction of the heaven and the earth; keep having disasters; so clearly we can see that these verses are misplaced in the text.

Similarly, we find other verses that speak of the same subject, for example:

A. Isaiah 34:1-4: "Come near, ye nations, to hear, and hearken, ye people listen. Hear all the earth and everything in it, the world and everything it produces. For the Lord is angry with all nations, and his fury upon all their armies, destroy them and delivered them to the slaughter. Their slain shall be cast out, and their stink shall come up carcasses, and the mountains shall be melted with their blood. And all the host of heaven shall be dissolved, and the heavens shall be rolled together as a scroll: and all their host shall fall, as the leaf falls from the vine, and as a falling fig from the fig tree".

* The Lord will be angry with all the nations gathered after the millennium to destroy Israel; of course, God himself will destroy it, and that's when Destroy the heaven and the earth we see today.

B. 2nd Peter 3:7; 10-13: "But the heavens and the earth which are now, are reserved by the same word for fire in the day of judgment and perdition of ungodly men.
10 But the day of the Lord will come like a thief in the night, in which the heavens will pass away with a roar and the elements will be dissolved, and the earth and the works that are therein shall be burned up. Since all these things shall be dissolved, what hastening the coming of the day of God, wherein the heavens elements ought you to be in holy conduct and godliness, looking for and hastening the coming of the day of God, because of which the heavens will be dissolved, being on fire, and the elements will melt with fervent heart? 13 Nevertheless we, according to his promise, look for new heavens and a new earth, in which righteousness dwells".

* The heaven and earth will be destroyed in the Day of Judgment, or day of the Lord, or day of God. When will this be? During the destruction of the wicked at the Last Judgment, before the New Jerusalem descends to the earth.

* In short, all these texts tell us where in the Revelation is that they must be located the reference verses.

C. Revelation 6:15-17: "And the kings of the earth, and the great , the rich, the captains, and the mighty men, every slave and every free man , hid themselves in the dens and in the rocks of the mountains, and said to the mountains and rocks, Fall on us and hide us from the face of him who sits on the throne and from the wrath of the Lamb: For the great day of their wrath has come , and who can stand?".

* There will be a great earthquake and the sign of the sun and moon will appear, and as a result of all this, the evil men will hide in bunkers or shelters that they have prepared to hide in case of major disasters or bombs. Let see other verses related to the theme:

A. Isaiah 2:10, 11, 19, 21: "Enter into the rock, and hide thee in the dust, for fear of the LORD and the splendour of his majesty. 11 The lofty looks of man be humbled, and the haughtiness of men shall be made low: and the LORD alone will be exalted in that day". 19 "And they shall go into the caves of the rocks and the holes of the earth, for fear of the Lord and from the glory of his majesty, when he shall arise to shake terribly the earth. 21 and will get into the clefts of the rocks and in the holes of the rocks, for fear of the LORD and the splendour of his majesty, when he ariseth to shake terribly the earth".

* When will the wicked are hide? When Jesus comes for the second time to earth to save Israel, as the verses 10, 19 and 21 show.

B. Luke 23:30: "Then shall they begin to say to the mountains, fall on us, and to the hills, cover us".

* The Lord Jesus prophesied this event on his way to his crucifixion, in the land of Israel.

C. Hosea 10:8: "And the high places of Aven will be destroyed, the sin of Israel, come up on their altars and thistle hawthorn. And they say to the mountains, Cover us, and to the hills, fall on us".

* It shows a context historical fulfilled, and one prophetic that has not yet been fulfilled; which implies us, that the

people of Israel preferred to go underground before the wrath of God.

D. Joel 2:11: "And the Lord shall utter his voice before his army: for his camp is very great, is strong that executes his word: for great is the day of the Lord, and very terrible, and who can stand"?.

* The sun and the moon are darkened before the coming of the day of wrath, the day of the Lord, and who can stand?

* These two verses bear no relation to the context, so must be ordered in proper place according to what other texts indicate.

3) In Revelation 19:1-6: John saw a great multitude in heaven, singing jubilant because God had already punished the great prostitute. We know that in Revelation 16:17-21 is when it holds its destruction.

Therefore, in Revelation 16:17-21 is destroyed, and then in chapter 19:1-6, takes place the celebration in heaven of that awaited revenge.

Looking back to earth, John sees the signal immediately before the return of Jesus Christ for the second time to Earth, to stay and rule for a thousand years. This is the announcement that finally reaches the consummation of God's wrath. **Here announces us that he will come, but not yet we see his coming.** (Revelation 6:12 B, 15-17). This will happen in Revelation chapter 16:11-21 where is consummate the wrath.

Compare with: **Matthew 24:29-30; Isaiah 2:10-12, 19, 21; Haggai 2:7-8; Amos 8:9; Luke 23:29-30; Joel 2:10-11; Revelation 6:12 and 15-17; Isaiah 13:5, 9-11 and 13; and Hosea 10:8.**

Matthew 24:29-30: "Immediately after the tribulation of those days shall the sun be darkened, and the moon shall not give her light, and the stars shall fall from heaven, and the powers of heaven shall be shaken. Then the sign of the Son of man in heaven: and then shall all the tribes of the earth will see the Son of Man coming on the clouds of heaven with power and great glory".

Isaiah 2:10-12: "Enter into the rock, and hide thee in the dust, for fear of the LORD and the splendour of his majesty. The lofty looks of man shall be humbled, and the haughtiness of men shall be made low: and the Lord alone shall be exalted in that day. For the day of the LORD of hosts shall come upon everything proud and lofty, exalted above all, and will be killed".

Isaiah 2:19 "And they shall go into the caves of the rocks and the holes of the earth, for fear of the LORD and the splendour of his majesty, when he ariseth to shake terribly the earth".

Isaiah 2:21 " ... and get into the clefts of the rocks and in the holes of the rocks, for fear of the LORD and the splendour of his majesty, when he ariseth to shake terribly the earth".

Haggai 2:7-8: "And I will shake all nations, and shall come to the Desire of all nations, and I will fill this house with glory, saith the Lord of hosts. The silver is mine and the gold is mine, saith the Lord of hosts".

Amos 8:9: "It shall come to pass in that day, saith the Lord, that I will cause the sun at noon, and I will darken the earth in the clear day".

Luke 23:29-30: "For behold, the days are coming when they will say, Blessed are the barren, and the wombs that never bore and the breasts that never nursed. Then shall they begin to say to the mountains, fall on us, and to the hills, Cover us"

Joel 2:10-11: "Before them the earth tremble, the heavens shall tremble: the sun and the moon are darkened, and the stars withdraw their shining. And the Lord shall utter his voice before his army: for his camp is very great, is strong that executes his word: for great is the day of the Lord, and very terrible, and who can stand"?.

Revelation 6:12 y 15-17: "And behold there was a great earthquake and the sun became black as sackcloth of hair, and the moon became as blood. And the kings of the earth, and the great, the rich, the captains, and the mighty men, every slave and every free man, hid themselves in the dens and in the rocks of the mountains, and said to the mountains and rocks, Fall on us, and hide us from the face of him that sitteth on the throne and from the wrath of the Lamb: For the great day of their wrath has come, and who can stand?".

Isaiah 13:5: "They come from a far country, from the end of the heavens, the Lord and the weapons of his indignation, to destroy the whole earth".

Isaiah 13:9-11: "Behold, the day of the Lord cometh, cruel both with wrath and fierce anger, to lay the land desolate and destroy out of it its sinners. As the stars of heaven and their constellations will not give their light: the sun be darkened, and the moon shall not give her light. I will punish the world for their evil, and the wicked for their iniquity and I will cause the arrogance of the proud, and will lay low the haughtiness of the terrible".

Isaiah 13:13: "Therefore I will shake the heavens and the earth shall remove out of her place, in the wrath of the LORD of hosts, and in the day of his fierce anger".

Hosea 10:8: "And the high places of Aven will be destroyed, the sin of Israel, come up on their altars and thistle hawthorn. And they say to the mountains, Cover us, and to the hills, fall on us".

This should not scare us to the degree of assuming the Earth will disappear. Why? Because this has already happened. When? Recently, when the Japanese earthquake occurred which caused this country to shift 4 meters to where it use to be. Geographically, Japan is not where it was before, it is four meters beyond. The rivers which were in the south-north are now north-south. Besides this, also caused the Earth to move 10 cm over its axis, causing shortening of time: Today the planet is eight minutes late, which will mean that the days are getting shorter as revealed in Matthew 24:22.

This leads us to consider that if it has already happened, it may happen tomorrow, but the earth will not yet be destroyed because it needs to pass the millennium and the last world war.

Verses 7 and 8 of Chapter 32 of the book of Ezekiel, similarly show how ancient Egypt was punished, and then there was darkening of the sun and moon. **For this reason, we conclude that the facts stated in Revelation 6:12 B, 15-17 happen in the battle of Armageddon, at the last bowl of the wrath of God, without the earth and the heavens being destroyed yet.**

4) Correction in Revelation 7:1-8: The first verse speaks of four angels who have nothing to do with the ones in the sixth trumpet in Revelation 9:14; nor are they equal to those of

Zechariah 6:5. These angels are individuals who are destined for a specific job.

* Revelation 7:1 : "After this I saw four angels standing on the four corners of the earth, holding the four winds of the earth , to not blow on the earth, neither the sea, nor on any tree".

* Revelation 9:14: "I said to the sixth angel which had the trumpet, Loose the four angels who are bound at the great river Euphrates".

* Zechariah 6:5: "And the angel answered and said unto me: These are the four spirits of the heavens, which go forth from standing before the Lord of all the earth".

* **As we know from the book of Daniel, Daniel's seventieth week is divided into two periods of three and a half years each. The first three and a half years are for the gentile church; the three and a half years later for the Jewish church, here is where the 144,000 are sealed and the two witnesses preach the gospel of the Name, to the Jews and the whole world . Today, the gentile church is doing this work.**

* <u>**In short, the 144,000 Jews will be sealed in the middle of the seventieth week of Daniel, still have a place where those verses.**</u>

5) Correction in Revelation 7:9-17: The crowd dressed in white robes, of all tribes, nations, peoples and languages, **is clearly referring to the church** confirms the question, "who are they...?". The response was immediate: "...they are the ones who came out of great tribulation ...". In Revelation 15:2 we see this crowd and say they have got the victory over the beast and his image and over his mark and the number of his name. In Revelation 14:9-13 the Bible says that those who receive the mark of the beast, will drink from the cup or bowls of the wrath of God, and finally concludes: "... **Blessed are the dead who die in the Lord ...**".

* Revelation 15: 2; 14:9-13: "And I saw a sea of glass mingled with fire: and them that had gotten the victory over the beast and his image and over his mark and the number of his name, stand on the sea of glass, having the harps of God".

"And the third angel followed them, saying with a loud voice, If any man worship the beast and his image and receives his mark on his forehead or on his hand, The same shall drink of the wine of the wrath of God, which is poured mixture into the cup of his anger, and he shall be tormented with fire and brimstone before the holy angels and of the Lamb: and the smoke of their torment goes up forever and ever. And they have no rest day or night, who worship the beast and his image, and whosoever receiveth the mark of his name. Here is the patience of the saints who keep the commandments of God and the faith of Jesus. I heard a voice from heaven saying to me, Write, Blessed are the dead who die in the Lord. Yes, says the Spirit, they will rest from their labours, and their works follow them".

* **Erroneously, references from the King James version lead us to Daniel 12:1 and Matthew 24:21:** "At that time Michael, the 5 great prince which stand for the children of thy people: and there shall be a time of distress such as never was since there was a nation, but at that time your people shall be delivered, every one that shall be found written in the book". "For then shall be great tribulation, such as has not been since the beginning of the world until now, nor ever shall be".

* We note that, clearly referring to the persecution that the Jewish people will suffer, in the middle of the seventieth week of Daniel, when the Antichrist sits in the temple to worship him, and starts the abomination of desolation.

* In other words, Revelation 7:9-17 must be ordered conformably with the events in the middle of the seventieth week of Daniel.

6) Revelation 8: The right thing is that followed by the seven seals of chapter six, will the seven trumpets of chapter eight. **If you read chapter six and follow to the eighth chapter, we will see that these chapters should be continuous.**

7) Revelation 9: Following Chapter eight is correct to continue with chapter nine as this is the correct order.

8) Revelation 10:1-11: These verses are a warning to the gentile church for this call upon them as he is announcing that the sound of the seventh trumpet, time the preaching of gospel to the Gentiles will be finished and the mystery that had been hidden for so long would be consummated. **What mystery? The mystery of the uprising of the church.** It orders that the gospel is preached to all nations for the last time , before closing the door to the Gentiles. Logically the seventh trumpet precedes the sixth of Revelation 9:13.

9) Revelation 11:1-13: These lines correspond to the gospel of the name, by the two witnesses of **-Jewish origin-** to the Jews and worldwide who have missed the rapture of the gentile church.

* As shown in the above texts, the beast is at its peak of power and glory when these two witnesses are preaching against him and the whole world is of the side of antichrist.

* In short, I do not think it is necessary to clarify that the two witnesses will appear on stage during the second half of the seventieth week of Daniel, precisely when the Antichrist is revealed as wicked and persecution is unleashed on the people of Israel.

10) **Revelation 11:14** *"The second woe is past: behold, the third woe cometh quickly".* In Revelation 8:13 an angel preaches about the three "WOE" that will happen with the sounding of the last three trumpets. In Revelation 9:12 spends the first woe that relates to the third trumpet. Revelation 11:14 is the second woe, and corresponds to the sixth trumpet. This verse cannot go in place of the two witnesses, for they will be preaching during the bowls of the wrath of God and never during the sounding of trumpets. The trumpets sound for the church, as the bowls are the only announcement for the Jewish people exclusively.

11) **Revelation 11:15-19**: The seventh trumpet should go in sequence after the sixth ring. **This is the correct order.**

The Bible clearly states that this is the time for rewarding the prophets, saints and those who fear His name. But this will only happen when we pass by the tribunal of Christ, immediately after the rapture of the gentile church; confirming once again, this will happen in middle of Daniel's seventieth week.

* We recall that so far have been two "woe", of the fifth and sixth trumpet, missing only the seventh, that as doesn't appear anywhere, it makes sense that go after the end touching the last trump: For this, I know that it goes here.

12) **Revelation 12:** This chapter will reveal to us what will happen to the people of Israel in the tribulation of Jacob.

13) Revelation 13: This chapter is a summary of the government of the antichrist and false prophet during the seven years of Daniel's seventieth week. The first ten verses correspond to the first half of the week and verses 11 to 18 correspond to the second half. **This summary is the transition between the seventh trumpet and the first cup of the wrath of God.**

14) Revelation 14:1-20: The 144,000 listed in these verses are the same 144,000 Jewish people sealed in Revelation 7:1-8.

Although the Bible does not explicitly specify, we can assume for several reasons:

A. The two groups are 144,000.

B. The apostle John not says "other", like often named "one" in Revelation, referring to a different kind of angel, signal, beast, and so on.

C. The two groups are sealed in their foreheads:

* **The Bible teaches us that every business must be evidenced by two or three witnesses, and here we have three valid reasons to believe that these two groups are one**. What happens then? We can conclude that the 144,000 of Revelation 7:1-8 are sealed before the ministry of preaching the gospel to the Jews and the world. In addition to the 144,000 Revelation 14:1-5 are the same, upon completion of his ministry in victory.

* Revelations 6-13 announce the gospel to the Jews and the incredulous world left behind in the rapture. The future and imminent destruction of the great whore, the punishment under the bowls of God's wrath to who put the mark of the beast; and bliss for those who die in exchange for living the gospel.

* Revelations 14-20 precisely verse 19 gives us understanding that this will happen during the wrath of God. What will happen? The earth and its inhabitants will be cut, blinded, and separated according to whether they have the mark of the beast or not.

* We can ensure, then, that these verses of Chapter 14 corresponding to the continuation of chapter 7:1-8, it clearly states that this will happen to those who do not hear the truth of the gospel so that they will be punished during the God's wrath.

* The 144,000 sealed will be allied with the two witnesses in preaching the gospel to the Jewish people and the world, for this reason, the texts are parallel.

15) Revelation 15: In these passages we can see several important respects:

A. The vision takes place at the beginning of God's wrath. Why? Because they are the seven angels with the seven last plagues which are given seven golden bowls full of the wrath of God. The cups are spread, but still the order to pour them is not yet given. (Revelation 15:7).

B. It is emphasized that no one could enter heaven until the last bowl of the wrath of God is poured out. **In other words, the gateway to heaven for the church compose by gentiles and Jews and for the whole world is closed.** It will only be opened when the judgment of the seventh bowl is complete for the Jews and Gentiles who have not been made by the antichrist mark may enter. At this point, the gentile church would have been lifted. (Revelation 15: 8).

C. When God's judgments are met through the seven vials, then all nations will come to Jerusalem to worship the Lord Jesus Christ during the millennium. (Revelation 15: 4).

16) Revelation 16:15: *"Behold, I come as a thief. Blessed is he who stays awake and keeps his garments, lest he walks naked, and they see his shame".*

This passage deserves a deeper study; because we can confuse us with the coming of the Lord Jesus Christ to raise the gentile church to meet Him in the clouds. But Revelation 16:15 is talking about his second coming; It is the time when he is coming the Gentile church to establish his millennial kingdom.

First of all, let's look at one of the signs left by the Lord Jesus Christ to the gentile church so that it is perceived in their encounter with him:

1st Thessalonians 5:2-9: "For yourselves know perfectly that the day of the Lord so cometh as a thief in the night, when they shall say, Peace and safety, then sudden destruction will come upon her, as labour pains on a pregnant woman, and not will escape. But ye, brethren, are not in darkness, that that day should overtake you as a thief. For all of you we are children of light and children of the day: we are neither of the night nor of darkness. Therefore let us not sleep as others do, but let us watch and be sober. For those who sleep, sleep at night, and those who get drunk, gets drunk at night. But we who are of the day be sober, putting on the breastplate of faith and love, and the hope of salvation as a helmet. For God hath not appointed us to wrath, but to obtain salvation through our Lord Jesus Christ".

We know the Lord Jesus Christ in this passage refers to the rapture of the gentile church, for three things:

a. Chapter 5:3: *"When they say peace and safety then sudden destruction cometh upon them ..."* This is half of the seventieth week of Daniel and happens when the abomination of desolation begins. In addition, it sets the tone in which the Antichrist will sit in God's temple to worship him. **And it is just at this moment when he break the covenant with the Jewish people.**

Daniel 9:27: *"And the other will confirm a covenant with many in the middle of the week he shall cause the sacrifice and offering. And for the overspreading of abominations he shall make it desolate, even until the consummation, and that determined shall be poured upon the desolate".*

b. Verse 9 confirms that God has not appointed the gentile church to go through the wrath of God, but save us from the coming wrath. How? !Lift up us before!.

For more clarity, we can see this text in other versions:

* 1st Thessalonians 5:9: *"For God did not choose us to suffer his punishment, but has chosen us for salvation through our Lord Jesus Christ"* (Word of God for all versions).

* "For God has not called us to punish, but to receive salvation through our Lord Jesus Christ". (Current Language Translation).

* "For God destined us to take the punishment, but to obtain salvation through our Lord Jesus Christ"(God speaks today).

c. The text tells that the Lord Jesus has left us signals for us to not be lost from the true path. We must not be mislead, much less let ourselves be surprised, because if we analyse the signs and follow them, then the rapture of the gentile church will not take us by surprise.

Revelation 3:3 "Remember therefore how thou hast received and heard, and hold fast, and repent. Well if you will not watch, I will come like a thief, and thou shalt not know what hour I will come upon thee".

The passage also refers to the exhortation which the Spirit makes the gentile church so that it is apperceived and watching for the time when the Lord Jesus Christ comes to lift us. This is a message to the gentile church in Sardis and the context and pretext indicate and emphasize that it is a message to the church and not to the Jewish people.

* Now let's analyze why this text of Revelation 16:15 actually refers to an appeal to the Jewish people to be ready regarding the second coming of Jesus Christ with the gentile church to establish His millennial kingdom:

A. Revelation 16:15: *"Behold, I come as a thief. Blessed is he who stays awake and keeps his garments, lest he walks naked, and they see his shame".* The context and pretext indicate that at this point of revelation is under the sixth bowl of God's wrath. Furthermore nations meet to invade Israel in the battle of Armageddon.

THIEF IN THE NIGHT: This title to the chief priests of the temple was granted, and who remained awake to monitor the fire of the altar of the temple so it will not go off, when they saw any of the Leviticus priests fall sleep, they sent a guard to set fire to his clothes and when Levites realized that the fire was spreading through his clothes, they began to strip away his clothes and said that his shame was discovered.

* Analyzing this verse also in the light of other scriptures, we can conclude much better the meaning of this text:

B. Matthew 24:37-39, 42-44: "But as the days of Noah, so shall also the coming of the Son of Man. For as in the days before the flood they were eating and drinking, marrying and giving in marriage, until the day that Noah entered into the ark, and knew not until the flood came and took it all, so shall also the coming the Son of Man".

"Watch therefore, for ye know not what hour your Lord doth come. But know this, that if the goodman of the house had known what hour the thief would come, he would have watched and not allowed his house. Therefore you also be ready, for the Son of man cometh at an hour when ye think not".

* As in the days of Noah shall also be the coming of the Son of Man, then did not believe it would rain water from the sky because it had never rained; now they do not believe that it will rain fire from heaven because it has never rained fire. **People then did not understand and now they do not understand either and are dedicated to earthly pleasures, and forget God.** The Lord Jesus Christ will come like a thief, he is not a thief, but he will come suddenly, when the world does not think or imagine. It will happen when they are enjoying themselves and enjoying carnal pleasures. This is what the Lord Jesus Christ tells the Jewish people and we know from the context in Matthew 24:29-30: *"Immediately after the tribulation of those days shall the sun be darkened, and the moon shall not give her light, and the stars fall from heaven, and the powers of heaven shall be shaken. Then the sign of the Son of man in heaven: and then shall all the tribes of the earth will see the Son of Man coming on the clouds of heaven with power and great glory".*

C. Translation King James refers us to other passages that have nothing to do with Revelation 16:15 because they are out of context; they are:

a. Luke 12:35-40: "Let your loins be girded and your lamps burning, and be like men who wait for their master to return from the wedding thirst, so that when he comes and knocks, they open right away. Blessed are those servants, whom the lord when he cometh shall find watching: verily I say unto you that he shall gird himself, and make them sit down to meat, and will come and serve them. And if he shall come in the second watch, or come in the third watch, and find them so, blessed are those servants. But know this, that if the goodman of the family that now the thief would come, he would have watched and not allowed his house. Be ye therefore ready also, for in an hour that ye think not the Son of man cometh".

* We can clearly see that this is a teaching through a parable, which indicates that it is not real, but as the same Lord Jesus Christ said, it is a likeness. That proves verse 36, where it says we should be like men who await for their lord "TO RETURN FROM THE WEDDING. "So if you are married and spent the honeymoon with your wife, why should we watch? Verse 37 is clearly speaking to the servants, not the wife, nor his Jewish people; these servants are those who must be vigilant to be invited to the table at the Wedding of the Lamb, and serve them himself. The servants are the guests, the guests, who sit at the table; are not the church compose by gentiles and Jews who is his wife.

b. 2nd Peter 3:10 *"But the day of the Lord will come like a thief in the night, in which the heavens will pass away with a roar and the elements will be dissolved, and the earth and the works that are therein shall be burned".*

This passage is very telling and refers to an event that will not happen in the middle of the seventieth week of Daniel, nor at the end of the week. This will happen after the millennium and in the day of judgment to the fallen angels with Satan at their head, in the judgment before the Great White Throne Judgment or angels. Why can we tell? Because that's when the heaven will be destroyed and the land we see today; not before the millennium.

* **Conclusion**: **We can conclude, thus, that Revelation 16:15 is where it should be in the book of Revelation and the Bible,** this verse is immovable, although is apparently in disagreement. Recall that one thing is the appearance and another is what it really is.

17) Revelation 16:1-16: The order is given to the seven angels to pour out on the earth the seven bowls of the wrath of God. This chapter 16 is chapter 17, but only in relation to the first six cups. Then there is an intermediate corresponding to Chapter 18, which tells how the great Babylon will be destroyed.

18) Revelation 16:17-21: Speaks of the seventh bowl and shows us the great catastrophes that will befall the earth and men who, by then, dwell in it. These texts must go after it tells how the great Babylon will be destroyed, which is Chapter 18. **We know this because in chapter 16:19 tells us that finally the great Babylon will be destroyed,** in addition, there is not place or another cup in which the punishment of the great prostitute is met. It is here and now, the moment of destruction.

19) Revelation 17: This chapter has a corresponding order after chapter 15. Why? Because in chapter 15: 1 says the word of God that John saw seven angels having the seven last plagues; this is the first time the seven angels appear. In Chapter 15: 7 it is where is recorded when the bowls are given to the seven angels, because Juan had seen before but without the bowls. In Revelation 17: 1 we are told directly that came one of the seven angels which had the seven vials; so the seven angels already had the seven bowls, which necessarily means that Chapter 17 has to go after Chapter 15, but before chapter 16, which already begin to pour out the bowls.

* Otherwise, this chapter shows us the meaning of the woman and of the beast that has seven heads and ten horns.

20) Revelation 18: This chapter tells how will be the destruction of the great whore and lamentation of the nations of the world because this abominable city has been destroyed in an hour. This chapter should go immediately ordered after that the six bowls of the wrath of God from chapter 16:1-16 spill. Chapter 18 is shown, how will be the destruction of the great whore; in chapters 16: 17-21 is finally shown itself destruction; why precisely chapter 18 goes first and then chapter 16: 17-21.

Revelation 16:19: **The big city has all the features of Sodom** (City destroyed for their sensual abominations);
Egypt (Country delivered to worship multiple gods);
Jerusalem (City of religious tradition, rebel to God and also incredulous);
Babylon (The cradle of pagan idolatry and moral corruption).

We can summarize that the big city has all the features decadent of Sodom, Egypt, Jerusalem and Babylon together, so it is the mother of harlots and abominations of the earth.

Great Babylon = The big city.

(Rev 18:2, 10, 16,18,19,21, 14:8, 16:19; 17, 5, 18).

There is an material Babylon = Rome and paganism. (Revelation 17).

Another spiritual Babylon = Jerusalem and rebellion. (Matthew 23:16-17; Luke 21:5; Exodus 28).

It was found: The blood of prophets, saints and the Son of God.

(Revelation 18: 24 = Matthew 23:34 = Luke 10:49 = Acts 7:52).

* Revelation 18:4 Urges the people to come out before the great Babylon be destroyed. It cannot refer to leave Jerusalem, because would have his people dispersed at the end of the seventieth week, and of course, would be contrary to what the Bible says; about Israel that will be all together in Jerusalem, when they are gathered nations in the valley of Megiddo; therefore it refers to leave Rome.

* Revelation 16:19: The great city was divided into three. Here you cannot be referring to Jerusalem, because only the Bible records that when the Lord Jesus Christ comes to save the people of Israel, his feet will stand on the Mount of Olives and it will split in two, creating two large valleys, this will be in the seventh bowl. **If Jerusalem is already divided in three parts into the sixth bowl, how, then, can be divided into two in the seventh bowl, with Jerusalem as small as it is today?**

* Matthew 24:15-21: The Lord Jesus Christ calls the Jewish people to leave Jerusalem only when the abomination of desolation, which will take place in the middle of the week when the peace treaty break.
In Matthew chapter 24:30-31 and Zechariah 14:4 tells us that after the Lord Jesus Christ stand on the Mount of Olives, all the nations shall see, and then He will send his angels to gather the people of Israel which it will be spread throughout the world because of his flight when the pact with the antichrist broke.

* We can conclude, then, that in any way the great city of Babylon of Revelation 17 and 18 is Jerusalem. Although apparently is similar as described in the top of this

reflection. Well, one thing is the appearance and another that is.

The great city of Jerusalem in Revelation 11:8 which is different from the great city of Babylon of Revelation 17:5 and 8.

Revelation 17:5: *"And upon her forehead was a name written, MYSTERY, BABYLON THE GREAT, THE MOTHER OF HARLOTS AND abominations of the earth".*

Revelation 17:8: *"And the woman whom you saw is that great city which reigns over the kings of the earth".*

Revelation 18:2: *"And he cried mightily with a strong voice, saying, fallen, fallen is Babylon the great, and is become the habitation of devils, and the hold of every foul spirit, and a cage of every unclean and hateful bird".*

Revelation 18:10: *"Standing afar off for the fear of her torment, saying, alas, that great city Babylon, that mighty city: for in one hour is thy judgment come".*

Revelation 18:16: *"And saying, Alas , alas, that great city, that was clothed in fine linen, purple and scarlet, and decked with gold, precious stones and pearls".*

Revelation 18:18: *"And I saw the smoke of her burning, they cried out, saying, what city is like unto this great city?".*

Revelation 18:19: *"And they cast dust on their heads, and cried, weeping and wailing, saying, Alas, alas, that great city, in which all who had ships at sea became rich by her wealth! For in one hour is she made desolate".*

191

Revelation 18:21: *"And a mighty angel took up a stone like a great millstone, and cast it into the sea, saying,* **with violence shall Babylon be thrown down, the big city, never to be found again"**.

Revelation 14:8: *"And another angel followed, saying, Fallen, fallen is Babylon the great city, because she made all nations drink of the wine of the wrath of her fornication"*.

Revelation 16:19: *"And the great city was divided into three parts and the cities of the nations fell: and great Babylon came in remembrance before God, to give her the cup of the wine of the fierceness of his wrath"*.

21) Revelation 19:1-6: John saw a great multitude in heaven singing jubilant because God had already punished the great prostitute. We know that in Revelation 16:17-21 is when it holds its destruction. Therefore, in Revelation 16:17-21 is destroyed and then in chapter 19:1-6 gives way to the celebration in heaven that awaited revenge.

22) Revelation 19:7-10: Precisely is here where the marriage of the Lamb is celebrated; which occurs once the New Jerusalem has descended. Therefore these verses must be located after the new heaven and new earth in Revelation 21 happens.

23) Revelation 19:11-21 in these verses it is revealed the outcome of the battle of Armageddon, which happens before the millennium and the outpouring of the seventh bowl of God's wrath. **The Lord Jesus Christ and his heavenly army will fight against the Antichrist, the false prophet and the kings of the earth and their armies.** As always, at the end of the battle, the Lord Jesus Christ is the winner and out of the way forever the antichrist, the false prophet and many kings and their armies. Now only Satan and his demons and other kings and their armies; all of them will be overcome in the final war, after the millennium. Revelation 19:11-21 is after the sign of the moon and the sun (Revelation 6:12B and 15-17), that announced the coming of the Lord Jesus Christ who overshadow his feet on the Mount of Olives, to save Israel of their enemies.

24) Revelation 20:1-6: We know from the prophet Zechariah (13:8) that only a third of humanity will survive the Battle of Armageddon. These nations entering the millennium or reign of Jesus Christ with the Church for a thousand years on earth. However, in the millennium God will be tested to the nations to see who is with him and who is against him. *Zechariah 13:9 "And I will bring the fire to the third party , and will refine them as silver is refined, and will I test them as gold is tested. Call on my name, and I will hear, and tell my people: and they shall say, The Lord is my God". Zechariah 14:16-19 "And all that is left of the nations which came against Jerusalem shall go up from year to year to worship the King, the LORD of hosts, and to celebrate the Feast of Tabernacles. And that whichever of the families of the earth do not go up to Jerusalem to worship the King, Jehovah of hosts, upon them shall be no rain. And if the family of Egypt does not go up and take part, they will have no rain; shall be the plague wherewith the LORD will smite the heathen that come not up to keep the feast of tabernacles. This will be the punishment of Egypt, and the punishment of all nations that come not up to keep the feast of tabernacles".*

* All this indicates that even in the millennium there will be own will. The nations will go to Jerusalem every year to celebrate the sacrifices of the Old Testament and the Jewish holidays. Every day, there will be burnt in the new temple, where the Lord Jesus Christ will be as a great High Priest that he is.

Isaiah 66:20, 23: *"And bring all your brethren from all the nations as an offering to the Lord, on horses, in chariots, in litters, on mules and on camels, to my holy mountain Jerusalem, says the LORD, to as the children of Israel bring an offering in a clean vessel into the house of the Lord. And month after month, and day of rest on the Sabbath, all flesh shall come to worship before me, saith the Lord".*

Isaiah 2:1-4: *"What Isaiah the son of Amos saw concerning Judah and Jerusalem. You pass in the last days, to be confirmed mountain of the house of Jehovah as chief among the mountains, and shall be exalted above the hills, and to him shall all the nations. And many people shall go and say, Come, and let us go up to the mountain of the LORD, to the house of the God of Jacob, and he will teach us his ways and walk in His paths. For out of Zion shall go forth the law, and the word of Jehovah Jerusalem. And he shall judge among the nations, and shall rebuke many people: and they shall beat their swords into plowshares, and their spears into pruning hooks shall not lift up sword against nation, neither shall they learn war any more".*

Here we also hear of the millennium and we explained that in this period there will be no more wars or rumours of wars. Similarly, Isaiah 11:1-10 speaks of this time period in which the Lord Jesus Christ will judge righteously and be peace between animals and between them and man.

Isaiah 65:25 *"The wolf and the lamb shall feed together, the lion shall eat straw like the bullock: and dust shall be the serpent's meat. Not hurt nor do poorly in all my holy mountain, saith the Lord. At this time the whole earth be filled with the knowledge of the gospel".* Isaiah 11:9 and Jeremiah 31:31-34 *And they shall teach no more every man his neighbour, and none his brother, saying, Know the Lord: for all shall know me, from the least of them to the greatest, says LORD: for I will forgive their iniquity, and I will remember their sin no more.* "People live a thousand years and a hundred years will a child live, in addition, the sinners who for a thousand years have not believed the gospel and keep sinning, will be cursed and saved to be deceived by Satan after the millennium. Isaiah 65:20: *"There shall be no more thence an infant of days, nor an old man that hath not filled his days: For the child shall die a hundred years old, and the sinner a hundred years old shall be accursed".* Satan will be bound during these thousand years for no more deception for the duration of this period. Revelation 20:1-3.

* **Finally, we can conclude that these texts of Revelation 20:1-6 must go after the outcome of the battle of Armageddon because this is when the millennium begins.**

* **Revelation 20:7-9** It shows the release of Satan and God's judgment on all nations, that were fooled after the millennium, to attacking Israel; **clearly, it is revealed that the punishment is with fire.**

This also corroborates the prophet Zechariah in chapter 14:12 *"And this shall be the plague with which the LORD will strike all the nations that fought against Jerusalem: Their flesh shall consume away while they stand upon their feet, and be consumed in the basins her eyes and their tongue shall consume away in their mouth".*

25) Revelation 20:10-15: it shows us the trial to Satan and the fallen angels, in addition to the Judgment before the great white throne or final Judgment; This will take place as we already saw in the theme of the resurrections; for all the pious and impious of all the times, from Adam until the final war of Revelation 20:9, but which have not been raised in previous resurrections. Here it is also confirmed to us the destruction of heaven and earth described in Revelation 6:13-14; 2nd Peter 3:7 and 10-12.

26) In Revelation 21:1-14: John sees heaven and new earth. He also sees the New Jerusalem coming down from heaven. In John 14:2 the Lord Jesus went to prepare a place for the Jew/Gentile church, after destroying the old Jerusalem with the firs heaven and earth.

Who will live in the New Jerusalem?

a. The fallen angels. (Hebrews 12:22).

b. The church compose by gentiles and Jews. (Acts 2:47 and Revelation 21:3-4).

c. The saints of Jesus Christ. (Hebrews 12:23).

d. Jesus Christ Himself. (Revelation 21:5-6).

e. The people of Israel left alive until the end of the world war. (Ezekiel 37:26-28).

27) Revelation 21:5-8: When he opened the fifth seal, the souls who had died for the witness of Jesus Christ cried out for vengeance and justice. When he opened the sixth seal something happened, and as we saw before, the verses 6:12B and 13-17 are in disagreement with the place and time of compliance, **therefore, is not that his place. It is therefore necessary to locate the exact texts that follow the sixth seal.** I believe by the Bible that Revelations 21:5-8 must go after Revelations 6:12 part (A) of the text; because part (B) is in disagreement as we have already explained earlier. In 21:5-8 tells us, how he was sitting on the throne is urging overcome whatever comes, because the sinners and cowards who are with the Antichrist will be cast into the lake of fire and brimstone, where there is no water.

The speaker is directly the Alpha and the Omega. He orders everything written and also gives a beatitude: He who have thirst, problems or tribulations; He will strengthen them.

28) Revelation 21:9-27 talks about the new Jerusalem where celebrate the wedding of the Lamb. will be perpetuated. Similarly, the dimensions of this great city are described. Its measurements correspond to 2222,4 km long by 2222,4 km and 2222,4 km wide high. It also has a wall of 70 meters approximately. **The city is built in the form of cube. The diameter of the moon is 2160 miles and the New Jerusalem will be 2600 miles.** In contrast to the tiny earthly Jerusalem, the heavenly is immensely large. Therefore, many people suggest it will be like a satellite on earth.

The earthly Jerusalem was called Sodom and Egypt for their high spiritual, moral and material corruption. Instead, the Jerusalem that comes down from heaven is called "The Great Holy City" and consequently is the New Jerusalem. In it there will be no temple because God himself is the temple of it, nor will the sun or moon because God himself will light with his glow. In other words, there will be no night.

The gates of the New Jerusalem will never be closed, and warned not to enter into it anything unclean or abominable liar ; enter only we are inscribed in the Book of Life.

There will also be an opportunity for nations that do not belong to the Jew/Gentile church but believed in the millennium and after millennium in the Lord Jesus Christ and His true gospel; to enter the New Jerusalem to worship and receive healing with the leaves of the tree of life that will be in the middle of the street in the Holy City. (Revelation 22:2).

We have to take into account that these nations are different than the ones that Zechariah named in 14:16-21; as these nations are ungodly and these ones will be the ones that are going to survive to the battle of Armageddon; which mercifully will enter into the millennium and will only require to go to Jerusalem once per year to worship, under the pain of the punishment without rain on their land.

Possibly these pagan nations will not take advantage of the latest offer of conversion offered by the Lord Jesus Christ; and which will be the ones that will fool Satan after the millennium to go to destroy Israel. (Revelation 20:7-8).

29) Revelation 22: In the first five verses continues by describing what will be in the New Jerusalem.
Verses 6-21 tell us that John was the one who saw and heard everything write in the book of revelation; and the Lord Jesus Christ sent his angel to show John what would happen in the future. Also coming soon explained by those who have washed their robes and ratified by his gospel with a list that cannot enter the New Jerusalem. **Finally, finishing by clarifying that no one can remove or add to this book, or will be cursed and excluded from the great salvation.**

CHRONOLOGICAL ORDER OF THE REVELATION

Chapters 1 +2 +3 +4 +5 + A + Chapter 6:1-12A

Chapter 21:5-8 + Chapter 8

Chapter 9+ Chapter 11:14

Chapter 10:1-11 + 11:15-19 (Third woe passed)

Chapter 7:9-17

Chapter 12 + Chapter 13

Chapter 7:1-8 + Chapter 11:1-13

Chapter 14:1-20 + Chapter 15:1-8

Chapter 17 + Chapter 16:1-16

Chapter 18 + Chapter 16:17-21

Chapter 19:1-6 + Chapter 6:12 B and 6:15-17

Chapter 19:11-21 + Chapter 20:1-9

Chapter 6:13-14 Chapter 20:10-15

Chapter 21:1-4 + Chapter 21:9-27

Chapter 19:7-10 + Chapter 22.

EXPLANATORY NOTE

In this occasion, is necessary to copy the book of Revelation without chapters or verses for better ordering and understanding. The corrections in terms of the ordering of the book, start at the sixth chapter.
(This, in case anyone wants to go directly to this chapter).

Revelation 22:18-19 *"I warn everyone who hears the words of the prophecy of this book: If anyone adds to these things, God shall add unto him the plagues that are written in this book. And if anyone takes words away from this book of prophecy, God shall take away his part from the Book of Life, from the holy city and from the things which are written in this book".*

Here we find a curse for those who remove or add to the book of Revelation. This curse does not extend to those who ordered by chapter and verse, for those who interpret or translate, much less for ordering this book for easy understanding by the church.

As we saw before, what we know today of Revelation is not the original, but rather a copy of a copy, because what we read today are copies of copies of copies of copies of copies ... etc. The original does not exist, and the ordering of the book does we do not know what the right order as we have no original to compare it.

We have today many mistranslations of the Bible, for example let's just put a few passages Casidoro version of Queen and revised by Cipriano of Valera, better known as Reina Valera:

Genesis 1:2 and the earth was without form and void ... (Something that this void cannot be without form).

The correct translation is: And the earth was found without form and void ...

Exodus 3:14 *And God said unto Moses, I AM THAT I AM* ... (God is only that which is?). **The correct translation is**: *I AM WHO I AM, THAT WAS AND THAT WILL...* (Revelation 1:4 and 8; Isaiah 44:6).

Matthew 6:13 *And lead us not into temptation, but deliver us from evil* ... (God never gets into temptation, nor tempt anyone that's what says James 1:13). **The correct translation is:** *And do not let us yield to temptation but deliver us from evil.*

Matthew 28:19 ... *baptizing them in the name of the Father and of the Son and of the Holy Spirit* (Baptismal Formula aggregate that does not appear in the original manuscript and the same bible confirms that there is no baptism done by the Apostles that contains this formula). **The correct translation is:** Go and make me urgently as you can so many disciples of all nations. The formula as stated is an added and there is another version made by Eusebius in the fourth century, says: ... *And make sure they are submerged in water in my name.*

1st Corinthians 1:12 ... *I am of Paul, and I of Apollos, and I of Cephas, and I of Christ.* (The Apostle Paul explains that we are all in Christ, so the discussion was not about who was Christ, or Paul, or Apollos, or Cephas, because if we are all Christ, cannot be no one else). **The correct translation is:** ... *I am of Paul, and I of Apollos, and I of Cephas, and I of CRISPO.*

1st John 5:7-8 because there are three that bear record in heaven, the Father, the Word, and the Holy Ghost: and these three are one. And there are three that bear witness on earth: the Spirit, the water and the blood: and these three agree. I note here including Apocrypha did the Roman Catholic Church to the official version, they used Bible, known as the Latin Vulgate, somewhere in the thirteenth century release. Minutes of the council Latera held by the Roman Catholic Church in 1215, is the first documentary record in Greek language; containing these apocryphal words. On the other hand one wonders: **Who is to be given witness of Heaven? To bear witness in heaven? Angels do not need evidence, because if you are in heaven, is because they are already saved.** The testimony should be given in the earth, where there is still a need of salvation through the testimony of the word. See: (Rev 12:11; 19:10; 22:16). **The correct translation is:** *There are three that bear witness: The Spirit, the water and the blood: and these three agree.*

1st Thessalonians 3:13 *So that He may establish your hearts blameless in holiness before our God and Father* <u>*at the coming of our Lord Jesus Christ with all His saints.*</u>

The Bible clearly teaches us that when Jesus comes with all the saints will be during the battle of Armageddon that will be at the end of the wrath of God (Rev 19:14 and 19; Zech 14:5).

By this time the gentile church will have been raised since 42 months ago; therefore the apostle Paul will not encourage the church to keep blameless to be able to go through the wrath of God.

The correct translation is given by the New Testament Interlinear Greek-Spanish of Francisco Lacueva:
"To secure to you the hearts, blameless in holiness before God and our father, <u>*in the presence of the Lord of us Jesus with all the his saints"*</u>.

In this stage Jesus Christ will come with the gentile church and with the angels. (Matt 16:27 and 24:31; Mark 8:38). The angels will also come to take part in the end of the world war; but the Jew/Gentile church will be excluded of this war. (2nd Thessalonians 1:7-9; Jude 1:14-15).

These are just a few examples of bad translations of the Bible we read today and we have no reason to doubt that the Apocalypse also has its Achilles heel. We also know that the Bible does not have the correct ordering of books by age and writing time, so for example the books of the Old Testament do not follow a chronological order and the New Testament are sorted by gender categories.

We assume that what we read today of Revelation is in the correct order, but the Bible is not based on assumptions or traditions, but on facts and realities.

REVELATION ORDERED WITHOUT CHAPTERS, NOR VERSES

"The revelation of Jesus Christ , which God gave him to show his servants what must soon take place and he sent by his angel unto his servant John: Who bare record of the word of God, and the testimony of Jesus Christ , and of all things that he saw. Blessed is he who reads and those who hear the words of this prophecy, and keep those things which are written therein: for the time is near.

John to the seven churches which are in Asia : Grace and peace to you who is and who was and who is to come, and from the seven spirits who are before his throne, and from Jesus Christ the faithful witness , the firstborn from the dead, and the ruler of the kings of the earth. At that loved us, and washed us from our sins by his blood and made us kings and priests unto God and his Father, to him be glory and dominion forever and ever. Amen. Behold, he cometh with clouds, and every eye will see Him, even those who pierced him: and all kindreds of the earth shall wail because of him. Yes, amen. I am the Alpha and the Omega, the beginning and the ending, saith the Lord, who is and who was and who is to come, the Almighty. I John, your brother and fellow partaker in the tribulation and kingdom and patience in Jesus, was on the island called Patmos because of the word of God and the testimony of Jesus Christ. I was in the Spirit on the Lord's day, and heard behind me a loud voice like a trumpet, Saying, I am Alpha and Omega, the first and the last. Write on a scroll what you see and send it to the seven churches which are in Asia: to Ephesus, Smyrna, Pergamum, Thyatira, Sardis, Philadelphia and Laodicea. And I turned to see the voice that spoke with me and turned, I saw seven golden candlesticks , and in the midst of the seven candlesticks one like unto the Son of man, clothed with a garment down to the foot , and girt about the breast with a golden girdle . His head and his hairs were white like wool, as snow, and His eyes like a flame of fire, and His feet were like bronze glowing in a furnace, and His voice as the sound of many waters. He had in His right hand seven stars, from his mouth came a sharp two-edged sword: and his countenance was as the sun shineth in his strength. When I saw him, I fell at his feet as dead. And he laid his right hand upon me, saying: Fear not, I am the first and the last: and he that liveth, and was dead, but here I am alive forever and ever, amen. And I have the keys of death and Hades. Write the things which thou hast seen, and they are, and the things which shall be hereafter. The mystery of the seven stars which you saw in my right hand and the seven golden lampstands: The seven stars are the angels of the seven churches, and feels lampstands are the seven churches.

To the angel of the church in Ephesus : He who holds the seven stars in his right hand, who walks among the seven golden lampstands , says this: I know your deeds, your hard work and patience, and you cannot tolerate evil , and thou hast tried them which say they are apostles and are not, and hast found them liars: and hast borne, and hast patience , and have laboured for My name, and hast not fainted . But I have against thee, because thou hast left thy first love. Remember therefore from whence thou art fallen, and repent and do the first works, or else I will come unto thee quickly, and will remove thy candlestick out of his place, except thou repent. But you have, that you hate the deeds of the Nicolaitans, which I also hate. He who has an ear, let him hear what the Spirit says to the churches. He who overcomes will I give to eat of the tree of life, which is in the midst of paradise of God. And to the

angel of the church in Smyrna write: The first and the last ,
which was dead, and lived , says this: I know thy works ,
and tribulation , and poverty, (but thou art rich) and the
slander of those which say they are Jews and are not, but
are a synagogue of Satan. Fear none of what you are
about to suffer. Behold, the devil shall cast some of you
into prison, that ye may be tried, and ye shall have
tribulation ten days. Be faithful until death, and I will give
thee a crown of life. He who has an ear, let him hear what
the Spirit says to the churches. He who overcomes shall
not be hurt of the second death.

And to the angel of the church in Pergamum write: He who
has the sharp two-edged sword sayzs this: I know your
works and where you dwell, where Satan's seat is : and
thou holdest my name, and hast not denied my faith ,
block before the children of Israel, to eat things sacrificed
to idols and fornication undertake. So hast thou also them
that hold the doctrine of the Nicolaitans, which thing I
hate. Repent, or else I will come unto thee quickly, and will
fight against them with the sword of my mouth. He who
has an ear, let him hear what the Spirit says to the
churches. He who overcomes will I give to eat of the
hidden manna, and will give him a white stone, and in the
stone a new name written, which no one knows except him
who receives it.

And to the angel of the church in Thyatira write: The Son
of God , who has eyes like a flame of fire, and like
burnished bronze , feet says this: I know your works, love,
and faith, your service and patience, and thy works are
more than the first . But I have a few things against you:
You tolerate that woman Jezebel, who calls prophetess, to
teach and to seduce my servants to commit fornication and
to eat things sacrificed to idols. And I gave her time to

repent, but she refuses to repent of her fornication. Behold, I will cast her into a bed, and great tribulation to them that commit adultery with her, unless they repent of their deeds. And I will kill her children with death, and all the churches shall know that I am he who searches mind and heart, and I will give to everyone according to your works. But you and the rest who are in Thyatira, who do not hold this teaching, who have not known what they call the depths of Satan , I tell you none other burden , but what you have, hold fast till I come . He who overcomes , and keeps My works until the end, to him will I give power over the nations: and he shall rule them with a rod of iron, and they shall be broken like pottery , as I also have received of my Father, and I will give the star morning . He who has an ear, let him hear what the Spirit says to the churches.

To the angel of the church in Sardis write: He who has the seven spirits of God and the seven stars, says this: I know thy works, that thou hast a name that thou livest, and art dead. Be watchful, and strengthen the things that are ready to die: for I have not found thy works perfect before God. Remember therefore how thou hast received and heard, and hold fast, and repent. Well if you will not watch, I will come like a thief, and thou shalt not know what hour I will come upon thee. Thou hast a few names even in Sardis which have not defiled their garments, and they shall walk with me in white, for they are worthy. He who overcomes shall be clothed in white garments, and I will not blot out his name from the book of life, I will confess his name before my Father and before his angels. He who has an ear, let him hear what the Spirit says to the churches.

To the angel of the church in Philadelphia write: He who is holy and true, who has the key of David , who opens and no one shuts , and shuts and no one opens : I know thy works : behold , I have set before thee an open door , and no man can shut it: for thou hast a little strength, and hast kept my word, and hast not denied my name. Behold, I will make them of the synagogue of Satan, which say they are Jews and are not, but do lie: behold, I will make them come and fall down at your feet and acknowledge that I have loved you. Because thou hast kept the word of my patience, I also will keep thee from the hour of trial which shall come upon the whole world, to try them that dwell upon the earth. Behold, I come quickly: hold that fast which thou hast, that no man take thy crown. He who overcomes will I make a pillar in the temple of my God, and he shall go out , and write upon him the name of my God , and the name of the city of my God, the new Jerusalem, which cometh down out of heaven from My God, and My new name. He who has an ear, let him hear what the Spirit says to the churches.

And to the angel of the church in Laodicea write: The Amen, the faithful and true witness, the beginning of God's creation, says this: I know thy works, that thou art neither cold nor hot. Wish you were cold or hot! But because thou art lukewarm, and neither cold nor hot, I will spew you out of my mouth. Because thou sayest, I am rich, have become wealthy, and have need of nothing: and knowest not that thou art wretched, miserable, poor, blind and naked. Therefore I counsel you to buy of me gold tried in the fire, that thou mayest be rich , and white clothes to wear , and that the shame of thy nakedness do not appear , and anoint thine eyes with eye salve , that thou mayest see . I rebuke and chasten I love, Therefore be zealous and repent. Behold, I stand at the door and knock: if any man hear my voice and opens the door, I will come in to him and dine with him, and he with me. To him that overcomes will I grant to sit with me in my throne, even as I also overcame, and am set down with my Father in his throne. He who has an ear, let him hear what the Spirit says to the churches.

After this I looked , and behold, a door was opened in heaven : and the first voice which I heard was like a trumpet speaking with me , said, Come up hither, and I will shew thee things which must be hereafter . And immediately I was in the spirit: and, behold, a throne was set in heaven, and upon the throne one sitting. And the one who was sitting was like a jasper and carnelian, and around the throne was a rainbow, resembling an emerald. Around the throne were twenty-four thrones, and seated on the thrones twenty-four elders, clothed in white robes, with golden crowns on their heads. And from the throne proceeded lightnings and thunderings and voices: and before the throne burn seven flaming torches, which are the seven Spirits of God. And before the throne there was a sea of glass like unto crystal: and in the throne, and round about the throne, were four beasts full of eyes before and behind. The first living creature was like a lion, the second was like an ox, the third had a face like a man, and the fourth was like a flying eagle. And the four beasts had each of them six wings about and within being full of eyes and no rest day and night, saying , Holy, holy , holy is the Lord God Almighty, who was and who is and which is to come . And whenever the living creatures give glory and honour and thanks to Him who sits on the throne, who liveth forever and ever, the twenty-four elders fall down before him who sits on the throne, and worship him who liveth forever and ever, and cast their crowns before the throne, saying, Lord, you are worthy to receive glory and honour and power: for thou hast created all things, and by your will they exist and were created.

And I saw in the right hand of him that sat on the throne a book written within and on the backside, sealed with seven seals. And I saw a strong angel proclaiming with a loud voice, who is worthy to open the scroll and break its seals? And no one in heaven or on earth or under the earth could open the book, neither to look thereon. And I wept much, because no man was found worthy to open the book and read it, neither to look thereon. And one of the elders saith unto me, Weep not. Behold the Lion of the tribe of Judah, the Root of David, has prevailed to open the scroll and its seven seals. And I looked, and saw between the throne and the four living creatures and among the elders, stood a Lamb as if slain, having seven horns and seven eyes, which are the seven Spirits of God sent throughout the land. And he came and took the scroll from the right hand of him that sat on the throne. And when he had taken the book, the four beasts and four and twenty elders fell down before the Lamb, each holding a harp , and golden bowls full of incense, which are the prayers of the saints, and they sang a new song, saying, Worthy you to take the book and to open its seals , because you were not slain, and with your blood you purchased men for God from every tribe and language and people and nation, and hast made us unto our God kings and priests: and we shall reign on earth. And I looked, and I heard the voice of many angels around the throne and the living creatures and the elders: and the number was thousands of thousands , saying with a loud voice : The Lamb that was slain is worthy to receive power and wealth and wisdom and strength and honour and glory and praise. And every creature which is in heaven and on earth and under the earth and on the sea, and all that is in them, singing: To him who sits on the throne and to the Lamb be praise and honour and glory and power , forever and ever. The four living creatures said, Amen, and twenty elders fell down and worshiped him that liveth forever and ever.

Chapter six

I saw when the Lamb opened one of the seals, and I heard one of the four living creatures saying with a voice of thunder, come and see. And I looked, and behold a white horse: and he that sat on him had a bow, and he was given a crown, and he went forth conquering, and to conquer. When he opened the second seal, I heard the second living creature saying, Come and see. And there went out another horse that was red: and its rider was given power to take peace from the earth, and that they should kill one another: and was given a large sword. When he opened the third seal, I heard the third living creature say, Come and see. And I looked and behold, a black horse, and its rider had a balance in his hand. And I heard a voice among the four living creatures saying , two pounds of wheat for a denarius , and three quarts of barley for a penny ; do not damage the oil and the wine . When he opened the fourth seal, I heard the voice of the fourth living creature saying, come and see. Look, and behold a pale horse , and its rider was named Death , and Hades followed with him and was given power over a fourth of the earth to kill by sword, famine and plague , and with the beasts of the earth. When he opened the fifth seal, I saw under the altar the souls of them that were slain for the word of God and for the testimony which they held. And crying out with a loud voice , saying, How long, O Lord , holy and true, dost thou not judge and avenge our blood on them that dwell on the earth ? And were given white robes and told to rest a little while, until the number of their fellow servants and brothers who were to be killed as they also had been completed. I looked when He opened the sixth seal, and he that sat upon the throne said, Behold, I make all things new. He said to me, Write: for these words are trustworthy and true. And he said, it is done. I am the Alpha and the Omega, the beginning and the end. To the thirsty I will give from the spring of the water of life. He who overcomes shall inherit all things, and I will be his God and he shall be my son. But the cowardly, unbelieving, abominable, murderers, sexually immoral, sorcerers, and idolaters, and all liars shall have their part in the lake which burns with fire and brimstone: which is the second death.

When he opened the seventh seal, there was silence in heaven for about half an hour. And I saw the seven angels who stand before God, and to them were given seven trumpets. And another angel came and stood at the altar, having a golden censer, and he was given much incense, with the prayers of all saints upon the golden altar which was before the throne. And the angel's had raised to the presence of God the smoke of incense with the prayers of the saints. And the angel took the censer, and filled it with fire of the altar, and cast it into the earth, and there was thunder, rumblings, flashes of lightning and an earthquake. And the seven angels which had the seven trumpets prepared themselves to sound. The first angel sounded, and there followed hail and fire mingled with blood, and they were cast upon the earth: and the third part of trees was burnt up, and all green grass was burned up. The second angel sounded, and as a great mountain burning with fire was cast into the sea: and the third part of the sea became blood. And the third part of the creatures which were in the sea, and the third part of the ships were destroyed died. The third angel sounded, and there fell a great star from heaven, burning like a torch, and it fell upon the third part of the rivers, and upon the

*fountains of waters. And the name of the star is
Wormwood. And the third part of the waters became
wormwood, and many men died of the waters, because
they were made bitter. The fourth angel sounded , and was
wounded a third of the sun, and the third part of the moon,
and the third part of the stars, so that the third part of
them was darkened , and there was no light in the third the
day and the night likewise . And I beheld, and heard an
angel flying through the midst of heaven, saying with a
loud voice, Woe, woe, woe to those who dwell on the earth,
because of the trumpet blasts about to be sounded by the
three angels!*

*The fifth angel sounded, and I saw a star fall from heaven
unto the earth: and to him was given the key of the
bottomless pit. And he opened the bottomless pit, and
smoke rose from it like the smoke of a great furnace, and
the sun and the air were darkened by the smoke of the pit.
And the smoke locusts came upon the earth and were given
power like the authority of scorpions of the earth. They
were told not to harm the grass of the earth, neither any
green thing, neither any tree, but only those men which
have not the seal of God on their foreheads. And I was
given, not to kill, but be tormented five months: and their
torment was as the torment of a scorpion when it strikes a
man. And in that day shall men seek death, and shall not
find, and long to die, but death will flee from them. The
appearance of the locusts was like horses prepared for war
in his head were crowns of gold, and their faces were as
the faces of men had hair as the hair of women, and their
teeth were like lions had breastplates like breastplates of
iron and the sound of their wings was as the sound of
chariots of many horses running to battle they had tails
like scorpions, and there were stings in their tails: and
their power was to hurt men five months. And they had a*

213

king over them the angel of the Abyss, whose name in Hebrew is Abaddon, and in Greek, Apollyon. One woe is past: behold, there come two ays! After this. The sixth angel sounded, and I heard a voice from the four horns of the golden altar which is before God, Saying to the sixth angel which had the trumpet, Loose the four angels who are bound at the great river Euphrates. And the four angels were loosed, which were prepared for an hour, day, month and year, for to slay the third part of men. And the number of the armies of the horsemen was two hundred million. I heard their number. I saw in vision the horses and their riders had breastplates of fiery red, hyacinth blue, and sulfur. And the heads of the horses resembled the heads of lions, and out of their mouths issued fire and smoke and brimstone. By these three was the third part of men, by the fire, smoke and sulfur that came out of his mouth. For the power of the horses is in their mouths and in their tails: for their tails were like unto serpents, and had heads, and with them they do hurt. And the men which were not killed by these plagues yet repented not of the works of their hands, that they should not worship devils , and idols of gold, silver , bronze , stone and wood , which neither can see, nor hear , nor walk: neither repented they of their murders, nor of their sorceries , nor of their fornication , nor of their thefts . The second woe is past: behold, the third woe is coming soon.

Down from heaven I saw another mighty angel in a cloud, with a rainbow over his head, and his face was like the sun, and his feet as pillars of fire. He had in his hand a little book open: and he set his right foot upon the sea , and his left on the earth, and cried with a loud voice as a lion roars : and when he had cried , seven thunders uttered their voices. And when the seven thunders had uttered their voices, I was about to write : and I heard a voice

*from heaven saying unto me, Seal up what the seven
thunders uttered, and write them not . And the angel which
I saw stand upon the sea and upon the earth lifted up his
hand to heaven , and swore by Him who lives forever and
ever , who created heaven and the things that therein are,
and the earth and things that are therein , the sea and the
things which are therein , that there should be time no
longer: But in the days of the voice of the seventh angel ,
when he shall begin to sound , the mystery of God finished,
as he announced to his servants the prophets. The voice
which I heard from heaven spoke unto me again, and said,
Go and take the little book which is open in the hand of the
angel which standeth upon the sea and upon the earth.
Went to the angel, telling him to give me the little book.
And he said: Take and eat, and thy belly bitter, but in your
mouth it will be sweet as honey. Then take the little scroll
from the angel's hand and ate it , and it was in my mouth
sweet as honey , but when I had eaten it , my belly was
bitter . And he said unto me, Thou must prophesy again
about many peoples, nations, languages and kings.*

*The seventh angel sounded: And there were loud voices in
heaven, saying, the kingdoms of this world have to make
our Lord and of His Christ, and He shall reign forever and
ever. The twenty-four elders who sat before God on his
throne, fell on their faces, and worshiped God , Saying, We
give thee thanks, O Lord God Almighty , which art, and
wast, and art to come , because you have taken your great
power and reigned. And the nations were angry, and thy
wrath is come, and the time for judging the dead, and for
rewarding your servants the prophets and the saints, and
them that fear thy name, small and great; and for
destroying those who destroy the earth. And the temple of
God was opened in heaven, and the ark of his covenant
was seen in his temple. And there were lightnings, noises,*

thunderings, an earthquake, and great hail. The third woe is past.

After this I looked, and behold, a great multitude which no one could count , from every nation, tribe, people and language, standing before the throne and before the Lamb, clothed with white robes, and palms in their hands , and cried with a loud voice, saying, salvation to our God who sits on the throne and to the Lamb. And all the angels stood around the throne and around the elders and the four beasts, and fell on their faces before the throne and worshiped God, saying, Amen. Blessing and glory and wisdom and thanksgiving and honour and power and might, be unto our God forever and ever. Amen. Then one of the elders answered, saying unto me, these that are clothed in white robes, who are they, and where did they come? I said, Lord, thou knowest. And he said to me, these are they which came out of great tribulation, and have washed their robes and made them white in the blood of the Lamb. Therefore are they before the throne of God, and serve him day and night in his temple: and he that sitteth on the throne shall dwell among them. They shall hunger and thirst , and the sun will not beat upon them, nor any heat : for the Lamb in the midst of the throne shall feed them, and shall lead them unto living fountains of waters : and God shall wipe away all tears from their eyes them.

It appeared in the sky a great sign: a woman clothed with the sun, the moon under her feet, and upon her head a crown of twelve stars. And being with child cried, travailing in birth, and pained to be delivered. Also another sign appeared in heaven: behold, a great red dragon, having seven heads and ten horns, and on his heads seven diadems his tail drew the third part of the

*stars of heaven and cast them to the earth. And the dragon
stood before the woman which was ready to be delivered,
for to devour her child as soon as it was born , and she
gave birth to a male child, who will rule with a rod of iron
to all nations , and his son I was caught up to God and to
his throne . And the woman fled into the wilderness, where
she hath a place prepared by God, that there a thousand
two hundred sixty days. And there was war in heaven:
Michael and his angels fought against the dragon, and the
dragon fought and his angels, and prevailed not, neither
was their place found any more in heaven. Was thrown out
the great dragon, that old serpent, called the Devil and
Satan, who deceives the whole world: he was cast out into
the earth, and his angels were cast out with him. I heard a
loud voice in heaven, saying: Now is come salvation, and
strength, and the kingdom of our God and the authority of
his Christ: for it has been released the accuser of our
brothers, who accuses before our God day and night. And
they overcame him by the blood of the Lamb and by the
word of their testimony and they loved not their lives unto
the death. Therefore rejoice, ye heavens, and ye that dwell
in them. Woe to the inhabitants of the earth and of the sea!
For the devil is come down unto you, having great wrath,
knowing that he has little time. And when the dragon saw
that he was cast unto the earth, he persecuted the woman
which brought forth the man child. And he gave the woman
the two wings of a great eagle , that she might fly from the
serpent into the wilderness , into her place , where she is
nourished for a time and times and half a time . And the
serpent cast out of his mouth after the woman water as a
river, that he might be dragged down by the river. But the
earth helped the woman, and the earth opened its mouth
and swallowed up the flood which the dragon cast out of
his mouth. And the dragon was wroth with the woman, and
went to make war with the remnant of her seed, which keep*

the commandments of God and have the testimony of Jesus Christ.

I stood upon the sand of the sea , and saw a beast rise up out of the sea , having seven heads and ten horns, and upon his horns ten crowns, and upon his heads the name of blasphemy. And the beast which I saw was like unto a leopard, and his feet like a bear, and his mouth as the mouth of a lion. And the dragon gave him his power and his throne and great authority. I saw one of his heads as it were wounded to death , and his deadly wound was healed: and all the world wondered after the beast , and they worshiped the dragon which gave power unto the beast: and they worshiped the beast , saying, who is like the beast, and who can fight against it ? The beast was given a mouth speaking great things and blasphemies, and he was given authority to continue forty and two months. And he opened his mouth in blasphemy against God, to blaspheme his name, and his tabernacle, and them that dwell in heaven. And he was allowed to make war with the saints and to conquer. And he was given authority over every tribe, people, language and nation. And worshiped all the inhabitants of the earth whose names were not written in the book of life of the Lamb slain from the foundation of the world. If anyone has an ear, let him hear. He that leadeth into captivity shall go into captivity: he that kills with the sword must be killed with the sword has. Here is the patience and the faith of the saints. Then I saw another beast coming up out of the earth, and had two like the horns of a lamb, and he spoke as a dragon. He exercised all the authority of the first beast before him, and causeth the earth and them which dwell therein to worship the first beast, whose deadly wound was healed. He performs great signs, so that he maketh fire come down from heaven to earth before men. And he deceives those

*who dwell on the earth by those signs which he was
granted to do in the sight of the beast, telling those who
dwell on the earth to make an image to the beast who was
wounded by the sword and lived . And he had power to
give life unto the image of the beast, that the image could
speak and cause all who refused to worship. And he
causeth all, both small and great, rich and poor, free and
slave, to receive a mark in their right hand , or in their
foreheads : And that no man might buy or sell, save he that
had the mark or the name of the beast, or the number of
his name. Here is wisdom. He that hath understanding
count the number of the beast, for it is man's number. And
his number is six hundred threescore and six.*

*After this I saw four angels standing on the four corners of
the earth , holding the four winds of the earth , to not blow
on the earth, neither the sea, nor on any tree . And I saw
another angel ascending from the rising sun , having the
seal of the living God : and he cried with a loud voice to
the four angels who had been given power to harm earth
and sea, saying, hurt not the earth, neither the sea, nor the
trees , till we have sealed in his face the servants of our
God. And I heard the number of them which were sealed
an hundred and forty -four thousand sealed from every
tribe of the children of Israel. Of the tribe of Judah were
sealed twelve thousand. Of the tribe of Reuben were sealed
twelve thousand. Of the tribe of Gad were sealed twelve
thousand. Of the tribe of Aser were sealed twelve
thousand. Of the tribe of Naphtali twelve thousand were
sealed. Of the tribe of Manasseh were sealed twelve
thousand. Of the tribe of Simeon were sealed twelve
thousand. Of the tribe of Levi were sealed twelve thousand.
Of the tribe of Issachar were sealed twelve thousand. Of
the tribe of Zebulun were sealed twelve thousand. Of the*

tribe of Joseph were sealed twelve thousand. Of the tribe of Benjamin were sealed twelve thousand.

Then I was given a reed like a measuring rod and was told: Go and measure the temple of God, and the altar, and them that worship therein. But the court which is without the temple leave out, and measures it not, for it is given unto the Gentiles, and they will trample the holy city for forty -two months. And I will give unto my two witnesses to prophesy for 1260 days, clothed in sackcloth. These are the two olive trees and the two candlesticks standing before the God of the earth. If anyone would harm them, fire comes from their mouths and devours their enemies: and if any man will hurt them, he must be killed the same way. These have power to shut heaven, so that no rain falls in the days of their prophecy: and have power over waters to turn them to blood, and to smite the earth with all plagues, as often as they want. When they finish their testimony, the beast that comes up from the Abyss will attack them, and overpower and kill them. Their bodies will lie in the street of the great city, which spiritually is called Sodom and Egypt, where also our Lord was crucified. And they of the people and kindreds and tongues and nations shall see their dead bodies three days and an half, and refuse them burial. And the inhabitants of the earth will rejoice over them and make merry, and shall send gifts to one another, because these two prophets tormented them that dwelt on the earth. But after three and a half days they entered into the spirit of life from God, and they stood on their feet, and great fear fell upon them which saw them. And they heard a great voice from heaven saying unto them, Come up hither. And they ascended to heaven in a cloud, and their enemies saw them. At that hour there was a great earthquake, and a tenth of the city fell , and in the earthquake were slain of men seven thousand: and the remnant were affrighted , and gave glory to the God of heaven.

Then I looked, and lo, a Lamb stood on the mount Sion, and with him an hundred forty and four thousand, having his name and his Father's name written on their foreheads. And I heard a voice from heaven like the roar of many waters, and as the voice of a great thunder: and the voice which I heard was like that of harpists playing their harps and sang a new song before the throne and before the four living creatures , and the elders : and no man could learn that song but the hundred and forty -four thousand who were redeemed from the earth. These are they which were not defiled with women, for they are virgins. These are they which follow the Lamb wherever he goes. These were redeemed from among men , being the first fruits unto God and to the Lamb , and in their mouth was found no guile: for they are without fault before the throne of God. I saw flying through the midst of heaven another angel , having the everlasting gospel to preach unto them that dwell on the earth, to every nation, kindred, tongue and people , saying with a loud voice, Fear God, and give glory to hour of his judgment is come: and worship him that made heaven and earth, the sea and springs of waters.

And another angel followed, saying, Fallen, fallen is Babylon the great city, because she made all nations drink of the wine of the wrath of her fornication. And the third angel followed them, saying with a loud voice, If any man worship the beast and his image and receives his mark on the forehead or on his hand, The same shall drink of the wine of the wrath of God, which is poured into the cup of his anger, and he shall be tormented with fire and brimstone before the holy angels and of the Lamb : and the smoke of their torment goes up forever and ever. And they have no rest day or night, who worship the beast and his image, and whosoever receiveth the mark of his name. Here is the patience of the saints who keep the commandments of God and the faith of Jesus. I heard a voice from heaven saying to me, Write, Blessed are the dead who die in the Lord. Yes, says the Spirit, they will rest from their labours, and their works follow them. I looked, and behold a white cloud, and upon the cloud one sat like unto the Son of man, having on his head a golden crown, and in his hand a sharp sickle. And another angel came out of the temple , crying with a loud voice to him that sat on the cloud, Thrust in thy sickle and reap, for the hour to reap has come , for the harvest of the earth is ripe . And he that sat on the cloud thrust in his voice on earth, and the earth was reaped. Another angel came out of the temple which is in heaven, he also having a sharp sickle. And another angel came out from the altar , which had power over fire, and cried with a loud voice to him who had the sharp voice, saying, Thrust in thy sharp sickle, and gather the clusters of the earth, because its grapes are ripe it . And the angel thrust in his sickle into the earth and gathered the vine of the earth, and threw the grapes into the great winepress of the wrath of God. And the winepress was trodden outside the city, and blood came out of the winepress up to the horses' bridles, for one thousand six hundred furlongs.

I saw another sign in heaven, great and marvellous, seven angels having the seven last plagues, for in them the wrath of God is complete. I saw something like a sea of glass mingled with fire: and them that had gotten the victory over the beast and his image and over his mark and the number of his name , stand on the sea of glass , having the harps of God. And they sing the song of Moses the servant of God, and the song of the Lamb , saying, Great and

marvellous are thy works, Lord God Almighty, just and
true are thy ways, thou King of saints. Who shall not fear
thee, O Lord, and glorify thy name? For you alone are
holy: for all nations shall come and worship before you,
for your righteous acts have been revealed. After this I
looked, and behold, it was opened in heaven the temple of
the tabernacle, and the temple came the seven angels
having the seven plagues, clothed in pure and white linen,
and girded around their chests with golden sashes. And
one of the four living creatures gave to the seven angel's
seven golden bowls full of the wrath of God who lives
forever and ever. And the temple was filled with smoke
from the glory of God and from His power, and no one
could enter the temple until they had the seven plagues of
the seven angels.

Then came one of the seven angels which had the seven
vials, and talked with me, Come, I will show you the
judgment of the great whore that sitteth upon many waters,
which have committed fornication with the kings of the
earth, and the inhabitants of the earth were made drunk
with the wine of her fornication. And he carried me away
in the spirit into the wilderness: and I saw a woman sit
upon a full of names of blasphemy, having seven heads and
ten horns scarlet beast. And the woman was arrayed in
purple and scarlet, and decked with gold, precious stones
and pearls, having in her hand a golden cup full of
abominations and filthiness of her fornication: And upon
her forehead was a name written, MYSTERY, BABYLON
THE GREAT, THE MOTHER OF HARLOTS and
abominations of the earth. I saw the woman drunken with
the blood of the saints and the blood of the martyrs of
Jesus: and when I saw her, I wondered with great
admiration. And the angel said unto me, wherefore didst
thou marvel? I will tell thee the mystery of the woman and

of the beast that carrieth her, which hath the seven heads and ten horns. The beast that you saw was, and is not, and will ascend out of the bottomless pit and go into perdition: and the inhabitants of the earth whose names have not been written from the foundation of the world in the book of life, when they behold behold the beast that was and is not and will come . These calls for a mind with wisdom: the seven heads are seven mountains on which the woman sits, and they are seven kings. Five have fallen, one is, the other has not yet come, and when he cometh, he must continue a short time. The beast that was, and is not, is an eighth, and is of the seven, and goeth into perdition. And the ten horns which you saw are ten kings who have not yet received a kingdom, but who for one hour will receive authority as kings with the beast. These have one mind, and shall give their power and strength unto the beast. War with the Lamb, and the Lamb will overcome them because he is Lord of lords and King of kings: and they that are with him are called and chosen and faithful. He said to me, the waters which you saw, where the whore sitteth, are peoples, multitudes, nations and languages. And the ten horns which you saw on the beast, these shall hate the whore , and shall make her desolate and naked, and shall eat her flesh , and burn her with fire, for God hath put in their hearts to do what he did : stand agree, and give their kingdom unto the beast, until the words of God are fulfilled . And the woman whom you saw is that great city which reigns over the kings of the earth.

I heard a loud voice from the temple saying to the seven angels, Go and pour out on the earth the seven bowls of the wrath of God. The first went and poured out his vial upon the earth, and there fell a noisome and grievous sore upon the men which had the mark of the beast and worshiped his image. The second angel poured out his vial

*over the sea, and it became blood as of a dead man: and
every living thing died that was in the sea. The third angel
poured out his vial upon the rivers and fountains of waters,
and they became blood. And I heard the angel of the
waters say, Thou art righteous, O Lord, which is, and
wast, and shalt be, because thou hast judged thus. For they
have shed the blood of saints and prophets, and thou hast
given them blood to drink as they deserve. And I heard
another out of the altar say, Even so, Lord God Almighty,
your judgments are true and just. The fourth angel poured
out his bowl on the sun, and power was given unto him to
scorch men with fire. And men were scorched with great
heat, and blasphemed the name of God, which hath power
over these plagues: and they repented not to give him
glory. The fifth angel poured out his bowl on the throne of
the beast, and his kingdom was full of darkness, and they
gnawed their tongues for pain, and blasphemed the God of
heaven because of their pains and their sores, and
repented not of their works. The sixth angel poured out his
bowl on the great river Euphrates, and its water was dried
up to prepare the way for the kings from the east. And I
saw from the dragon's mouth , and the mouth of the beast ,
and the mouth of the false prophet , three unclean spirits
like frogs , they are the spirits of devils, working miracles,
which go forth unto the kings of the land around the world,
to gather them to the battle of that great day of God
Almighty. Behold, I come as a thief. Blessed is he who
stays awake and keeps his garments, lest he walk naked
and they see his shame. And they assembled them at the
place that in Hebrew is called Armageddon.*

*After this I saw another angel coming down from heaven,
having great authority, and the earth was lightened with
his glory. And he cried mightily with a strong voice,
saying, Fallen , fallen is Babylon the great , and is become*

*the habitation of devils , and the hold of every foul spirit ,
and a cage of every unclean and hateful bird . For all
nations have drunk of the wine of the wrath of her
fornication , and the kings of the earth have committed
fornication with her , and the merchants of the earth are
waxed rich through the abundance of her delicacies. And I
heard another voice from heaven , saying, Come out of
her, my people, that ye be not partakers of her sins and
receive of her plagues , for her sins have reached unto
heaven , and God hath remembered her iniquities . Reward
her even as she rewarded you, and repay her double
according to her works: in the cup which she hath filled fill
to her double. How much she hath glorified herself , and
lived deliciously, so much torment and sorrow give her :
for she saith in her heart, I sit a queen, and am no widow,
and shall see no sorrow so in one day her plagues will
come , death and mourning and famine, and she shall be
utterly burned with fire: for strong is the Lord God who
judges her . And the kings of the earth who committed
adultery with her and shared her delight in will weep and
lament for her , when they see the smoke of her burning ,
Standing afar off for the fear of her torment, saying, Alas,
alas , that great city Babylon , that mighty city : for in one
hour is thy judgment come And the merchants of the earth
weep and mourn over her because no one buys goods
merchandise of gold, silver , precious stones, pearls, fine
linen , purple, silk and scarlet , all expensive wood , all
articles of ivory , all articles of costly wood, bronze , iron
and marble, cinnamon and aromatic spices, incense ,
myrrh, frankincense , wine, oil , fine flour , wheat, cattle ,
sheep, horses and chariots, and slaves, and souls of men.
The fruit you longed for is gone from you, and all your
riches and splendour have vanished, never to be
recovered. The merchants of these things, which were
made rich by her, shall stand afar off for the fear of her*

torment, weeping and wailing, saying, Alas, alas, that
great city, that was clothed in fine linen, purple and scarlet
, and decked with gold and precious stones and pearls !
For in one hour such great riches. And every shipmaster ,
and all the company in ships , and sailors, and as many as
trade by sea , stood afar off, and they saw the smoke of her
burning , they cried out , saying, What city is like unto this
great city ? And they cast dust on their heads , and cried,
weeping and wailing, saying, Alas , alas, that great city, in
which all who had ships at sea became rich by her wealth ,
for in one hour she was desolate ! Rejoice over her, thou
heaven, and ye holy apostles and prophets, for God hath
avenged you on her. And a mighty angel took up a stone
like a great millstone, and cast it into the sea, saying, Thus
with violence will Babylon be thrown down, that great city,
and never be found again. And the voice of artists,
musicians, flutists, and trumpeters shall not be heard in
you again, and no craftsman of any craft shall be found in
you, and the sound of a millstone shall be heard in you.
Light lamp will never shine in you, and the voice of
bridegroom and bride will be heard in thee: for thy
merchants were the great men of the earth, for by your
sorceries were all nations deceived. And in it the blood of
prophets and saints was found, and all that were slain
upon the earth.

The seventh angel poured out his bowl into the air, and
there came a great voice out of the temple of heaven, from
the throne, saying, it is done. Then there were lightnings
and voices and thunders and a great earthquake, such a
large earthquake, which it never occurred since men were
upon the earth. And the great city was divided into three
parts, and the cities of the nations fell: and great Babylon
came in remembrance before God, to give her the cup of
the wine of the fierceness of his wrath. And every island

fled away and the mountains were not found. And from heaven fell upon men a great hail, like a talent: and men blasphemed God because of the plague of the hail, since that plague was exceedingly great.

After these things I heard a great voice and a great multitude in heaven, saying: Alleluia! Salvation and glory and power belong to our God, for his judgments are true and righteous because He has judged the great harlot who corrupted the earth with her fornication. It has avenged the blood of his servants at her hand. Again they said, Alleluia! And her smoke rose up forever and ever. And the four and twenty elders and the four living creatures fell down and worshiped God that sat on the throne, saying: Amen! Hallelujah! And a voice came from the throne, saying, Praise our God, all you His servants and those who fear him, both small and great. And I heard the voice of a great multitude, as the sound of many waters, and as the voice of mighty thunderings saying, Alleluia: for the Lord God Omnipotent reigns!

And behold there was a great earthquake and the sun became black as sackcloth of hair, and the moon became as blood. And the kings of the earth, and the great , the rich, the captains , and the mighty men, every slave and every free man , hid themselves in the dens and in the rocks of the mountains , and said to the mountains and rocks, Fall on us, and hide us from the face of him that sitteth on the throne and from the wrath of the Lamb: For the great day of their wrath has come , and who can stan?

Then I saw heaven opened, and a white horse, and he that sat upon him was called Faithful and true, and in righteousness He judges and makes war. His eyes were as a flame of fire, and on His head many diadems, having a name written that no one knew except Himself. He was clothed with a robe dipped in blood, and His name is called The Word of God. And the armies in heaven, clothed in fine linen, white and clean, followed Him on white horses. From his mouth comes a sharp sword with which to strike down the nations and he shall rule them with a rod of iron and treads the winepress of the fierceness and wrath of Almighty God. On his robe and on his thigh a name written: KING OF KINGS AND LORD OF LORDS. Y saw an angel standing in the sun on his feet , and cried with a loud voice, saying to all the fowls that fly in the midst of heaven, Come and gather together for the great supper of God , that ye may eat the flesh of kings , generals, and mighty men , of horses and their riders , and the flesh of all people, free and slave, small and great. And I saw the beast and the kings of the earth and their armies gathered together to make war against the rider on the horse and against his army. And the beast was taken, and with him the false prophet that wrought miracles before him, with which he deceived them that had received the mark of the beast and those who worshiped his image. These both were cast alive into a lake of fire burning with brimstone. And the rest were killed with the sword which proceeded from the mouth of the rider on the horse, and all the fowls were filled with their flesh.

I saw an angel coming down from heaven, having the key of the bottomless pit and a great chain in his hand. He seized the dragon , that ancient serpent , who is the devil and Satan, and bound him a thousand years, and cast him into the bottomless pit, and shut him up , and set a seal upon him . that he should deceive the nations no more , until that thousand years should be fulfilled : and after that he must be loosed a little time. And I saw thrones , and they sat upon them, and judgment was given, and I saw the

*souls of them that were beheaded for the witness of Jesus
and for the word of God, and which had not worshiped the
beast or his image , and had not received his mark on their
foreheads or their hands : and they lived and reigned with
Christ a thousand years. Rest of the dead lived not again
until the thousand years. This is the first resurrection.
Blessed and holy is he that hath part in the first
resurrection , the second death has no power over them,
but they will be priests of God and of Christ and will reign
with him a thousand years. When the thousand years are
expired, Satan shall be loosed out of his prison and will go
out to deceive the nations which are in the four corners of
the earth , Gog and Magog, to gather them together to
battle: the number of whom is as the sand of the sea. They
marched across the breadth of the earth and surrounded
the camp of the saints and the beloved city: and fire came
down from heaven and devoured them.*

*And the stars of heaven fell unto the earth, as a fig tree
casts its unripe figs when shaken by a strong wind. And the
heaven departed as a scroll when it is rolled up, and every
mountain and island was removed from its place.*

*And the devil that deceived them was cast into the lake of
fire and brimstone, where the beast and the false prophet
are, and shall be tormented day and night forever and
ever. And I saw a great white throne and Him who sat on
it, from whose face fled the earth and sky, and no place
was found for them. And I saw the dead, great and small,
standing before God, and books were opened: and another
book was opened, which is the book of life: and the dead
were judged out of those things which were written in the
books according to their works . And the sea gave up the
dead that were in it, and death and Hades gave up the
dead which were in them: and they were judged every man*

according to their works. And death and hell were cast into the lake of fire. This is the second death. And whosoever was not found written in the book of life was cast into the lake of fire.

I saw a new heaven and a new earth: for the first heaven and the first earth passed away, and the sea was no more. And I John saw the holy city, New Jerusalem, coming down out of heaven from God, prepared as a bride adorned for her husband. And I heard a great voice out of heaven saying, Behold, the tabernacle of God is with men, and He will dwell with them, and they shall be his people, and God himself will be with them as their God. He will wipe every tear from their eyes, and death shall be no, nor will there be mourning nor crying nor pain anymore, for the former things are passed away.

And there came unto me one of the seven angels which had the seven vials full of the seven last plagues , and talked with me , saying, Come hither, I will shew thee the bride , the Lamb's wife . And he carried me away in the spirit to a great and high mountain, and showed me the holy city Jerusalem coming down out of heaven from God, having the glory of God. And its light was like a most precious stone, like a jasper, clear as crystal. Had a great, high wall with twelve gates, and at the gates twelve angels, and names written thereon , which are of the twelve tribes of the children of Israel to the east three gates, on the north three gates, on the south three gates ; the west three gates . And the wall of the city had twelve foundations, and on them the twelve names of the twelve apostles of the Lamb. The one who spoke with me had a measuring rod of gold to measure the city, its gates and its wall. The city was foursquare, and the length is as the breadth: and he measured the city with the reed, twelve thousand furlongs:

the length, height and width are equal. And he measured its wall, one hundred forty-four cubits, and the measure of man, which is of an angel. The construction of its wall was of jasper: and the city was pure gold, like clear glass, and the foundations of the city wall were adorned with every precious stone. The first foundation was jasper, the second sapphire, the third chalcedony, the fourth emerald, the fifth sardonyx, the sixth carnelian, the seventh chrysolite, the eighth beryl, the ninth topaz, the tenth chrysoprase , the eleventh hyacinth , the twelfth amethyst. The twelve gates were twelve pearls: each individual gate was of one pearl. And the street of the city was pure gold like transparent glass. And I saw no temple therein: for the Lord God Almighty is its temple, and the Lamb. The city has no need of sun or moon to shine in it: for the glory of God did lighten it, and the Lamb is its lamp. And the nations shall walk by its light, and the kings of the earth bring their glory and honour into it. Its gates will never be shut by day: for there shall be no night. And they shall bring the glory and honour of the nations into it. Not enter into it anything that defiles, or causes an abomination and a lie: but they which are written in the book of life of the Lamb.

Let us be glad and give him glory, because they have reached the Lamb, and his wife has prepared. And to her was granted that she should be arrayed in fine linen clean and white: for the fine line is the righteousness of saints. And the angel said unto me, Write, Blessed are they which are called unto the marriage supper of the Lamb. And he said to me, these are true words of God. I fell at his feet to worship. And he said to me, do not: I am thy fellow servant, and of thy brethren that have the testimony of Jesus. Worship God: for the testimony of Jesus is the spirit of prophecy.

And he showed me a pure river of water of life, clear as crystal river, flowing from the throne of God and of the Lamb. In the middle of the city street, and on either side of the river stood the tree of life, bearing twelve fruits, yielding its fruit every month: and the leaves of the tree were for the healing of the nations. And there will be no more curse: but the throne of God and of the Lamb shall be in it, and His servants shall serve Him and see His face, and His name shall be in their foreheads. There will be no night there and they need no light of lamp or sunlight, for the Lord God gives them light: and they shall reign forever and ever. He said to me these words are trustworthy and true. And the Lord, the God of the spirits of the prophets sent his angel to show his servants what must soon take place. Behold, I am coming soon! Blessed is he who keeps the words of the prophecy of this book. I, John, who heard and saw these things. And when I had heard and seen, I fell down to worship before the feet of the angel who showed me these things. But he said to me, See thou do it not because I am a fellow servant of thy brethren the prophets, and of them which keep the sayings of this book. Worship God. And he told me, Seal not the sayings of the prophecy of this book: for the time is near. He that is unjust, let him be unjust still: and he who is filthy, let him be filthy still: and he that is righteous, let him be righteous still: and he that is holy, let him be holy still. Behold, I am coming quickly, and my reward is with me, to give to everyone according to his work. I am the Alpha and the Omega, the Beginning and the End, the First and the Last. Blessed are those who wash their robes, that they may have right to the tree of life, and may enter through the gates into the city. But outside are dogs and sorcerers and sexually immoral and murderers and idolaters, and whosoever loveth and maketh a lie. I Jesus have sent mine angel to testify unto you these things in the churches. I am the root and the offspring of David, the bright morning star. And the Spirit and the bride say, Come. And let him that heareth say, Come. And let him who thirsts come and whoever wishes, let him take the water of life freely. I warn everyone who hears the words of the prophecy of this book: If anyone adds to these things, God shall add unto him the plagues that are written in this book. And if anyone takes words away from this book of prophecy, God shall take away his part from the Book of Life, from the holy city and from the things which are written in this book. He who testifies to these things says, surely I come quickly. Amen, come, Lord Jesus. The grace of our Lord Jesus Christ be with you all. Amen".

ORDER OF THE FINAL EVENTS

1. The world is plunged into an economic, moral and spiritual crisis. There is a combination of disasters on the planet: Earthquakes, tsunamis, terrorist attacks, bacteriological, wars and rumours of wars, occurrence of solar flares, and last but not least, it has been destroying the ozone layer which has already caused major disasters, even an asteroid threatens to destroy the earth.

Moreover, the EU is divided and the world cries out for a leader who will bring peace, order, and solve global problems.

2. There are only ten countries integrating the European Union. (Daniel 7:23-24).

3. The antichrist will knock down three kings of the ten that will make up the European Union. In this way, will the European Economic State with seven countries, himself the eighth. (Daniel 7:23-24 and Revelation 17:7-8).

The fourth beast is the antichrist.(Revelation 17:7 -8).

• The 10 horns are the European Economic Status. (Revelation 17:2).

• The seven hills is Rome. (Revelation 17: 9) and are seven kings. (Revelation 17:10).

• Five kings have fallen are: Egypt, Assyria, Babylon, Persia and Greece of Alexander, Iran and Iraq today.

• The ruling was Rome.

• The soon to come and would be short -seven years- would be the antichrist.

• The Antichrist will be the seventh and eighth, of only eight countries that finally will form the European Economic Status. (Revelation 17:11).

In Daniel 7 we are told of the four beasts that will rise from the sea, which are:

a. Babylon was like a lion with eagle's wings: The symbol of the U.S. is the eagle and the UK is the lion, which means capitalism.

b. Medes and Persians: Such a bear, symbol of Russia; means atheism.

c. Greece: Represented by a leopard, symbol of speed, violence, toughness and vengeance; muslin people attributes.

d. The fourth beast was terrible and awful it had all the features of the previous beasts: Like a leopard, feet like a bear, and a lion's mouth, a monster in itself; it is the sum total of all empires that are considered like beasts chapters 13 and 17.

The Babylonian and Persian lion bear had one head, the Greek leopard had four heads and terrible beast had a head. The Babylonians, Medes and Persians had no horns on their heads, but the fourth beast had ten horns. **Together the four beasts had seven heads and ten horns, corresponding to the beast of Revelation 13 and 17.**

e. As God anointed Jesus with the Holy Spirit; Satan will anoint with his diabolical spirit the antichrist.

f. Just as Jesus was called Immanuel, which means "God with us", the Antichrist will be Satan ruling the men through a man.

g. Just as Jesus Christ was born of a woman, Son of God, the Antichrist will be a man born of ten nations, however, his true origin will be the abyss or hell.

h. The offer rejected by Jesus when he was tempted by the devil (Matthew 4:8-11), will be accepted by the antichrist.

4. Antichrist as president of the European Common Status takes possession.

5. Signing a peace treaty between Israel and the world.

6. So far, we have been using the mark of the beast or barcode **and have used the number of the beast "666".** When the antichrist as president of the European community takes office, **the name of the Antichrist will be known.** Thus, the requirement is complete to mark humanity, so, no one can buy or sell, only those that had the mark or the name of the beast or the number of his name. (Revelation 13:17).

7. Begins to open the seven seals.

8. The antichrist flattery, advanced ideas and deceptive powers seizes the world including Jews. Only this power escapes the gentle church, which will be preaching to not allow to be market by money, nor by power, or health or welfare, etc. For this reason, the gentile church will be persecuted as in the days of its inception; in this way, the true gospel of the Name of Jesus Christ to the world will expand.

9. The world will be experiencing happiness, joy, mirth.
Will have money, power, will be eating, drinking at parties; there will be healing for cancer, AIDS; there will be no blind, or maimed. All will be for the world happiness in exchange for implanted microchip voluntarily.

10. It proliferate selfishness, falsehood, indifference.
Everything will be for interest, vanity and pride.

11. Will sell to each other and there will be no secrets, some by fear and others by living well.

12. There will be signs in the sky, on land, at sea, but it will be hardly serious consequences, it will just be a warning of the wrath to come.

13. Antichrist as Wicked be revealed, as the son of perdition, as a leader and world dictator, and all that are not written in the book of life will worship him, and serve him faithfully will continue.

14. The peace treaty by the antichrist breaks and when the world is saying peace and security shall come upon all the people, including Jewish, there will be sudden destruction.

15. The gentile church is built by the Lord Jesus Christ to pass by the judgment seat of Christ.

16. Begins the gospel to the Jews by Elijah and Enoch and the 144,000 sealed Jews.

17. It already has been open the 7 seals and the 7 trumpets have sounded; now will be spilling the 7 bowls of God's wrath.

18. When poured out the seven bowl, the nations come together to destroy Israel in the battle of Armageddon.

19. Judgment to Israel.

20. The beast and the false prophet were cast alive into the lake of fire burning with brimstone.

21. Judgment to the nations.

22. The gentile church is lifted by the Lord Jesus Christ to pass by the judgment seat of Christ.

23. The Millennium government of Jesus Christ on earth begins with the church already composed by Gentiles and Jews. **Satan is bound during these thousand years.**

24. The millennium ends. The church of gentiles and Jews raised in the past two resurrections is lifted, together with the combined church of gentiles and Jews who are raised in this resurrection and those who are alive at the time of the lifting; but they have not risen in the previous two resurrections.

25. Satan is loosed and goes out to deceive the nations.

26. War doomsday.

27. Trial to Satan and the fallen angels.

28. Judgment before the great white throne, or final judgment.

29. New heaven and a new earth.

30. The New Jerusalem.

31. The wedding of the lamb.

32. The Jews/Gentile church and the only true God, living in the New Jerusalem; and the nations which are saved, living outside the New Jerusalem.

THE COURT OF CHRIST

1. Who is the judge in the tribunal of Christ?

The church will be judged by the Lord Jesus Christ. Who is your lawyer today, tomorrow will be your judge. What can you hide?

John 5:22: *"For the Father judges no man, but hath committed all judgment unto the Son".*

John 5:26-27: *"For as the Father has life in Himself, so He has granted the Son to have life in Himself, and has given him authority to execute judgment, because the Son of Man".*

2. Who will go by the court of Christ?

A) The dead in Christ and then to live when lifting the Church occurs; mainly gentiles.
(1st Corinthians 15:51-52, 2nd Corinthians 5:10).

Romans 14:10: "But you, why do you judge your brother? Or you, why do you despise your brother? We shall all stand before the judgment seat of Christ".

2nd Corinthians 5:10 "For we must all appear before the judgment seat of Christ , that each one may receive the things done while in the body, whether good or bad".

1st Peter 4:17: "For the time is come that judgment must begin at the house of God: and if it first begins at us, what shall the end be of them that obey not the gospel of God"?.

B) The dead in Christ and the living in Christ after the battle of Armageddon; mainly Jewish converts. (Revelation 20:4).

C) The dead in Christ and those who are alive when the uprising of the Church occur, at the end of millennium.

* It is necessary to clarify the resurrected after these three resurrections; they will not go through the judgment seat of Christ; If not for the trial before the Great White Throne. (Rev. 20: 11-15).

* The judgment seat of Christ is to reward, to govern; while the trial before the Great White Throne is to assign punishment those who are condemned, and assign services to all who are saved, which will be always governed.

* People in the first two phases of the first resurrection will be rewarded reigning with Christ in the millennium and also as priests of God and of the Lamb. (Revelation 20:6).

* When the Bible speaks to **ALL** stand before the judgment seat of Christ; **ALL** this refers to the members of the church in three stages: Middle and end of the seventieth week of Daniel, and millennium. (Ro 14:10 and 2nd Co 5:10).

* The judgment seat of Christ has three phases; each phase after each phase of the first resurrection.
(1st Corinthians 15:51-52; Revelation 20:4-6).

* The people of Israel who lived completed the 70th week of Daniel; they will enter the millennium with his body unprocessed. The Jewish church of the same period, enter the millennium with his transformed body; but only if he died in Christ. The Jewish church, who do not died in the millennium; they will be transformed his body in the resurrection of the end of the millennium.

3. Where will be the court of Christ?

A) The judgment seat of Christ to the Gentile church will be in the clouds, in the air; possibly in the second heaven. (1st Thessalonians 4:16-17).

B) The judgment seat of Christ to the Jewish church will be on earth; more exactly in the nation of Israel, headquarters of Jesus Christ and his saints including Gentile church. Jerusalem will not have been transformed in the New Jerusalem yet. (Revelation 20:4).

C). The judgment seat of Christ for the dead and alive in Christ who complete the millennium; It will be possibly in the second heaven as the first fruits; but I say possibly because the Bible does not reveal. It could also be in Jerusalem, once the millennium ended and before go to sky. I do not know, only God knows. (Revelation 20:5).

4. When will be the court of Christ?

A) To the Gentile church it will be finished the wrath of Satan; half of the 70th week of Daniel. (1st Thess 2:1-4).

B) To the Jewish church It will be completed the battle of Armageddon. (Revelation 20:1-4).

C) To the church of gentiles and Jews leaving the millennium; It will be when the millennium ended. (Rev. 20:5).

Revelation 20:4-5 "*And I saw thrones, and they sat upon them, and judgment was given, and I saw the souls of them that were beheaded for the witness of Jesus and for the word of God, and which had not worshiped the beast or his image and had not received his mark on their foreheads or their hands and they lived and reigned with Christ a thousand years. Rest of the dead lived not again until the thousand years. This is the first resurrection".*

5. What will be judged at the court of Christ?

As useful or useless, dignity or indignity had during our life in the church. All will be saved and will be judged by seven main things:

1) The useless that I was because of the sins I committed.
2) Those who were lost because I did not shared the gospel.
3) The damage not restored because of sin I committed.
4) Those who stumbled, fell and lost because my fault.
5) The time that I lost, preventing that God's will, will take place in my life.
6) What I did that God did not command me to do.
7) What I did not do that God asked me to do.

Romans 14:12: *"So then every one of us shall give account of himself to God".*

6. What is the court for?

The trial is not for punishment, but to receive awards:

Critérium = judgment to condemn = Final Judgment.

Bima = Awards Judgment = Court Judgment of Christ.

A) The prizes for the Gentile church are: Coronas, awards, reigned with Christ a thousand years, take part of the heavenly army, be priests of him, to be his wife.

B) The prizes for the Jewish church are: Coronas, awards, reigned with Christ a thousand years, take part of the heavenly army, be priests of him, to be his wife.

C) The prizes for the millennial Jewish-Gentile church are: Coronas, awards, to be his wife. They will not receive the other prizes.

Revelation 22:12 *"Behold, I am coming quickly, and my reward is with me, to give to everyone according to his work".*

1st Corinthians 3:8-15 *"And he who plants and he who waters are one: and every man shall receive his own reward according to his own labour. For we are God, and ye are God's husbandry, God's building. According to the grace of God which is given unto me, as a wise master builder I laid a foundation, and another builds on it but each careful how he builds. For other foundation can no man lay than that is laid, which is Jesus Christ. And if upon this foundation gold, silver, precious stones, wood, hay, straw, each man's work shall be made manifest: for the day shall declare it, because the fire will be revealed, and the work of each man is the fire shall try. If any man's work abides which he hath built thereupon, shall receive a reward. If any man's work shall be burned, he shall suffer loss: but he himself shall be saved, yet so as by fire".*

1st Corinthians 4:5 *"Therefore judge nothing before the time, until the Lord comes, who will bring to light the hidden things of darkness and reveal the counsels of the hearts: and then shall every man have praise of God".*

2nd Corinthians 5:1 "For we know that if our earthly house of this tabernacle were dissolved, we have a building from God, a house not made with hands, eternal in the heavens".

2nd Corinthians 10:18 "because it is not approved that commends itself, but whom the Lord commends".

1st John 4:17 *"In this is love perfected with us, that we may have boldness in the day of judgment: because as he is, so are we in this world".*

Revelation 21:4 *"He will wipe every tear from their eyes, and death shall be no, nor will there be mourning nor crying nor pain anymore, for the former things are passed away".*

7. What crowns will we receive?

1st Corinthians 9:25 *"Whosoever fight, in all things; them to do it to receive a perishable wreath, but we an incorruptible".*

2nd Timothy 4:8 *"Finally, I a crown of righteousness, which the Lord will give me just judge in that day: and not to me only, but unto all them also that love his appearing".*

Philippians 4:1 *"Therefore, my brethren beloved and longed for, my joy and crown, so stand fast in the Lord, beloved".*

1st Thessalonians 2:19 *"For what is our hope, or joy, or crown of rejoicing? Are not even ye, before our Lord Jesus at his coming".*

James 1:12 *"Blessed is the man that endureth temptation: for when he is tried, he shall receive the crown of life that God has promised to those who love Him".*

1st Peter 5:4 *"And when the chief Shepherd shall appear, ye shall receive a crown of glory"*.

Revelation 2:10 *"Do not fear what you are about to suffer. Behold, the devil shall cast some of you into prison, that ye may be tried, and ye shall have tribulation ten days. Be faithful until death, and I will give thee a crown of life"*.

Revelation 3:11 *"Behold, I come quickly: hold that fast which thou hast, that no man takes thy crown"*.

8. Reward for the winners:

Revelation 2:7 *"He that hath an ear, let him hear what the Spirit says to the churches. He who overcomes will I give to eat of the tree of life, which is in the paradise of God"*.

Revelation 2:11 *"He that hath an ear, let him hear what the Spirit says to the churches. He who overcomes shall not be hurt of the second death"*.

Revelation 2:17 *"He that hath an ear, let him hear what the Spirit says to the churches. He who overcomes will I give to eat of the hidden manna, and will give him a white stone, and in the stone a new name written, which no one knows except him who receives it"*.

Revelation 2:26 *"To him who overcomes, and keeps my works until the end, to him will I give power over the nations"*.

Revelation 2:28 *"and I will give him the morning star"*.

Revelation 3:5 *"He who overcomes shall be clothed in white garments, and I will not blot out his name from the book of life, I will confess his name before My Father and before His angels".*

Revelation 3:12 *"To him that overcomes will I make a pillar in the temple of my God, and he shall go out, and write upon him the name of my God , and the name of the city of my God, the new Jerusalem, which cometh down out of heaven from my God, and my new name".*

Revelation 3:21 *"To him that overcomes will I grant to sit with me in my throne, even as I also overcame , and am set down with my Father in his throne".*

Revelation 21:7 *"He who overcomes shall inherit all things, and I will be his God and he shall be my son".*

9. How the gospel is preached will be considered :

1st Corinthians 10:31 *"So whether you eat or drink, or whatsoever ye do, do all to the glory of God".*

2nd Corinthians 4:5 *"For we preach not ourselves, but Christ Jesus as Lord, and ourselves as your servants for Jesus' sake".*

1st Corinthians 9:16 *"For if I preach the gospel, I have nothing to glory of: for necessity is laid upon me, and woe is me if I preach not the gospel".*

1st Peter 4:11 *"If any man speak, let him speak as the oracles of God: If any man minister, the strength God provides, so that in everything God may be glorified through Jesus Christ, to whom be praise and dominion for forever and ever . Amen".*

10. What will not be judged in the court of Christ?

Past sins are not judged, for they were already forgiven when upon us the Name of Jesus was invoked, in the baptismal waters. (Acts 2:38, 4:11-12).

Hebrew 8:12 and 10:17 *"For I will be merciful to their unrighteousness, and never again remember their sins and their iniquities".*

John 5:24 *"Verily, verily, I say unto you, He that heareth my word, and believes Him who sent me has everlasting life and shall not come into judgment, but has passed from death to life".*

Romans 8:1 *"There is therefore now no condemnation to them which are in Christ Jesus, who walk not after the flesh but after the Spirit".*

11. Awards: *"And behold, I am coming quickly, and My reward is with Me, to give to everyone according to his work.* (Rev 22:12).

Regarding about the awards is necessary to take into account that during the judgment seat of Christ; we will receive more or less awards, or no award. This does not mean that we will lose salvation; but rather we will occupy a lesser rank in the reign of the millennium and in the new Jerusalem. Also it must be said that the awards are earned according to what we have done for God while we were alive. (Job 31:2; Psalm 19:9-11 and 58:11; Proverbs 11:18; Matthew 5:11-12; Luke 6:22-23 and 35; 1st Corinthians 9:16-18; Hebrew 10:34-39 and 11:24-26; 2nd John 8; Rev 11:18 and 22:12).

THE COURT OF CHRIST REFLECTIONS

1. The Jew/Gentile church will be judged by the Lord Jesus Christ who is your lawyer today, tomorrow He will be your judge.

2. The Jew/Gentile church will not live forever in heaven, we will live in the New Jerusalem.

3. The Jew/Gentile church will rule the earth in accordance with the awards it has received.

4. The heaven was not made for the man to live eternally in him.

5. Whoever receives Jesus Christ just before he dies, is like one who lived many years with Christ and does not meet the Commission; they are saved, but have no awards.

6. **To die in Christ is gain, but as long as the race is over.**

7. He who dies without Jesus Christ has fulfilled the purpose in him; his death will be gain in terms of eternal life, but will be loss as to receiving awards.

8. You know the souls who did not convert because of your testimony? Why not preach to them? ... No time to waste time. Also consider the time you were misled and did not do the will of God.

9. What have stolen, murdered, abused, insulted, slandered ... How do I restore it? Return four times as Zacchaeus? How to rebuild notoriety? How do you rebuild death...?

Sin is erased, but the damage is rebuilt by you.

10. In many cases, even doing good things, we are against the will of God; therefore the Holy Spirit hinders us, because He needed elsewhere, not where we want to go.

"And going through Phrygia and the region of Galatia, they were forbidden by the Holy Spirit to speak the word in Asia, after they were come to Mysia, they tried to enter Bithynia, but the Spirit suffered them not. And they passing by Mysia came down to Troas. And Paul had a night vision a man of Macedonia was standing beseeching him and saying, Come over into Macedonia and help us. When he saw the vision, immediately we sought to go to Macedonia, concluding that God had called us to preach the gospel". (Acts 16:6-10).

11. We did many things for God, many good works, but never the will of God. (As is the case of David with the Temple, or Saul and sacrifices).

12. When we stand with the work we have done: Hay, stubble, gold, silver, precious stones ... if it burns, it will mean that the work was not approved, because we didn't the will of God. The awards are not by works, but by the character of the works. If it were by works, all the credit would for the Holy Spirit; because is the one who reveals, gives grace, sign, turns, making wise, healthy, and well. In conclusion, if the award is for work then the Holy Spirit deserves it all, because we did nothing. Fortunately, **for God obedience is more important than great sacrifices.**

13. Preaching the gospel, evangelize, speak of salvation. *Matthew 16:15-16: "He said unto them, But whom say ye that I am? Simon Peter answered and said, Thou art the Christ, the Son of the living God".*

14. In every congregation there are several types of people:

a. Those who make that things happen.

b. Those who go against that things happen.

c. Those who see as the things happen.

d. Those who do not care whether things happen or not.

e. Those who do not even realize when the things happen.

TO WHICH OF THESE FIVE GROUPS YOU BELONG TO?

GOG AND DAMASCUS REFLECTIONS

Satan will be released after the millennium and will go out to deceive the nations which have entered the millennium, these nations entered according to the help which they had given to Israel.

The first event, after the millennium will be the invasion of Gog and Magog and their subsequent destruction by the Lord Jesus Christ. Israel will then picking up the bodies of their invaders for 7 months and the weapons of his enemies for seven years. At this time Satan will tempt the nations who were in the millennium, but will soon forget about the benefits obtained by the Lord Jesus Christ. Satan exploited the discomfort that will come against the Jews, to come together to destroy the people of Israel. (Ezekiel 39:1-14).

Many years after seven years, there will be a war in the Middle East and Israel will destroy the city of Damascus and off the map. This will give rise to Satan to give the final blow to deceive the unbelieving nations. The Bible says that after Israel destroys Damascus, the Jewish people will be rejected by many nations. (This is a hypothesis concerning the possible date of the destruction of Damascus since the Bible gives no clues about it and any date is a guess. Some believe that the destruction of Damascus will be before the 70th week of Daniel which would lead to a war that would lead to the possession of the antichrist. Who is right? Only time will tell). These nations that will reject the Jews are the ones who go against Israel in the final battle, but will be destroyed along with Satan. Clearly, between the destruction of Damascus and the War of the End of the world will take several years. (Is 17:1; Je 49:23-27; Am 1:3-5; Zech 9:1).

MYSTERY OF THE WEDDING OF THE LAMB

1. Who will be the participants of the Wedding of the Lamb?

A) Groom.

Matthew 9:15 *And Jesus said to them, "Can the friends of the bridegroom mourn as long as the bridegroom is with them? But the days will come when the bridegroom will be taken away from them, and then they will fast.*

John 1:29 *"The next day John seeth Jesus coming unto him, and saith, Behold the Lamb of God who takes   away the sin of the world".*

John 3:29 *He who has the bride is the bridegroom; but the friend of the bridegroom, who stands and hears him, rejoices greatly because of the bridegroom's voice. Therefore this joy of mine is fulfilled.*

Matthew 9:15 *"Jesus said unto them, is Can the wedding guests mourn as long as the bridegroom is with them? But the days will come when the bridegroom will be taken from them, and then they will fast".*

Revelation 19:7 *Let us be glad and rejoice and give Him glory, for the marriage of the Lamb has come, and His wife has made herself ready."*

Revelation 22:17 *And the Spirit and the bride say, "Come!" And let him who hears say, "Come!" And let him who thirsts come. Whoever desires, let him take the water of life freely.*

B) Wife or Church Composed of Gentiles and Jews.

All risen in all three phases of the first resurrection, together with which they would be alive when the uprising of their respective Gentile church, before the wrath of God or Jewish before the millennium; We are part of the body of the church of Jesus Christ.

Hosea 2:16, 19, 20 *"In that day, saith the Lord, call me Ishi, and shalt call me no more Baali. I will betroth you to me forever will betroth you in righteousness and justice, kindness and mercy. I will betroth you in faithfulness, and you shall know the Lord".*

Isaiah 54:5 *"For your Maker is your husband, the LORD of hosts is his name, and thy Redeemer, the Holy One of Israel, God of the whole earth shall be called".*

Romans 11:25-28" *For I would not, brethren, have you ignorant of this mystery, lest you be wise in yourselves: Israel has experienced a hardening in part until the full number of the Gentiles: and so all Israel will be saved, as it is written: "come out of Sion the Deliverer, and shall turn away ungodliness from Jacob. And this is my covenant with them when I take away their sins. "As concerning the gospel, they are enemies for your sakes: but as touching the election, they are beloved for the fathers' sakes".*

1st Corinthians 10:32 *Give no offense, either to the Jews or to the Greeks or to the church of God,*

2nd Corinthians 11:2 *"For I am jealous over you with godly jealousy: for I have espoused you to one husband, to present you as a chaste virgin to Christ".*

Ephesians 5:25, 27 and 32 *"Husbands, love your wives, even as Christ also loved the church, and gave himself for it. And might present himself a glorious church, not having spot or wrinkle or any such thing, but holy and blameless. This is a great mystery: But I speak concerning Christ and the church"*.

1st Thessalonians 2:14-16 *For you, brethren, became imitators of the churches of God which are in Judea in Christ Jesus. For you also suffered the same things from your own countrymen, just as they did from the Judeans, 15 who killed both the Lord Jesus and their own prophets, and have persecuted us; and they do not please God and are contrary to all men, 16 forbidding us to speak to the Gentiles that they may be saved, so as always to fill up the measure of their sins; but wrath has come upon them to the uttermost.*

1st Peter 4:17 *For the time has come for judgment to begin at the house of God; and if it begins with us first, what will be the end of those who do not obey the gospel of God?*

C) New Jerusalem.

Revelation 21:2, 9 *"And I John saw the holy city, New Jerusalem, coming down out of heaven from God, given as a bride adorned for her husband. And there came unto me one of the seven angels which had the seven vials full of the seven last plagues, and talked with me, saying, Come hither, I will shew thee the bride, the Lamb's wife"*.

Look at the text of Revelation 21:9 in other versions:
• Reina Valera Antigua Translation:
"Come I will show you the bride, the Lamb's wife ..."

• God Speaks Today Translation:
"Come, I will teach the bride, the Lamb's wife ..."

• Current Language translation:
Come, I will show you the bride, to be the wife of the Lamb..

The New Jerusalem has the mansions of the Jewish / Gentile church and is also the place where they will live forever the honeymooners. Therefore the New Jerusalem is also considered as part of the bride of Jesus Christ.

2. Who will be invited to the Wedding of the Lamb?

A. the Old Testament saints and among them patriarchs and prophets, and those who do not belong to the church, but who practiced holiness and had a good reputation.

John 3:29: *"He who has the bride is the bridegroom: but the friend of the bridegroom, which standeth and heareth him, rejoiceth greatly because of the bridegroom's voice; therefore this joy of mine is fulfilled".*

John 15:15 *"I no longer call you servants, for the servant knoweth not what his Lord, but I have called you friends, for all things that I heard my father I have made known".*

Matthew 8:11 *"I tell you, many will come from east and west, and shall sit down with Abraham and Isaac and Jacob in the kingdom of heaven".*

Mark 9:38-41 *"And John answered him, saying, Master, we saw one casting out devils in thy name, and he followeth not us: and we forbad him, because he followeth not us. But Jesus said, forbid him not: for no one who does a miracle in my name, that can lightly speak evil of me. For he that is not against us is for us. And whosoever shall give you a glass of water in my name because you belong to Christ, verily I say unto you not lose his reward".*

B. The nations which are saved after the final war.

Revelation 21:24 *"And the nations shall walk by its light, and the kings of the earth bring their glory and honour into it".*

Revelation 22:2 *"In the midst of the street of the city, and one to the other side of the river stood the tree of life, bearing twelve fruits, yielding its fruit every month: And the leaves of the tree were for the healing of nations".*

C. Those without the use of reason and aborted.

Luke 14:15-24 *"Hearing this one of those who sat with him at meat, he said: Blessed is he that shall eat bread in the kingdom of God. Then Jesus said, a certain man made a great supper, and bade many. And at dinner he sent his servants to tell the invited, Come, everything is ready. And they all alike began to make excuses. The first said: I have bought a field, and I must go and see it: I pray thee have me excused. Another said I have bought five yoke of oxen, and I go to prove them: I pray thee have me excused. And another said, I have married a wife, and therefore I cannot go. The servant returned, he reported this to his master. Then the parent angry, said to his servant, Go out quickly into the streets and lanes of the city, and bring in the poor, the maimed, the lame, the blind. And the servant said, Lord, it is done as thou hast commanded, and yet there is room. The lord said unto the servant, Go out into the highways and hedges, and compel them to come in, that my house may be filled. For I tell you that none of those men which were bidden shall taste of my supper".*

D. Those who gave themselves to the Lord Jesus Christ before death but were not baptized in water or in spirit.

Luke 23:39-43 *And one of the malefactors which were hanged railed on him, saying, if thou be Christ, save thyself and us. 40 But the other answering rebuked him, saying, dost not thou fear God, being in the same sentence? 41 And we, indeed, justly, for we receive the due reward of our deeds: but this man hath done nothing amiss. 42 And he said unto Jesus, remember me when you come into your kingdom. 43 And Jesus said unto him, Verily I say to you today you will be with me in paradise.*

E. Those who did not get market by the beast during the 70th week of Daniel. These people helped in different ways to the Jew/Gentile church or to the people of Israel when they were in anguish or persecution.

Revelation 19:9 *And he saith unto me, Write, Blessed are they which are called unto the marriage supper of the Lamb. And he saith unto me, These are the true sayings of God.*

Matthew 22:14 For many are called, but few are chosen.

F. The Virgins

Psalm 45:14-15 *"With embroidered dresses will be brought to the king; Virgin goes after her, her companions will be brought to you. They shall be brought with gladness and rejoicing shall they enter into the king's palace".*

Matthew 25:1 and 10 *"Then the kingdom of heaven will be like ten virgins who took their lamps and went to meet the bridegroom. And while they went to buy, the bridegroom came, and those who were ready went in with him to the marriage: and the door was shut".*

G. The angels will be present, either as spectators or as guests. But they will be there along with archangels, seraphim and cherubim.

Hebrews 12:22-24 *"But you have come to Mount Zion and to the city of the living God, the heavenly Jerusalem, to an innumerable company of angels, to the congregation of the firstborn who are enrolled in heaven, to God the judge of all, to the spirits of just men made perfect, to Jesus the mediator of the new covenant, and to the blood of sprinkling, that speaketh better things than that of Abel".*

1st Corinthians 4:9 *"For I think that God has exhibited us apostles last, as men condemned to death: for we are made a spectacle to the world, to angels and men".*
Revelation 4:6: *"And before the throne there was a sea of glass like unto crystal: And in the throne, and round about the throne, were four beasts full of eyes before and behind".*

Revelation 5:11 *"And I looked and heard the voice of many angels around the throne and the living creatures and the elders: and the number was thousands of thousands".*

3. Where will the wedding of the Lamb?

In the New Jerusalem:

Revelation 21:2, 3, 9, 10 *"And I John saw the holy city, New Jerusalem, coming down out of heaven from God, given as a bride adorned for her husband. And I heard a great voice out of heaven saying, Behold, the tabernacle of God is with men, and He will dwell with them, and they shall be his people, and God himself will be with them as their God. And there came unto me one of the seven angels which had the seven vials full of the seven last plagues, and talked with me, saying, Come hither, I will shew thee the bride, the Lamb's wife . And he carried me away in the spirit to a great and high mountain, and showed me the holy city Jerusalem coming down out of heaven from God".*

4. When will the Wedding of the Lamb be?

The Marriage of the Lamb will take place when there is new heaven and new earth.

Revelation 21:1, 2, 9, and 10 *"I saw a new heaven and a new earth: for the first heaven and the first earth passed away, and the sea was no more. And I John saw the holy city, New Jerusalem, coming down out of heaven from God, prepared as a bride adorned for her husband. And there came unto me one of the seven angels which had the seven vials full of the seven last plagues, and talked with me, saying, Come hither, I will shew thee the bride, the Lamb's wife . And he carried me away in the spirit to a great and high mountain, and showed me the holy city Jerusalem coming down out of heaven from God".*

THE WEDDING OF THE LAMB REFLECTIONS

1. The Lord Jesus Christ is the same Lamb of God.

2. The Lamb of God is the same groom.

3. The bride is formed of the Gentile/Jew church and the new Jerusalem where they will spend the honeymoon and will live for all eternity; occupied mansions that Jesus promised his church, to be where he is. This is the future home of God that speak John 14: 2-3.

4. The groom is the one inviting, therefore he is not invited.

5. The bride is also the one inviting, therefore, is not invited.

6. Some are invited, and others guests.

7. One thing is the wedding supper of the Lamb, and another the Wedding of the Lamb.

8. Neither the groom nor the bride is serving the guests table

9. The bride and groom can sit at the table with the guests, but guests never guests themselves but the party hosts.

10. The bride may not be the servant; therefore the servants talking Revelation 22: 3 are saved according to their works; but they deserve to be in the New Jerusalem; serving the Bridegroom, the Queen and the kingdom. These servants are also different from the saved who live outside the New Jerusalem of Revelation 21:24.

11. First, the couple who become husbands marry, then held a great dinner and a party.

Finally, they will honeymoon.

ORDER OF EVENTS TEXT TO TEXT

1. Revelation 6:1-2: The first seal represents the power of the Antichrist on the world. Perhaps this is where the Antichrist receives the mortal wound and makes parody of his resurrection. This can tell by what the Bible tells us in Revelation 13: 1-5 which speaks to the beast rising from the sea and the dragon gave him his throne. Once the beast was empowered, John saw the antichrist wounded of death; this is surely when fighting toppling three kings, by not agree with their policies and approaches. Verse 4 confirms that it is in a battle where this evil is mortally wounded. Revelation 6: 2 says that the antichrist went out conquering and to conquer, and this time only defeats in battle or war; as Revelation 13: 4 reveals that after this event all the world wondered after the beast and wondered: Who can fight against her?.

2. Revelation 6:3-4: The second seal: *"And ye shall hear of wars and rumours of wars: See that ye be not troubled, for all this must happen, but the end is not yet. For nation shall rise against nation, and kingdom against kingdom: and there shall be famines, and pestilences, and earthquakes in various places. All these are the beginning of sorrows. Then they will deliver you up to tribulation and kill you, and ye shall be hated of all nations for my name's sake. And because iniquity shall abound, the love of many will grow cold".* (Matthew 24:6-9, 12).

3. Revelation 6:5-6: The third seal depicts the global food shortage.

4. Revelation 6:7-8: The fourth seal refers to the death by starvation, wars and plagues of a quarter of humanity; approximately 1,500 million people.

5. Revelation 6:9-11: The fifth seal refers to the dead in Christ, awaiting the redemption of the body.

6. Revelation 6:12A and Revelation 21:5-8 "I looked when He opened the sixth seal, *and he that sat upon the throne said, Behold, I make all things new. He said to me, Write: for these words are trustworthy and true. And he said, it is done. I am the Alpha and the Omega, the beginning and the end. To the thirsty I will give from the spring of the water of life. He who overcomes shall inherit all things, and I will be his God and he shall be my son. But the cowardly, unbelieving, abominable, murderers, sexually immoral, sorcerers, idolaters, and all liars shall have their part in the lake which burns with fire and brimstone: which is the second death".*

Here we reveal who is speaking, and we are encouraged to overcome in order to inherit. Recall that are only the children who will inherit, the slaves not inherit. Furthermore, let us clear who cannot inherit all things of the kingdom of God.

7. Revelation 8:1-6: The opening of the seventh seal shows the seven angels with the seven trumpets were ready to play them. It also alludes to the prayers of the saints, in the fifth seal, clamouring for justice.

8. Revelation 8:7 The first angel sounded his trumpet, and a terrible punishment on material things on earth broke loose. In Exodus 9:23-25 had already announced it to come to earth, like the punishment of Egypt.

9. Revelation 8:8-9 The Second Trumpet indicates that trade and communication breaks throughout the land on their third part; also peace is completed in a third part of the earth.

10. Revelation 8:10-11 The Third Trumpet references a possible meteorite falling on the third part of the waters of the earth and makes them bitter and unpalatable for humans. It can also refer to the man continue without respecting decontamination protocols and because of this, the rivers and fountains no longer resist and will pay back with death to man.

Note that in the second trumpet the third part of the sea was useless; the third trumpet meanwhile, will useless the quarter part of sweets or drinkable water.

11. Revelation 8:12-13 The fourth trumpet states that the days are very short , maybe eight hours or less , in addition, the evening will be in total darkness for the third part , without seeing the light of the moon. May be considered to succeed continuous electrical and technology blackouts.

12. Revelation 9:1-12: The fifth trumpet announces reaching a torment, which will last five months on the men who have rebelled against God and his gospel in these five months, men will seek death because of pain, but not die ... may be the only time when Death will rest of his job to kill.

13. Revelation 9:13-21: The sixth trumpet is unleashed because of the prayers of the righteous that are still crying for justice. Evidenced by the fact that the order leaves the altar Revelation 6:5 and 8:3. The four angels mentioned here are different from those holding the four winds in Revelation 7:1.

This judgment only comes upon the third part of men; (4/4 parts were, but 1/3 was destroyed in Revelation 6: 8 in the opening of the fourth seal); here nature is not touched only the man, seeing such calamities do not repent of their iniquities; on the contrary, they strengthen their alliance with satanic works.

14. Revelation 11:14 The second "woe" happened.

15. Revelation 10:1-11: the consummation of the mystery of God in the seventh trumpet is announced and is urged to continue to preach the gospel to every person.

16. Revelation 11:15-19 : The seventh trumpet reveals that has come finally, the moment awaited by the righteous to receive the award which is received in the tribunal of Christ, when the gentile church has already been lifted. It is also time to avenge the blood of the saints in the wicked that made suffer. Finally, the prophecy of revelation 10:7 is fulfilled; the gentile church is raised from earth to heaven to go through the judgment seat of Christ. (The third "woe" happened).

17. Revelation 7:9-17: John sees those who have come out of the great tribulation: The same people who have suffered at the hands of the antichrist. These being the church, they belong to the whole world. **Therefore, the church is universal.**

18. Revelation 12 speaks of the persecution to which is subjected the people of Israel by the antichrist, and corresponds to the second half of the 70th week of Daniel.

19. Revelation 13 tells the government of the antichrist and false prophet during the 70th week of Daniel. Lets us see the power they have over humanity does not believe in Jesus Christ.

20. Revelation 7:1-8: Until it has not completed the number of the 144,000 sealed of Israel, will not start the wrath of God.

21. Revelation 11:1-13: Enoch and Elijah begin to preach the gospel to the Jews. The struggle they have against the Antichrist and his subsequent victory over this is observed.

22. In Revelation 14:1-20: We read the song of the 144,000 who had the name of the Lamb and his Father written on their foreheads. This is the promise Jesus made to the Church of Philadelphia in Revelation 3:12 to those who overcome. These firstfruits are different from the 144,000 of the 12 tribes of Israel; they are holy as John or Paul through 7 dispensations. These firstfruits in turn, are different from those named in James 1:18 and 1 Corinthians 15:23 where he speaks of the Gentile church.

We also see here the three angels message: One has the everlasting gospel, which is not to say that he is the one who preaches; for angels they are not sent to preach. The second angel announces the coming destruction of the great whore. The third angel proclaims the punishment for those who worship the beast and his image, or have been marked. **The final message of this chapter is to tell how will be the destruction of the wicked during the stage of God's wrath.**

23. Revelation 15:1-8: We see here how the gateway to heaven is completely closed and only opens when the seven bowls of the wrath of God are met.

24. Revelation 17 reveals who is the great harlot and who their followers are. On this with God's help, we will do a deeper study in another book.

25. Revelation 16:1-2: The first bowl speaks of punishment on the men who had the microchip, at that time, it shall be mandatory.

26. Revelation 16:3: In the second bowl die 2 /3 of the creatures that were in the sea; after that 1/3 were destroyed in Revelation 8:8, in the second trumpet.

27. Revelation 16:4-7: The third poured bowl causes all the rivers become blood; not anymore drinking water in the world because man rejected the warning of the third trumpet; when only part of the water was contaminated.

28. Revelation 16:8-9: In the fourth bowl, the sun heated seven times, fulfilling the prophecy of Isaiah 30:26. Moreover, ozone is completely destroyed and for this reason, the sun shines directly on the ground. Despite all these great signs, warnings and sorry state of the earth, not even men repent of their wickedness, and continued allied with Satan and his minions.

29. Revelation 16:10-11: In the fifth bowl Everyone with the microchip suffer pain and sickness in his mouth and tongue and become more wicked.

30. Revelation 16:12-16: The Euphrates River is dried and the stage for the invasion of China on Israel is prepared. In addition, all the world's nations are deceived by Satan, the Antichrist and the false prophet, to meet in the valley of Armageddon and well disposed to destroy Israel.

31. Revelation 18: We see that the destruction of the great whore, is in an hour and is believed to be destroyed by an atomic bomb by the antichrist.

32. Revelation 16:17-21: The seventh bowl shows the disappearance of the islands and the high altitude, perhaps as a result of the atomic bombs. But men, as usual, they blame God for the errors and evils that they commit. It takes place the great battle of Armageddon. Judgment is also given to the nation of Israel and the judgment to the nations.

33. Revelation 19:1-6: Praise Him in heaven for a big crowd, who are not identified.

34. Revelation 6:12 B; 6:15-17: Signs in the sun and the moon, the inhabitants of the earth, at this stage of the wrath of God, hide in underground shelters because of the destructions that are happening.

35. Revelation 19:11-21: It begins and ends the battle of Armageddon between Jesus Christ, the Jew/Gentile church and people of Israel; against the antichrist, the false prophet and the pagan nations.

36. Revelation 20:1-6: The millennium. The government of the Lord Jesus Christ with Jew/Gentile church here on earth.

37. Revelation 20:7-9 Satan out of prison where he has been bound for 1000 years (The same reign of Jesus Christ with the Jew/Gentile church on earth) and goes out to deceive the nations which have been as Judas Iscariot; making smiles ahead to Jesus Christ and the church, and then try to bury the knife in the back.

It is exactly at this time, Revelation 20:8, when Russia launched to invade to Israel along with other nations more. (Hezekiah 38:2-6).

Gog and Magog = Russia and Moscow

Cush = Sudan   Fut = Iraq

Gomer = Sugeríos = Several Soviet republics in Asia

Beth- Togarmah = Turkey

Ezekiel 30 and 39 describe the invasion of Russia and its allies against Israel, however, should take into account several important factors to know when will this invasion. **The Bible itself is the one who reveals:**

a. Ezekiel 38:8 says that the invasion will be when Israel more confidently, and here you would think that refers to the three and a half years of the seventieth week of Daniel, but the Bible reveals much more and makes it clear that this is exactly during the millennium.

Compare also 14:8-9, 11 and Zechariah 14:12-21.

b. Ezekiel 38:8 also tells us that Israel will have been saved from the land and out of the nations. **When did this happened?** Before the millennium there will be another invasion on Israel in the battle of Armageddon, delivered by Jesus Christ Himself; then all Israel will return to Israel to live the millennium.

c. In Ezekiel 38:11 the Bible tells us that the people of Israel will dwell securely, without walls, bars or gates ... We know that during the seventieth week of Daniel rely only live three and a half years; but not so bold as to leave their doors open, to break down its walls, ramparts and even let them in and out of the homes all peoples of the world. Israel will have peace, but will always retain some suspicion in your heart and never leave their weapons, or destroy them.

Only during the millennium, really live in safety and will turn their weapons into ploughshare. (Isaiah 2:2-4).

d. Ezekiel 39:12 states that Israel will be burying the bodies of their invaders for seven months which could be in the initial three years and half of the seventieth week of Daniel.

e. According to Ezekiel 39:9 definitively rule out any doubt regarding the time of the invasion of Russia and its allies may arise. The Bible says that the people of Israel will be for seven years burning the weapons of the invaders. We know that the seven years of Daniel's seventieth week, they can only collect weapons in the initial three and a half years since then come and persecution but will not have only time to run and run. In Revelation 20:8 we are told that after the millennium, Satan will deceive the nations, Gog and Magog to go on destroying Israel.

Therefore, we can conclude, without fear of mistakes, that this invasion will occur after the millennium.

38. Revelation 6:13, 14: the heaven and earth that we see today will be destroyed.

39. Revelation 20:10-15: Will be the judgment of Satan and the fallen angels. And also the judgment of the great white throne or final judgment.

40. Revelation 21:1-4 and 21:9-27 and 19:7-10: They are held the wedding between the Lamb Jesus Christ (the husband) and the Jew/Gentile church (who are the wife). The wedding will be in the New Jerusalem.

41. Revelation 22:1-5 shows us a pure and clean river. But on both sides the river is the tree of life, the tree that hid

God from man in the Garden of Eden. (Genesis 3:22-24). The leaves of the tree are for the healing of the nations who have been on the side of Jesus Christ and the Jew/Gentile church, and not have ceased deceived by Satan and his demons after the millennium. In the New Jerusalem there will be no night nor day because God Himself will be the glow of the city.

42. Revelation 22:6-17 tells us to be prepared for the coming of the Lord Jesus Christ when he comes to raise the gentile church. **Also tells us who will not be in the New Jerusalem.**

43. Revelation 22:18-19 Here we find a curse for those who remove or add to the book of Revelations. It does not reach those who ordered by chapters and verses, which translate or interpret, let alone those who ordered this book for easy understanding by the Jew/Gentile church.

44. Revelation 22:20-21 The Lord Jesus reminds us that He is coming soon and will not delay.

SUMMARY ORDER OF THE FINAL EVENTS

As we did a thorough explanation of the final events, now we will only give a brief summary of the events of the seventieth week of Daniel:

1. The European Economic Community is made up of ten countries. A common president for all eight countries by appointing seven years.
(Revelation 17:12-13, Daniel 7:24-25,8:23-25).

2. The antichrist destroys three of the ten kings of the European Economic Status, leaving only seven, then he will become the eighth. (Daniel 7:7-8, Revelation 17:8-11).

3. A peace treaty between Israel, Europe and the rest of the world is signed. (Daniel 9:27).

4. The seven seals are opened. (Rev 6:1 and 8:1-5 -12A).

5. Sound the seven trumpets.
(Revelation 8:6-13, 9:1-21, 10:1-11, 11:15-19).

6. Covenant or peace treaty is broken.
(Daniel 8:11-12, 9:27).

7. The false prophet takes over the power of the Antichrist. (Revelation 13: 11-12).

8. The gentile church is lifted up to meet the Lord in the air, and immediately go through the judgment seat of Christ. (1st Cor 15-51-52; Rev 10:7, 2; 2nd Thess 2:2-8, 2nd

Cor 5:10; 1st Thess 4:16-17).

9. The seven bowls of God's wrath are poured.
(Rev 16:1-21).
Here occur the following outstanding events:

a. **The Euphrates River dries** to China and his minions prepare to invade Israel. (Revelation 16:12).

b. **The great whore** by ten kings of the European Economic status is destroyed. (Rev 16:19; 17:16,18 and 18:8).

10. Nations to invade Israel meet. (Revelation 19:19).

11. Trial of Israel by God. (Ezekiel 20:33-38).

12. Judgment the antichrist and the false prophet.
(Revelation 19: 19-20).

13. Trial nations. (Revelation 19:21; Matthew 25: 31-46).

14. Millennium reign of Jesus Christ or the Jew/Gentile church on earth. Also, here Satan is bound.
(Revelation 20:1-6, Isaiah 65:18-25).

15. Satan is loose and goes out to deceive many of the nations who were in the millennium. (Revelation 20:7-8).

16. Early events after the millennium:

a. **Invasion of Gog and Magog.**
(Zechariah 14:9-11, Zechariah 14:12-21, Ezekiel 38:8-10, Ezekiel 39:1-2,4 and 9, Ezekiel 39:11-13).

b. **Israel collects weapons and spoils** of their enemies to the north, for seven years. (Ezekiel 39:9).

17. Israel destroys Damascus and lose popularity.
To make matters worse, he is criticized by other countries.
(Isaiah 17:1-4, Jeremiah 49:23-27, Amos 1:3-4).

18. All nations come together; for the final war.
(1ˢᵗ Peter 3:10-12; Revelation 20:9).

19. Destruction of heaven and earth. (Revelation 6:14-15).

20. Judgment of God, Satan and the fallen angels.
(Revelation 20:10).

21. Judgment at the Great White Throne. (Rev 20:11-15).

22. New heaven and new earth. In addition, the New Jerusalem descends. (Revelation 21:1-3).

There are many who wonder why Isaiah and Peter speak of the destruction of the heavens, as if they were many; taking Juan to clarify saying only be destroyed the first of the three heavens. As Isaiah prophesied that the light of the moon will be as the light of the sun and the light of the sun will be sevenfold; this will be accomplished during the shedding of the 4th bowl of the wrath of God and is a warning of the destruction of heaven and earth in the war of the end of the world. The sun and the moon disappear and that is why John did not see in the New Jerusalem; but it will be illuminated by the glorious light of God.
(Isaiah 30:26, 65:17, 66:22; 2 Peter 3: 5-7, 10-13; Romans 1: 18-20 and 8:21; Revelation 16: 8-9, 21: 1-2 and 23).

23. The Marriage of the Lamb. (Rev 19:7-8, 21:2 y 9).

SMALL SUMMARY OF CONTROVERSIAL CONTENT OF THE BOOK

So that you can understand in a slightly easier way, I will give a short summary of the content that is controversial book. As is widely discussed and supported with their Bible verses right through the pages of this, then I'll just deal with what could be more confusing to the reader.

1) The order of events would come according to the Bible, as follows:

A. According to the revelation that was given to the prophet Daniel, 70 weeks are determined for the millennium begins. (Daniel 9:24) . We are in week 69. Each day is equal to one year, so that the 7 days is equal to 7 years. This 7 year period is known as THE GREAT TRIBULATION. Week 70 is divided into two periods of three and a half years. The first three and a half years are called SATAN 'S WRATH (7 seals and 7 trumpets) and the final three and a half years called THE WRATH OF GOD. (7 vials of the wrath of God).

B. The wrath of Satan **BEGINS** with the signing of the peace treaty, by the aid of the antichrist between Israel and the Arab world. (The Antichrist will deceive all nations will be submerged in a huge crisis, owing to the great violence, social disorder, disease, unknown viruses, lack of food, lack of water, overpopulation, etc. This charismatic, intelligent, billionaire and powerful man, have the cure for AIDS, cancer and other diseases will control viruses; convert sea water into drinking water; invented a new transport system and advocated for human rights, for such reasons will be hailed by the worldwide as the messiah, The saviour and receive the Nobel peace prize When the remaining European Common Market made up of 10 nations, this man brought down three nations that do not agree with their plans, policies and thoughts, then stay the Union European made only for 7 piss and the same shall become the eighth). The wrath of Satan **ENDS** with the lifting of the Gentile Church to meet with the dead in Christ and meet face to face with the Lord Jesus Christ in the clouds, and immediately go through the judgment seat of Christ. (The false messiah will already sitting in the temple rebuilt by the people of Israel and where they would be making sacrifices to YHWH. Upon this phony itself known as the son of perdition , as a man of sin and worship him as ordered god or die, at which time the gentile church is raised (2nd Thessalonians 2:1-3). The door of the revelation of the gospel to the Gentiles closes and opens to the Jews. Begins also the mark of the beast to be compulsory as for now had only been voluntarily in exchange for welfare, health, power and wealth, but now it has to be put on or death.

C. The wrath of God, also known as Jacob's trouble; **BEGINS** when the antichrist is furious that the Jews refuse to worship him as a god, which unleashes a great persecution against these people, known as the abomination of desolation, in this stage the Euphrates river is dried, thus setting the stage for the invasion of China and its allies over Israel, which occurs during the sixth bowl, and the seventh bowl is carried out the destruction of the great whore. The Wrath of God **ENDS** when all nations are gathered in the valley of Megiddo to destroy Israel, and this is known as the battle of

Armageddon, the Jews cry out to God for help and when descending from the heavens the Lord Jesus Christ together with the church of Jesus Christ on the Mount of olives, and divides it into two large valley is formed.(Zechariah 14:3-5). And to end, the trial of the nation of Israel; the beast and the false prophet, who appeared on stage at the beginning of the wrath of God, are cast alive into the lake that burns with fire and brimstone, and finally the judgment the nations. (Revelation 16:12-16 and 19:19-21).

D. The millennium **BEGINS** when Satan is bound in the abyss for a thousand years, and **ENDS** when Satan is released from his prison and goes out to deceive the nations. During these thousand years the Lord Jesus Christ with the Church, will have a government of complete peace on earth. (Revelation 20:1-7, Isaiah 65:17-25).

E. The Final Judgment **BEGINS** with the invasion of Gog and Magog and its allies over Israel, and continues with the destruction of Damascus, which triggers the end of the world war, where they destroyed the earth and the first heaven. COMPLETE with the trial of Satan (who be cast alive into the lake of fire and brimstone), the trial of the fallen angels, and the final judgment and/or trial before the great white throne (Revelation 20:7-10).

F. Finally we have the Wedding of the Lamb. A period **BEGINS** with new heaven and new earth, where the New Jerusalem descends, with dwellings that Jesus Christ has prepared for us, and COMPLETE with the coveted wedding of the Lamb. (Revelation Chapter 21 and 19:7-9).

In this period, I would remember that The **WEDDINGE OF THE LAMB** will be held in the **New Jerusalem** as the Bible says. Regarding this point, it is important to discuss the following:

a. The Bride of the Lamb composes: The gentile Church, the Jews church and the New Jerusalem.

b. It is impossible to imagine as a kind, loving and just God may be able to be enjoying themselves, enjoying and partying, while his people loved Israel is suffering, dying, and suffering persecution.

c. Scripture quotations relating to this subject, confirming the above, can read the chapter called "The Wedding of the Lamb".

2) With regard to when the church will be raised; so I will summarize as follows:

The theory that traditions have taught us is that the church will be up before the 70th week of Daniel, but the Bible does not support that assertion , nor is there even a Bible verse that says that the church will not go through the great tribulation. Because this theory is deeply rooted in our hearts, I will explain some verses they use to support this tradition:

A. Revelation 3:10 When here the expression "I also will keep thee from the hour of trial" is used, it is using the Greek (TEREO EK), which means (WATCH DE). This means that God will save INSIDE the hour of trial. As in John 7:15 Jesus prayed that his disciples were SAVED IN THE

WORLD (TERO EK). Not be taken out of the world but SAVED In THE WORLD: As we see in Revelation 3:10 as in John 7:15 promises. A proof of this is that in Revelation 9:4 when the fifth trumpet sounds the bottomless pit is opened and came locusts that were ordered was injured every man who did not have the seal of God on their foreheads. This stamp is received when we are baptized by the Holy Spirit.

B. Isaiah 26:20 This verse applies to say that the church did not go through the 70th week of Daniel, but as we will see anything this text refers to the church. **First** of all we see in verse 1 that this chapter 26 is a song of the people of Israel in Judah. **Second,** we see in verse 19 as a figure of the resurrection as a restoration of Israel from spiritual ruin which is submerged in use; well confirms Daniel 12:1-2. **Third**, verse 20 says literally: Come, my people, (What people is this? obviously this refers to Israel) enter into thy chambers, and shut thy doors about thee; (already in verse 2 had opened doors for to enter the righteous people of Israel), hide a little, for a moment, until the indignation is past. In the original text says while passing the IRA. (What is this anger? Verse 21 and all of chapter 27 shows us that relates to the WRATH OF GOD). On the other hand , if this verse is referring to the church, claiming that the church would not suffer the WRATH OF GOD, that is the three and a half years late Daniel 's 70th week, which is what we say in this book. **Finally**, when is that God's people must hide a little bit? Verse 21 teaches him to say: "Behold, the Lord cometh out of his place to punish the inhabitants of the earth for their iniquity". When God punishes the inhabitants of the earth during the Great Tribulation? During the Wrath of God, so in the final three and a half years; because in the initial three and a half years the church will be troubled and punished by Satan and his minions; while the earth shall enjoy peace and quiet. When God leave his place, dwelling or palace? When he leaves to get to the church in the air, and then begins the Wrath of God God's punishment on the inhabitants of the earth, you who have not been sealed to the tribes of Israel, and those who have not fled to Petra. Remember that when you feel the antichrist in the temple of God and calls worship, the Jews then understand that this is not a Messiah and refuse to worship him, then begins the period known as THE ABOMINATION OF DESOLATION, a terrible persecution against the people of Israel, who will have to flee to a city called Petra, which is located in southeast red mountains of Israel. Writing Petra identifies with: Mount Seir, Mount Hor, Sela, and the strong city of Edom. Clarify that according to the story, Jacob is the father of Israel, and Esau the father of the Edomites. Daniel 11:41 tells us that even though the Antichrist dominate the world during the 70th week of Daniel still Edom , Moab and Amon; escape from his hand. Therefore Israel is believed to escape to Petra, to shelter from the terrible persecution of the Antichrist during the abomination of desolation.

Revelation 12:6 and 13-14 talks about the place God has prepared for His people to be supported during this difficult period.

Revelation 18:4 In the sixth bowl of God's wrath, God commands his people to leave Rome in literal sense, and idolatry in the spiritual sense, that they are not destroyed along with the great whore.

Revelation 7:2 God seals 144,000 from all the tribes of Israel, that they do not suffer any punishment from his angels, but suffer at the hands of the Antichrist. The 144,000 sealed and the two witnesses did not flee to Petra, but Israel continued in preaching the gospel to his people and to the world, for this reason suffers persecution, torture and suffer to die at the hands of the Antichrist.

When the gentile church is lifted, the gateway to the kingdom of God to the Gentiles is closed, and opens to the Jews church. (The door to the understanding of the revelation of the gospel).

C. Matthew 24:3-28 The first 14 verses speak of the church. The end of that talk in verses 6, 13 and 14; is to preach the gospel to the Gentiles. Verse 15 begins the WRATH OF GOD or tribulation of Jacob, until verse 28; this is for the Jewish, the people of Israel and the church that have become the rapture of the Gentile church.

D. 1st Thessalonians 5:9 For God did not appoint us to wrath, but to obtain salvation through our Lord Jesus Christ. The Bible is clear on this point the church NOT PASS THE WRATH OF GOD, will be lifted before God pours out the 7 bowls of wrath, or in the middle of the week.

3) I want to clarify a little about 2nd Thessalonians 2:1-3

2:1 Now concerning the coming of our Lord Jesus Christ and our being gathered to him, we beseech you, brethren,

2:2 will not be soon shaken in your thinking, or be troubled, neither by spirit, nor by word, nor by letter as from us, to the effect that the day of Christ is at hand.

2:3 Let no man deceive you by any means: for that day shall not come, except there come a falling away first, and that man of sin, the son of perdition is revealed.

They wanted to confuse the church into believing that these verses are talking about the day of the Lord, and not the lifting of the gentile church. Nothing is further from reality as verse 1 clearly says here that it is the coming of our Lord Jesus Christ and our being gathered to him**. But the day of the Lord encompasses three major events:** Start with the lifting of the church continues with the trial during the battle of Armageddon, and ends with the trial of war doomsday.

Verse 2:3 tells us that this lifting of the gentile church does not take place UNTIL the man of sin, the son of perdition is revealed. When will the Antichrist be manifested as man of sin? As evil? As a murderer? As perverse? When you show it really is? Right, when you sit in the temple and asked to worship him as if he were the one true God. When is this? In the middle of the 70th week of Daniel.

4) Also is necessary to clarify who or what is what prevents the antichrist is revealed?

2nd Thessalonians 2:7-8.

2:7 For the mystery of iniquity, only he who now restrains will do so until he is taken out of the way.

2:8 And then shall that Wicked be revealed, whom the Lord shall consume with the spirit of his mouth, and shall destroy with the brightness of his coming.

One thing is clear: Is not the gentile church that holds the manifestation of antichrist. The Bible explains this when he says in verse 3 that the gentile church will be raised after the Antichrist is revealed as a man of sin or evil , **then first manifests or discloses the antichrist as wicked and then the gentile church is raised.** Verses 7-8 tell us that when holding the manifestation of the wicked is out of the way, then the wicked will manifest. **Clearly we see that the gentile church is not preventing the manifestation of the wicked , because for the gentile church to be lifted must first manifest the Antichrist as wicked , and for the Wicked be revealed, first has to be removed which prevents manifest.** We have already said in this book with biblical evidence, that what prevents the Wicked be revealed, it's time to preaching the gospel to the Gentiles, when this happens, then the antichrist will manifest as wicked.

5) To end this mini summary I would like to leave you with these texts:

4:13 But we, brethren, concerning them which are asleep, that ye sorrow not, even as others which have no hope.

4:14 For if we believe that Jesus died and rose again, even so God will bring with Him those who sleep in Jesus.

4:15 Wherefore I say this word of the Lord, that we who are alive, who are left till the coming of the Lord shall not prevent them which are asleep.

4:16 For the Lord himself with a shout, with the voice of the archangel and with the trumpet of God, will descend from heaven and the dead in Christ shall rise first.

4:17 Then we who are alive, who are left, will be caught up together with them in the clouds to meet the Lord in the air: and so shall we ever be with the Lord. 15:51 Behold, I show you a mystery: We shall not all sleep, but we all shall be changed.

15:52 In a moment, in the twinkling of an eye, at the last trump: for the trumpet shall sound, and the dead shall be raised incorruptible, and we shall be changed.

There is talking here that when Jesus Christ comes to raise the gentile church will with God's trumpet and trumpet.

What is the trumpet of God? And when the last trump shall sound?. **Revelation 10:6-7 is the answer:**

10:6 and swore by Him who lives forever and ever , who created heaven and the things that therein are, and the earth and the things that therein are, and the sea and the things which are therein , that there should be time no longer,

10:7 But in the days of the voice of the seventh angel, when he shall begin to sound, the mystery of God should be finished, as he hath declared to his servants the prophets.

When the seventh angel begins to sound (Voice of the Archangel), at the last trumpet (The seventh trumpet is the last). After this trumpet sound, the gentile church is going with Jesus.

CONCLUSION

I cannot conclude this book without first devote a few sentences to analyze the ten horns of the beast will be something short and that, God willing, in a forthcoming book discuss in depth the seven heads, ten horns and ten crowns of beast.

There are several theories about these ten horns:

1. Ten European Economic Status: This is the most common thought and known by all. Particularly, I am inclined to this theory, considering the following reasons:

a. It was the first to form and have everything in common.

b. In Brussels there is already a gigantic supercomputer dominating the digital economy in the world, and even themselves call it "the Beast".

c. All computers work with 666.

d. The European Economic State is the revived Roman system. No matter where the antichrist is or what country of the world comes, some say it is of European origin, others say it will be the Middle East ... etc. . . But the truth is that it will be of Jewish origin and of the tribe of Dan (Genesis 49:16-17), and will be sworn in as President of the European Economic Status. The tribe of Dan is not listed among the hundred and forty four thousand sealed in Revelation 7. The prophecy that Dan shall judge his people have not yet attained so far and therefore must be met in the future.

2. New World Order: Global Reorganization of all nations.

a. North America
b. Western Europe
c. Japan
d. Australia, South Africa and the rest of the economy of the developed world market.
e. Eastern Europe, including Russia
f. Latin America
g. North Africa and the Near East
h. Tropical Africa
i. South and Southeast Asia
j. China

3. Continentals Unions:

a. Union European (EU)
b. Union American (NAU)
c. Unión Mediterranean (UM)
d. Unión African Union (AU)
e. Unión of South America (UNASUR)
f. Central American Union (SICA)
g. Union of the Gulf (GCC)
h. Unión the Caribbean (CARICON)
i. Unión Asian (ASEAN)
j. Union the Pacifism (TBA)

4. The courts and the international judiciary ten countries:

Are they really the ten horns pre-existing kings? Why is said to receive authority as kings? Perhaps they are not? The ability of the justice system resembles reign.

Is it possible that the ten horns are human tribunals that are embedded in the territories of the political powers?

Apparently, it is the courts that are exposing the whore, and are those who have the legal authority to prosecute her. Politically speaking, it is not right that governments judge religions as it is considered as violation of human rights. However, if religions are accused of criminal acts, the courts and the judiciary are the ones who have the authority to sanction, sue and punish.

There is a possibility that the ten horns are really the great courts that exist in the territories of the political powers. There are kings, but receive power as kings one hour. These give authority to the beast.

Here is the list of the main countries in which you are suing or being studied sue the Vatican:

a. United States
b. England
c. Canada
d. Australia
e. Ireland
f. Mexico
g. Austria
h. Poland
i. Germany
j. Spain

5. Ten U.N. Global Zones

a. The NATO
b. Ten nations around the country Israel

c. Ten not permanent the council of safety of the UN.
d. Ten nations of the Union European Western
e. Roma and/or Roman Empire Revived

**Finally, I want to make a brief reference to the
NEW WORLD ORDER,** which again has nothing, as
it has been articulated since the 12th century. In fact,
there are many secret, such as corporations: The
Bilderberg, the Trilateral Commission, the World
Health Organization and the United Nations, among
others, who have been preparing the ground. All lead
to the Illuminati who are controlling the world and are
infiltrated all governments, religions and doctrines,
including the doctrine of Name.

**Yes , my dear brother, and no wonder, for Satan
himself masquerades as an angel of light, the Bible
also speaks of false brethren, false teachers, false
prophets and false shepherds brought into the
church.**

The Illuminati are the ones who decide about wars ,
invasions, and the global economy are the controlling
religions, those with money and power to control
everything, plus those who will take office as the
Antichrist world dictator, ostensibly to bring peace,
security and equality to the citizens of planet earth.

**You can _research_ more about it on the internet at
about: The Illuminati, New World Order, HAARP,
Conspiracy Theory, Bilderberg Group,
Freemasons, The Mark of the Beast, among others.**

These revelations that the Lord Jesus Christ has given me, are not to keep them for me; but to make them known to the Jewish / Gentile church and the world, because they also need to know the truth of what is going to happen in the future.

The book of life is the bible, and is a book that God began to write in the Garden of Eden and will end of be written with The War of the End of the World; when will be destroyed the first heaven and the earth by fire.

The book of life continues to be written today by those who are part of the Gentile church, it will be written by the Jewish church, continue to be written during the millennium and will end writing with the human last living that has entered into the New Jerusalem; when carrying out The War of the End of the World.

What the Bible says is what should prevail over what the man says; this is why you will find in this book many biblical references, to check the veracity of what is written in this book; because what is written here it is tested and proven according to the doctrine that teaches the Bible, and it is done even the man did not believe it.

God bless and prosper abundantly rich, a Spiritual level, Moral and Material. "Prove all things, hold fast what is good and evil cast aside".

THIS BOOK IS A COPY OF THE ORIGINAL ONE IN SPANISH: "APOCALIPSIS MISTERIO REVELADO".

you can find this books in the whole world in paper and ebook by: "www.amazon.com and Kindle eBooks".

AUTHOR'S BIBLIOGRAPHY

Author of the book "The Holy Spirit" Eivar Galindez was born in Colombia in 1965. In the year 1993 gave his life to the Lord Jesus Christ. Neiva was the city where he grew up and began to serve the Lord Jesus Christ in the evangelistic field, social work and finally before departing to Europe, served as a leader of the prison labour.

In 2000 he moved to Spain, where God together with his family used him to start two beautiful works:
one in Torrelavega (Cantabria) and another in Malaga (Andalucia).

In 2010 he travelled to England, where he currently lives with his wife and five children and serves at the church of London.

Eivar Galindez is available for conferences at your city, organization, university or study group.

For more information write to:
 pleyverstown@hotmail.co.uk

Made in the USA
Charleston, SC
20 July 2015